# Our Proud Mountain Roots and Heritage

*Martha Ellen Arbogast married Isaac Perry Vance; Ida Jane Arbogast married Perry Clark Arbogast; Christena Arbogast married Bernard Dellard Powers; Laura Susan Arbogast married George Triplett; James William Arbogast married Ruth May Coberly; Etta Arbogast married Minard Summerfield; Lemuel Earl Arbogast married Mary Margaret Howell; Anna M. Arbogast married John Peters; Jenny Florence Arbogast married William Fansler; Benjamin Harley Arbogast married Amanda E. Sacks; George Hobart Arbogast married Florence Smith.*

## George R. Triplett

International Standard Book Number 0-87012-708-X
Library of Congress Control Number 2003112793
Printed in the United States of America
Copyright © 2003 by George R. Triplett
Elkins, WV
All Rights Reserved
2003




McClain Printing Company
Parsons, West Virginia 26287
www.mcclainprinting.com
2003

# Table of Contents

# Foreword

Full credit and recognition is to the prior writers who provided materials to pull the description of "Mountain State" experiences together. There is a most well-researched and written book by Don Rice, titled *Randolph 200, a Bicentennial History of Randolph County, West Virginia, 1787-1987* that provides a detailed history and pictorial description of Elkins and Randolph County to which I refer all readers for more details.

Don Rice was a teacher at Durbin School in 1951 and 1953. I have used many of Don Rice's photos and research to prepare this informal, incomplete introduction to early life on the Upper Cheat River Basin.

There have been two narrative histories, H.W. Maxwell's *History of Randolph County, West Virginia* and Dr. A.S. Bosworth's *History of Randolph County*, which have been accepted as the bases of subsequent study and discussion of our Randolph County history since their publications came to print more than seventy years ago.

Roy B. Clarkson, a Green Bank High School teacher who went on to teach for thirty-six years at West Virginia University, and author of *Tumult on the Mountains* and *On Beyond Leatherbark: The Cass Saga,* has provided several photographs from his two publications. Roy Clarkson was born and raised in Cass, graduated from Green Bank High School and taught science there for one year. Roy injured his back at the Cass Mill and decided to attend college. The severe back injury continues to cause him difficulty. Roy is a retired member of the West Virginia University Faculty and resides in Morgantown, West Virginia.

Another Green Bank High School teacher, Warren E. "Tweard" Blackhurst wrote *Riders of the Flood* which was published the year after the class of 1953 graduated.

There is *Mountain Heritage*, edited by B.B. Maurer, which contains the article by Dr. O. Norman Simpkins, "An Informal Incomplete Introduction to Appalachian Culture" that has been completely copied as Part II of this book. The article, represented in *Mountain Heritage*, is adapted from Dr. Simpkins address at the Huntington Galleries, Mountain Heritage Week June 19-24, 1972, by B. B. Maurer.

Part IV of this book is adapted from Chapter XVI, "Family History" origins or surnames from Dr. A.S. Bosworth's *History of Randolph County* with permission granted by Madeline Crickard, widow of Owen Crickard, who wants Randolph County's history to remain alive.

No literary merit is claimed in the presentation of this book for an informal incomplete introduction to early life on the Upper Cheat River Basin. The purpose of the writer is to present facts and if any event of historical value will be saved for future generations, the author will feel compensated for his labors. An undertaking embodied within this book involves labor, research and a life-style understood by the average individual. Encouragement and assistance have been received from many sources not practical to enumerate, but nonetheless cherished and appreciated.

I acknowledge gratitude for and assistance from Roy Clarkson, Don Rice, Red Payne, Mary Armentrout, Arlie Arbogast, Peck Vance, Calvin Shifflett, Wanda Powers Sharp, Lori DiBacco, Lars Byrne, Booche Cussins, Madeline Crickard, Michelle Mullenax-McKinnie, my assistant Nanette Nelson Trammell and all my family and all surviving descendents of all the families from the Upper Cheat River Basin mentioned or unmentioned in this book.

I only pray my three grandchildren, George Andrew Triplett, Robert Charles Triplett and Sofia Frances Triplett, are instilled, taught and ingrained by their parents with the same positive mental attitude, work ethics, hope, faith and love handed down from all the Upper Cheat River Basin families. That they, if ever down, will climb to the top of Cheat Mountain and look down at the beautiful valley and Cheat River flowing below, and that will help them find "peace of mind."

# Part I

## Brief Summary of Elkins Railroad History

The population of Randolph (including other territories) was 751 according to the 1790 Census. The only access to Randolph County was by Indian Trails known as the Shawnee and Seneca Indian Trails, which provided some limited access to the Monongahela River, South Branch of the Potomac Valley and Virginia.

When George Washington, during the 1780s, put out the call to arms against the British, "Rally around me men of West Augusta and we shall raise this bleeding nation from the sand," the mountain men responded.

The men of West Augusta (Randolph County), in 1794, resisted the Federal Revenue Laws, known in history as the "Whiskey Insurrection".

In 1792, the present territory of Randolph County had a population of 305 and 260 horses. The population of Elkins in 1910 was 5,260.

The West Virginia Supreme Court of Appeals ordered the removal of the county records from Beverly, where they had been domiciled since 1787, to Elkins. The records were then stored in the offices of the Coal and Coke Building in Elkins. During the latter part of the 1890s, a bitter feud between Beverly and Elkins erupted which almost led to a shooting war between the communities on May 6, 1899, when Elkins supporters threatened to forcibly remove the records from Beverly.

1

The first passenger train arrived in Elkins (Leading Creek) on August 18, 1889 as a result of the economic and political influence of United States Senator Henry Gassaway Davis and Stephen B. Elkins.

## Western Maryland Railway–Durbin Branch

The Durbin Branch of the Western Maryland Railway extended from Elkins eastward to Bowden on Shaver's Fork of Cheat River; then southward up Shaver's Fork to Cheat Junction; then eastward to Glady on Glady Fork of Dry Fork of Cheat; then southward up Glady Fork to the Pocahontas County line at the divide between Glady Fork and Greenbrier River; and then southward down West Fork of Greenbrier to Durbin, Pocahontas County. It was originally built by the late Senator Henry G. Davis and associates under the name of Coal and Iron Railway. It was completed to Durbin August 1, 1903, and was bought by the Western Maryland November 1, 1905. In Randolph County it had 28.76 miles of mainline tracks and 3.76 miles of sidings; in Pocahontas there were 17.62 miles of main track and 2.01 miles of sidings. At first this road was mainly used for hauling lumber, but it became an important carrier of coal from the Cheat Mountain coal fields. At Durbin it connected with the Greenbrier Division of the Chesapeake and Ohio Railway, and in later years received and carried eastward heavy consignments of through freight from the latter system.

## R. Chaffey Railroad

The R. Chaffey Railroad, tributary to the Durbin Branch of the Western Maryland at Glady, Randolph County, was originally the property of the Glady Manufacturing Company which built a lumber mill at Glady in 1912. It was acquired by Mr. Chaffey in 1925. In the autumn of 1926, this road comprised fourteen miles of forty-two-inch gauge track. Its route was southward up the East Fork of Glady and then eastward to the headwaters of Laurel Fork of Cheat River. It was mainly used for hauling logs to the Chaffey Mill at Glady.

## Western Maryland Railway– Elk River Branch

The Elk River Branch of the Western Maryland Railway consisted of acquired portions of the Greenbrier, Cheat and Elk Railroad and West Virginia Maryland Railroad. It started at Cheat Junction, Randolph County, and extended southward up the valley of Shaver's Fork of Cheat River to Spruce, Pocahontas County, where it turned westward across Cheat Mountain and passed through the divide between Tygart's Valley River and Big Spring Fork of Elk River to Mace. From Mace it followed down Big Spring Fork to its mouth at Slaty Fork town and then down Elk River to Bergoo and Webster Springs, Webster County. There were, in the Greenbrier, Cheat and Elk portion, 41.67 miles of main track and 3.79 miles of siding in Randolph County; 23.71 miles of main track and 2.94 miles of siding in Pocahontas; and 8.93 miles of main track and 0.17 miles of siding in Webster. The portion of the line from Cheat Junction to Bergoo was originally built and owned by the Greenbrier, Cheat and Elk Railroad Company, having been completed about 1917, but was purchased by the Western Maryland Railway March 3, 1927. The portion from Bergoo to Webster Springs, about 10 miles long and not included in the Webster County mileage figures above quoted, was built as a narrow-gauge by the West Virginia Midland Railroad Company in 1927 or 1928, but later a third rail was added to make a standard-gauge road and the line was purchased by the Western

Maryland on May 31, 1929. After this change 17.51 miles of main track and 2.74 miles of sidings were acquired, including certain lines around Webster Springs.

Between Cheat Junction and Bergoo certain trackage rights were retained by the West Virginia Pulp and Paper Company, who formerly owned the Greenbrier, Cheat and Elk Railroad, and a line operated from Spruce to Cass, Pocahontas County, as well as numerous lumber spurs. Between Bergoo and Webster Springs the West Virginia Midland, largely owned by the Pardee and Curtin Lumber Company, retained the narrow-gauge track together with certain operating rights.

## Western Maryland Railway—Main Line

The main line of the Western Maryland Railway extended from Baltimore, Maryland, westward to Belington, West Virginia, a distance of 292.3 miles. It entered Randolph County near Montrose and extended down Leading Creek to Elkins, and down the eastern side of Tygart's Valley River to Norton and Belington. The latter point being in Barbour County. It was first merged into a trunk line August 6, 1906, by the completion of a connection 60 miles long, between what was formerly known as Western Maryland Railroad Company at Big Pool, Maryland and West Virginia Central and Pittsburgh Railway Company at Cumberland, Maryland. The latter line having been previously absorbed by the parent company November 1, 1905. The line from Elkins to Belington, however, was first built as the Belington and Beaver Creek Railroad, being purchased by the Western Maryland Railway November 1905. The original railroad extended through Mineral, Grant and Tucker counties and was first organized as the Potomac and Piedmont Coal and Railroad Company in 1866, but was recognized under the name of West Virginia Central and Pittsburgh Railway June 25, 1881. Construction from Piedmont westward was begun about April 20, 1880, completed to Elk Garden October 29, 1881; to Thomas and Davis November 1, 1884; to Parsons early in 1889; to Elkins August 18, 1889; and to Belington May 1, 1891. This system contained 54.92 miles of main-line trackage and 19.70 miles of sidings in Randolph County.

## Early Workers Compensation and Job Security

Jay White, an Elkins section gang hand, was injured on the Western Maryland. The railroad company kept Jay on the payroll and made him the South Davis Avenue Railroad watchman at the location where the Tygart Valley Special picks up and drops off passengers in Elkins for transportation to "High Falls".

Wy Pritt, Lonnie Bennett and Owen Fansler were early Western Maryland section gang foremen in Elkins and on the Cheat River Basin side of the first tunnel where the Bowden Section began. The section gang tool house was on the opposite side of the tracks from the pick up and drop off stop.

## The Start of Passenger Train Trips to High Falls

Elkins Bartlett was a freight station supervisor. The freight station building was situate from the pick up and drop off stop to South Davis Avenue, Elkins. The railroad freight shipments were received, stored, shipped and routed to and from Elkins. Jesse Robinson was also a long-time supervisor at the freight station, as was "Bus" Robinson, track supervisor office clerk.

After commencing your train trip to High Falls you pass over the Tygart River Railroad Trestle and see the 11th Street Bridge. You next cross a railroad overpass for US 219 and US 250 and observe the US 33 Intersection on your left.

US 250 and US 33 begin in Richmond, Virginia, and cross in Elkins. US 250 is the northern route that ends at Lake Erie. US 33 is the southern route and passes through Elkins to Weston and Glenville and exits West Virginia near Ravenswood. The two highways were the subject of early political controversy.

You can also observe the home of former West Virginia Governor Herman Guy Kump on the left side of the train. You can barely see up "Triplett Hollow" at the motel on your left and the tan brick house. Charlie Triplett and Geneva Triplett constructed a 28 x 34 feet 3-bedroom house, partially from wide boards of Western Maryland houses torn down at Spruce during the 1950s. Charlie hauled the lumber from Spruce to Cheat Bridge by "push truck" pulled by a motorcar.

After rounding a sharp curve and a railroad crossing is the residence of Arthur Woods. Arthur is the son of Jim Woods, who was a railroad section gang hand. Jim had a large family and lived on Poe Run. Jim never owned an automobile. He and his family would carry their groceries on payday to Poe Run either over the old Seneca Indian Trail or along US 33. Arthur is a "jack of all trades" and is married to Leah Turner Woods.

There were two locomotive engineers, Liedy Bohon and David Bohon, who lived on the left just before you crossed over the US 33 overpass. David married "Leafie" White from Bemis and Liedy married Cressie White, daughter of Lonnis White.

## Canfield Crossing–Osner Creek

Canfield Crossing, which is referred to as Poe Run Hollow, was home to several Western Maryland Section Gang hands who lived there with their families, including, Frank "Snuffie" Hedrick, his son David Hedrick, Jim Woods and Vernon Hedrick.

Section gang hands, "gandy dancers" or trackmen are synonymous words. They are the hard working laborers who kept the railroad tracks in good repair and safe for trains to travel.

Canfield Crossing, also known as the Poe Run Crossing, is the site of the Coastal Lumber Company Mill, which was started by Calvin Mongold after his mill burned on the Cheat side of Tunnel Mountain in the early 1960s. Calvin Mongold started his first sawmill in Glady after moving from Pendleton County.

Coy Lambert, whose home stands in the hollow above the Isner Loop, was a locomotive engineer, and two of his sons were the strongest young men in the Elkins area. Coy and Jack Lambert would lift a Crosley car off the ground at lunch time for entertainment at Elkins High School. Both were football players and US Marine Corps veterans.

Boss Bell, son of Martin Bell, also lived in the Isner Creek Hollow and had a large family.

## Tunnel No. 1

The Elkins Train Yard had a large locomotive repair shop, roundhouse, turn table, railroad coal car construction shop and numerous sidetracks to store or park loaded and empty railroad cars being transported to and from the coal fields and lumber mills. You will observe the "Corridor H," a four-lane highway, which hopefully will be US Interstate 66, connecting Weston via Elkins to the US 495 Beltway around Washington, DC.

There was a 1,200 foot siding on the Elkins side of the Tunnel No. 1, which allowed parking of train cars and/or locomotives for storage or passing of oncoming trains or motorcars. The US Mail Trains and fast "war freight" trains had first priority for use of the tracks and tunnel.

Tunnel No. 1 is 1,716.5 feet in length and is "S" shaped. It passes under Cheat Mountain to the Shavers Fork of Cheat River along old US 33 before construction of the four-lane.

7

New US 33, is above the railroad tracks until you arrive at Bowden Station. There is no major highway access from Bowden until the train arrives at the US 250 Crossing at Cheat Bridge. Old timers used to refer to Cheat River as one of the "Seven Wonders of the World," because it flowed such a long distance in the mountains.

Shaver Fork drops 2,800 feet from the Beaver Creek, Randolph-Pocahontas County Line to the Tucker-Randolph County Line, more than in the remainder of the flow to the Gulf of Mexico.

## Lumber

A railroad stop was established here on the Durbin Branch of the Western Maryland Railroad six miles east of Elkins and one mile east of the tunnel on Kelly Mountain. A logging railroad was extended from this point north along Shaver's Fork to serve a logging operation maintained by D.D. Brown.

# Cheat Mountain

Cheat River and Cheat Mountain got their names for "cheating" so many men out of their lives while they were working on the railroad and in the coalmines and timber industry. Early Faulkner, Bowden, Cheat Mountain and Cheat River Basin settlers included the Tygarts, Chenoweths, Files, Tripletts, Isners, Raines, Arbogasts, Calains, Kimbles, Flints, Powers, Summerfields, Vances, Phares, Woods, Champs, Revelles, Taylors, Hedricks, Sponaugles, Coberlys, Conrads, Weeses, Whites and many others.

A few of the family cemeteries in the path of U.S. Rt. 33 caused the relocation of several family burial sites, including the Taylor, Triplett, Calain and Isner cemeteries about 1970. The West Virginia Department of Highways originally offered $1 compensation to some of the families for the cemeteries. The good citizens of Randolph County, as members of the Petit Jury, awarded substantially more in the Jury's verdict to the landowners.

*George Washington's Diary from 1745-1795*, obtained from the Library of Congress, disclosed the close friendship between Francis Triplet, William Triplet and Thomas Triplet in Northern Virginia (diary spells "Triplet" and "Triplett"). A substantial land grant was conveyed to the Triplet Family from the Washington Estate after the Revolutionary War. John Triplett, son of William Triplett, came to Randolph County about 1790 to settle the Triplett land ownership grant. William was the main builder of Mt. Vernon.

# Faulkner

Bill Flint was a Presbyterian minister and his two-story frame home is visible above the railroad tracks after passing the "Triplett Home;" the two-story frame house above the railroad crossing near the Triplett homesite at a camping trailer park. The Swiss settlers, Knutti, Hertig, Cunninghams–Schmiedlen, Senic, and Ogdens, often stayed overnight with the Tripletts and Flints traveling to and from Beverly or Elkins from the Alpena Swiss Settlement.

The Stone Quarry was owned and operated by an Italian immigrant, who was an intelligent, self-taught businessman, Sam G. Polino, Sr. Charlie Triplett, at the age of thirteen, was employed at the quarry, to help support his family and helped mine the limestone. The Quarry caverns are visible above the railroad and Rt. 33.

Charlie was a water boy for Railroad Section Gang Foremen George Kimble and Harl "Cub" Coberly, after his Stone Quarry employment.

## Faulkner School–1920 Roster

George Cunningham was the early teacher. The textbook was the *McGuffey Reader and Spelling Books*, authored by Professor William H. McGuffey, University of Virginia. Barnabus Harris' son, Nehemiah Harris, married Anna McGuffey, sister of William McGuffey. Faulkner, Bowden, Taylor Run, Woodrow, Nydegger Stone, Kight, Revelle and Weese Crossing students walked to school. Arlie Arbogast was a custodian at Bowden School and earned enough money to purchase a workhorse and milk cow for his brothers and sisters.

The areas near Faulkner, Bowden, Alpena, Dailey, Glady, Harman, Elkins, Gilman, Canaan Valley, and Dolly Sods were

WWII training grounds for the US Army's "Mountain Fighters" for D-Day to liberate Europe. The Infantry Assault Climbers trained on the face of Seneca Rocks and Blackwater Canyon. It was a settlement in which Creed Isner, grandfather of J. Herman Isner, owned one of the first stores or trading posts, "Cheat River Cash Store" J. Herman Isner's father was Jefferson Isner, who was the son of Creed Isner who was the son of Henry Isner.

## Bowden

The railroad station and post office were named for Harry L. Bowden, a local merchant and postmaster in 1908. It is located eight miles east of Elkins, on the Western Maryland Railroad line going up the Shaver's Fork River. The station closed May 31, 1967, with the last scheduled passenger train from Elkins going to Bowden and to Durbin at that time. The passenger train from Elkins to Durbin stopped at Bowden Station. There was a six-day-a-week passenger train service from Elkins to Durbin leaving Elkins about 11 am and returning from Durbin about 5 pm. It connected the Cumberland, Western Maryland passenger trains to Elkins with the C & O Railroad passenger train from Ronceverte at Durbin about 2 pm. Both Revelle's and Bowden's operated stores. The lumber company was Cheat River Lumber Company.

Mrs. Revelle, grandmother of Hansel Bazzell, operated a general store in Bowden and was the postmistress for many years. Revelle Campgrounds are named after the Revelle Family.

My cousin Arlie Arbogast who owned a service station for many years is the son of Will Arbogast, who was a brother to my grandmother, Lora Susan Arbogast Triplett. Arlie, after being reasonably successful by hard work and good business practices, tore down the service station and constructed a church with his own money. Cousin Arlie told me that Ben White, the Randolph County jailer allowed him to stay overnight with his dad, Uncle

11

Will, in the jail during a visit. Arlie didn't want to leave his dad. The correctional system was a lot different in the 1920s than the 2000s.

Taylor Run was the source for numerous moonshine making operations from Bowden across the river below US 33 traveling East. My grandaddy, George Washington "Pud" Triplett, Uncle Earl and Uncle Will Arbogast and some of their offspring have been said to have manufactured some of the county's best "white lightning".

Moonshine whiskey had several different names among mountain folks, including, "white lightning," "fire water," "spirits," "tonic" "the recipe," and "The Devil's Brew". "Pud" Triplett may have been a short-time boarder at the Randolph County Jail for possession and manufacture of the "spirits".

During a hunting trip up Wolfe Run near Montes during the early 1970s the late Jim Rhodes pointed out to me and my doctor son where the manufacturing took place in a "laurel thicket," with rockcliff cover and good cold spring flow of pure mountain water. I understand a few of their most trusted clients were government officials sworn to prohibit, arrest and prosecute the manufacturers of "illegal spirits".

### Revelle

Lemuel Arbogast married Ellen Rexrode and they had thirteen children. Ellen's grandson, Ira Vance, a section gang foreman, ran over Ellen one night with a motorcar during her late years while she was walking the tracks. The Lemuel Arbogast home was on the river side of the railroad tracks as you pass Revelle.

# *L*ogging *O*perations

There was a shortage of ministers to perform wedding ceremonies. The young couples would "take up" housekeeping together and have a "sarvice" wedding ceremony under a Sarvis tree until the circuit rider could get there to legalize the marriage. If a child was born before the nine months and any derogatory comment was made about the young mother, both families defended her "integrity".

If a male classmate visited his male friend who had a sister or sisters in a four-room company house with two bedrooms (there was one bedroom for the parents and one bedroom for the children, with two beds – one for the boys and one for the girls), there was an unwritten "Code of Mountain Ethics" that male visitors stayed in the designated male bed and didn't cross the boundary line.

A mountain girl was taught right by her mother's guidance how to "make do with what she had" and if necessary, when she loved her man to move under a rock cliff and make a warm, soft nest for her husband and family and not complain.

Mountain women were very clean, saving, thrifty, loving, sharing, caring and family-oriented homemakers to the very best of their ability with what means they had. They prepared good "vittles," aimed to keep the place "red up" and prepared plenty to "et".

Lora Susan Arbogast Triplett was a most beautiful young lady. Pud Triplett's father, Jasper, wouldn't allow him to marry Susan because of Civil War grudges. Lora and "Pud's" three sons, Charlie, Ira and Harry (Charlie was born April 24, 1905) were born at Revelle at the Lemuel Arbogast home out of wedlock.

Charlie was never accepted by Jasper as his grandson for the same reasons he didn't want "Pud" to marry Lora. It is said some of the Arbogasts may have been members of the Northern Home Guard or "Swampers" that fatally wounded Oliver Triplett and

13

severely wounded Jasper in the Sinks of Gandy after the raid on Tucker County of the Union Army "pay train" while they were asleep by the campfire. Job Triplett, Oliver's father, hauled Oliver's body by horse and sled to Faulkner and buried his body in the Triplett Cemetery. Jasper carried the grudge to his grave. U.S. Rt. 33 construction caused the Triplett Cemetery to be moved to Maplewood Cemetery in Elkins.

"Pud" Triplett was a logging teamster. He was on Log Drives from Cheat Bridge to Point Marion, Pennsylvania, when Red Spruce logs were floated down Shavers Fork of Cheat River, prior to railroad construction, commencing at Cheat Bridge to Point Marion, PA. The logs were cut to float and drive to Point Marion with Spring thaws and ice jam breaks.

Gaylord Harris was the general woods superintendent for the logging operations for the log floating drives from Upper Cheat River Basin to Point Marion. Gale left Randolph County eventually, after the log drives to Point Marion, were losses and the company went "belly up". Gale never returned. He spent the remainder of his days in Abingdon, Virginia.

There were usually three wooden constructed log rafts in the log drive operation:
1. cook raft–housed the cook, dining room and food
2. horse raft–kept the horses, hay, oats and teamsters
3. sleeping raft–bunkhouse for the log drivers and river men

The Cheat River log drives lost too many logs and lives which caused the company to "go broke".

The "Moonshine" making and sale by mountain people only beat the government out of a little revenue. It stems from our "Celtic" culture that we don't like big government, neither control from Washington, DC, nor Charleston, WV. That holds true today by "mountain people".

Mountain people believe what is good for Washington, DC, inside the "Beltway Circle" and Charleston, WV, isn't necessarily

14

good for Randolph, Tucker, Pendleton and Pocahontas county residents. Remember the State Motto– "Mountaineers are always free". Mountain people, Celtic culture - *Don't want the outside law enforcement interference* or "meddling". They want to be left alone to mind their own affairs.

US Supreme Court Justice Tom Clark once told me, "We have enough laws on the books if they were enforced. Government operates on placing people in fear, and pass laws against something new before they learn much about it."

## *You Can't Legislate Morality*
## *A Must Be Taught and Practiced in the Home*

Mountain people don't believe in "warehousing people" in long term correctional or mental institutions unless completely necessary. They had and have their own communication system between themselves with one another by word of mouth. Respect must be earned from mountain Celtic people and can't be demanded.

Real mountain people were and are a proud group and have their own welfare system to look after one another and share among themselves. The successful mountain men leaders led by example. They were bold risk takers, but not reckless. They never asked another man to do a job they wouldn't do themselves.

## *Mountain People Never Give Up*

### *Woodrow*
This is a railroad siding and abandoned village on the old Coal and Iron Railroad (later Western Maryland) on the Shaver's Fork of Cheat River midway between Bowden and Flint. Two sawmills were operated here early in the century.

15

Woodrow had two lumber mills, C.T. Nelson and Company and Woodrow Lumber Company. The train stops for the first time and you observe trees in the bottom on the sidetrack toward the river, including apple trees. Fields now grown up were once cleared. Hay crops, gardens, potato patches and cornfields were harvested and farmed with horses.

Bob Hedrick and the Honorable Robert E. Maxwell were delegates to the 1960 National Democratic Convention held in Los Angeles, California and returned to Elkins with John F. Kennedy, whose plane landed in Elkins. Bob Hedrick was given the title "Judge Hedrick" at the convention.

Robert Hedrick, a deceased Elkins businessman, told me about Harness Kerns. Harness Kerns was a respected "moonshiner". The revenuers could never find his still. His wife lived on one end of the field and Harness lived on the other end. His wife would take shots when anyone came around there and everyone thought Harness and his wife were real enemies. She was thought to be a real mean, vicious, vindictive, ruthless mountain woman to be feared by all.

Harness furnished moonshine to government officials during "Prohibition". He is reputed to never have sold anything that he wouldn't drink. When the two houses were torn down, a basement was found under the wife's house where Harness made the "white lightning" at night, while the rest of the world was sleeping, under the vigilant watchful eye of his wife for any government revenue officers.

Harness always wore a wide-brim hat, red wool Ritchie coat, duck back pants and high-top shoes. His mustache was white and he was small in stature. He always peddled his moonshine on the Western Maryland passenger train from Woodrow to Elkins in burlap sacks. Harness was an election official and walked to Bemis to yell the opening of the polls to vote on every Election Day. I don't believe he was ever arrested or prosecuted. His son,

16

Doris, was a section gang foreman for the Western Maryland Railroad. Harness has descendents in Randolph County. Colonel Calhoun of the West Virginia State Police always tried to "bust" the Cheat River operations during the years of prohibition, but wasn't ever successful.

I am told that "look-outs" in Pendleton County around the "Smoke Hole" area used smoke signals from the top of the mountains to warn of the government revenue officers attempted intrusions.

## Montes

Montes, at the mouth of Wolfe Run, is owned by Arlie Arbogast, who has a camp in the bottom across Cheat River from Flint. A lumber mill was established here by D.D. and M.M. Brown in 1907 six miles south of Bowden on the Western Maryland Railroad. It was built on the east side of Shaver's Fork River opposite the WMRR railroad tracks and was connected to the railroad line by a bridge and a railroad spur.

## Flint and Walker

Flint and Walker was the start of the "sewell" underground coal mining operations. Howard Triplett, a railroad trainman, had an arm amputated at Flint in the early 1930s.

Jake Leary was an early radio mountain music entertainer, who with his family lived at Flint for a period of time. "Jake" is said to have been in the "spirits" manufacturing business. One of his daughters, Wilma Lee, a most beautiful mountain lady married a Dry Forker, Stoney Cooper and they became famous Grand Ole Opry entertainers in Nashville, Tennessee.

The Walkers from Pennsylvania started the coal business at Flint, Walker and Bemis. Mrs. Walker is said to have been the better business family member and carried on the coal business, after her husband's demise. She raised the family after her husband's death. I believe the Erickson Family in Elkins, Lobbs, Parsons, Sanders and Burnes families are related to the Walker Family.

Upper and Lower Pond Lick near Flint has native Brook Trout. Jim Rhodes was one of the best hunters to set foot on Cheat Mountain. He married Bethel Vance and knew lower Cheat Moun tain like the back of his hand. He had an Indian walk to travel up a mountain and down a mountain at the same pace without changing his stride or pace. No young man could ever keep up with Jim Rhodes in his late seventies. He lived at Glady, worked the coal mines and hunted all over Cheat Mountain. Jim and Bethel were married sixty-five years before their demise.

# *B*emis

It was formerly called Fishinghawk and is located at the mouth of Fishinghawk Creek on Shaver's Fork of Cheat River. It was named for J.M. Bemis who formed the Bemis Lumber Company in 1906 at the mouth of Fishinghawk Creek.

There were five lumber mills in Bemis: J.M. Bemis and Son, Coketon Lumber Company, John L. Rumbarger and Sons, Harry C. Bemis and Bemis Lumber Company. The train station was located on the north side of the railroad crossing. Bemis also had a two-year high school until about 1936. Walker Coal Company mined Sewell Coal. Billy Green also had coal mining operations near Bemis.

Joe Erickson and Carl Erickson, brothers of Swedish descent owned two general stores that were situate on opposite sides of the road at the Bemis railroad crossing. Many of their children were born at Bemis. One daughter was Sandra Erickson Sanders, wife of Tom Sanders. Lars Byrne, *Barbour Democrat*, Philippi, is another Walker descendent.

Adam Dahmer married Jewel Lantz, the daughter of Charlie Lantz. He operated a general store in Bemis in a two-story brick building. Charlie had several children including Beulah Lantz Dahmer, Fred, Henry, Charlie, Jr., Raymond, Blackie, Brad, Meggan Lantz Montoney, Rose Lantz Armentrout Ogden, grandmother of Mary Armentrout and mother of Harold "Goog" Ogden and Helen Ogden. The Bemis square dances were held at Dahmers or Bemis School.

Joe Shifflett, a "gandy dancer," had five sons, Ronald,

Maynard, Orville, Clarence and Calvin. They all played musical instruments for the square dances. Joe was a railroad section gang hand on the Bemis section.

Orville married a most beautiful lady from Glady, Nellie Phares, and always lived in Bemis. Orville commuted weekly to Baltimore to work after his US Navy WWII service and on *USS Yorktown* aircraft carrier in South Pacific and raised his family in Bemis. Two of Orville's daughters are Lynn Pugh and Roxanne Webley; both work in Elkins.

The Tool House is located on the mountain side of the railroad. Hub Bodkins was the Bemis section gang foreman. He has two sons, "Leslie" and "Punk," who are retired from the Western Maryland Railroad.

The Bemis Section extended to Cheat Junction. There are a few company houses remaining that were two stories, consisting of a kitchen, living room and two bedrooms. One bedroom was for the kids and one was for the parents. The bath had a path and "Sears and Roebuck," "Montgomery Ward," "Speigels Catalogs" or Saturday *Evening Post*, *Life* magazine or, even occasionally, store-bought toilet paper. Jack Adams, son of Kenny Adams, owns houses across the tracks on the Fishinghawk side of the railroad.

There was a two-room school at Bemis, which still stands. The schoolteachers were usually the most important and respected persons in Bemis. Schoolteachers were the only college book learned people on the mountain and river basin. Mountain people believe in book learning. They realized education is accumulated experience and you learn something from every job you perform and person you meet, if you are interested in learning.

There was one church in Bemis. Bemis residents were hard working, beer drinking, fun loving, caring people, who made their own entertainment.

Electricity came to Bemis about 1949. Bemis is two miles from Glady across Shavers Mountain. The Shavers Mountain Trail which starts at Guardineer Fire Tower and follows the top of Shavers Mountain, and ends on top of Tunnel Mountain above Glady is sixteen miles long. Early Bemis families included: Ericksons, Shiffletts, Simmons, Whites, Adams, Taylors, Lobbs, Thompsons, Hedricks, Bodkins, Dahmers, Cravens, Walkers, Rhodes, Davis, Nelsons, Whites, Vances and Adams, among many others.

There were not enough beautiful women to go around. Usually, there were Saturday night fights but no criminal charges were filed or prosecuted–victims took their whippings, went home and healed up for the next "weekend toot". Often the fights started at school between kids on Friday and carried through to the weekends, even between brothers, uncles, parents and grandparents.

Calvin's Place is the poor man's Elk's Club of Randolph County. During the early 1970s, a couple young state police officers visited Calvin's Place, which should have been off limits to law enforcement. Dick Cave could throw his voice across the room. So, Dick, by throwing his voice, made comments about the "Boy Scouts" in their pretty uniforms and big hats, which aroused the curiosity of the young police officers. One of the officers put his hands on a quiet mountain man, who "cleaned their plow," took their pistols and hats and sent them packing to Elkins. This caused all law enforcement in several counties to return to Calvin's Place and arrest all occupants and lodge them in the Randolph County Jail. I was the Randolph County Circuit Judge and was out of town at the time. When I returned there was a call from Calvin to me from the Randolph County Jail. Upon visiting the Randolph County Jail filled with Bemis and Glady residents, I quickly understood that Dick Cave, a relative and childhood friend had been responsible. Calvin later told me Dick was stuffed in a garbage can with his cap pulled over his eyes, helpless during the real "knock-down-drag-out" free-for-all between Calvin's customers and law enforcement.

Court was convened with the sheriff, Prosecuting Attorney

James Cain and Jack Nuzum, defense lawyer. I dismissed the charges against Calvin and the Glady-Bemis residents. A court direction was made to law enforcement to clean up the illegal slot machines and illegal sale of whiskey at the Elks Club in Elkins before they would press charges against Calvin Shifflett and "Poor Man's Elk Club" members at Bemis. David Fletcher negotiated the return of the officer's hats and pistols from Calvin without further difficulty. Calvin continuos to operate and is postmaster at Glady.

"There was a railroad junction two miles south of Bemis, which separated the two branches of the Western Maryland Railroad as they extended to Durbin in Pocahontas County and to Webster Springs in Webster County." On September 27, 1910, the railroad that would become the most famous logging railroad in the East was formed. The Greenbrier, Cheat and Elk River Railroad Company was formed to commence near Bemis to a point near Webster Springs. The authorized capital to fund the project was $50,000. Charlie Cromer, an engineer, took Shay #3 over the C&O and Western Maryland to Cheat Junction in 1917 and construction was started to meet the line being built down Cheat River from the South.

Ola Rhodes harvested a six hundred pound black bear about 1946 between Cheat Junction and High Falls. The Airedale and Black and Tan hounds Cross Breed was Ola Rhodes' special breed of bear dogs for Cheat Mountain bear hunting. His sons, Lloyd, Jim and Clellan didn't need bear dogs to harvest their bear usually every fall season. Ola had several wives and fathered twenty-seven children.

Jim married Bethel Vance, one of Ira Vance's eighteen children and my cousin, through the Tripletts, Vances and Arbogast ancestry. A visitor never left Bethel Rhodes' home hungry and she was one of the county's best cooks and homemakers.

Evelyn Bell Davis was born to Elmer and Willa Davis at Cheat

Junction and delivered by a Dr. Miller from Bemis. Elmer was a track walker and sometimes rode a "Speeder" or walked to inspect the railroad tracks for safe passage for trains over the treacherous mountain railroad.

As a young man I ran behind the bear dogs up and down the mountains through laurel thickets in addition to working in the log woods with a double-bitted ax and crosscut saw, which made me tough as a "pine knot" for college football by fall. The lyrics to the song "Life's Railroad" are so true and were my Uncle Ira Triplett's favorites so appropriate as you travel from Cheat Junction to Spruce over the GC&E (Greenbrier, Cheat and Elk Branch). It was sung at Uncle Ira's funeral service and many Cheat River Basin railroad worker's funerals, who most always want to be buried in the family plot. They were even to be returned from sister states for mountain burial.

## Life's Railroad

Life is like a mountain railroad with an engineer that's brave
You must make the run successful from the cradle to the grave
Watch the curves, the fills, the tunnels, never falter, never fail
Keep your hand upon the throttle and your eyes upon the rail.

Chorus:

Blessed Savior Thou will guide us
Till we reach that blissful shore
Where the angels wait to join us
In Thy praise forever more

You will roll up grades of trial, you will cross the bridge of strife
See that Christ is your conductor on this lightning train of life
Always mindful of obstructions do your duty, never fail

23

Keep your hand upon the throttle and your eye upon the rail

Chorus. . .

As you roll across the trestle spanning Jordan's swelling tide
You behold the Union Depot into which your train will glide
There you'll meet the Superintendent God the Father, God the Son
With a hearty joyous greeting "Weary Pilgrim welcome home"

Chorus. . .

## The Point

From Cheat Junction to High Falls, the canyon is very deep and has cost the lives of many men, both from timbering and working on and for the railroads. The stream was called Wilmoth's River for a number of years in the early history of the county for the reason that the Wilmoth's were the first settlers on its banks.

The normal Western Maryland train crew consisted of the engine men engineer (operator), fireman (shoveled the coal, greased and oiled locomotive), flagman (watched for oncoming or following trains when stopped), conductor (in charge of the train), brakeman (usually the newest or youngest member of the crew). It was the brakeman's job to walk the tops of the moving freight cars loaded with coal, timber or logs to set the "Detainers" or brakes. At night he would perform his duties while holding a kerosene lantern. This was a very dangerous job especially during the cold, icy, snowy, sub-zero weather conditions.

I remember as a small boy at Cheat Bridge, seeing the ambulance from F. E. Runner Funeral Home, Elkins, WV, or Wallace and Wallace, Lewisburg, WV, pickup and load the fatally or severely mangled bodies from the train. Dan Poe, a Western Maryland flagman, who was a kind gentleman, met his fate as a flagman before dawn on a coal train en-route from Spruce to Elkins during the early 1940s. Walking the frozen coal cars he was fatally thrown from the fast moving train. A severly injured victim was Sam Waugh, an engineer who was thrown from the cab of a 700 Steam Engine above Cheat Bridge above Mile Post 28 and below the Water Tank at Cabin Fork and lower Hopkins Siding River Trestle. He survived the injury.

There were several log camps situated along the railroad by West Virginia Pulp & Paper Company that transported logs from High Falls to the Cass Mill by way of Spruce. There was a pulpwood peeling mill at Spruce during the early 1900s. A passenger on the train will observe the mountain laurel, steep hillsides, deep canyon and heavy water. The only transportation was by walking, riding a motorcar, speeder or handcar.

## Glady

Geneva Harris Triplett was born on June 12, 1912. She married Charlie Robert Triplett on September 12, 1929, and moved to Triplett. Raphael "Raph" Simeon Harris was her father and Lena Bowers Harris was the mother of Geneva and operated the R.S. Harris General Store, saloon and cattle farm. "Raph" supplied the log camps, coal mines and railroad camps with groceries, dry goods and all necessities. Most deliveries were by railroad transportation.

This once active lumber town flourished on Glady Fork River some nine miles south of U.S. Route 33 from 1901 to 1911 with the operation of Glady Fork Lumber Company, The McClure, Tyson and Irwin Company, and the nearby Wheeler Lumber Company. Glady had nine lumber mills: Wheeler Lumber Company, McClure, Tyson and Irvin, Glady Fork Lumber Company,

Glady Manufacturing Company, McMillan Lumber Company, Chaffey Lumber Company, J. Roy Lilly, Lewis Brothers and Campbell Brothers. The Glady Railroad Tunnel of the Western Maryland Railroad and a natural gas compressor station are nearby. Glady large sawmill burned to the ground.

Early settlers were the Harris, Thompsons, Phares, Arbogasts, Strawders, Bonnells, Kerns, Rhodes, Lantz, Rennix, Montoney, Spears, Armentrouts, Gatowoods, Buzzells, Stewarts, Bowers, Hedricks, Davis, Shiffletts, Bennetts, Whitecottons, Caves, Taylors, Spears, Tinglers, Louks, Vance, Summerfields, Cosners, Linkenfelters, Nelsons, Whites, Sponaugles, Teters, Mallows, Kettermans, Flints, Chaffeys and many others.

Cheat Mountain and Cheat River Basin girls were never overweight because they had to walk and work. There were no vehicles.

## *It Is Better to Try and Fail– Than Not Try at All!*

Charlie Triplett was promoted to section gang foreman in 1927 at "Triplett" on the GC & E when the Western Maryland took over. He was in charge of the section from Cheat Junction to near Helmick. He had a model "T" Ford and got the name "Zip" because he zipped through Glady and won the privilege of marrying Geneva Harris at age seventeen and moved her to Triplett. "Raph," in granting Charlie the right to marry his daughter, who was seven years younger than Charlie, said, "Take her for life and never mistreat Geneva." Charlie honored "Raph's" request until his death of a heart attack on a cold day in January 1970, when he died with his rubber boots on in the barn lot with his pony hooked up to a sled. A few days before his death Charlie expressed to me while I was shoveling snow in Triplett Hollow for him early one morning, "Bud, I always wanted to make this world a little better place to live in during my life, but I don't think I have. My only

26

fear of death is the kind of world I'm leaving my grandsons to grow up in."

Mary Armentrout, who is a hostess on the Tygart Flyer Special Train, is the daughter of Bill Armentrout and Goldie Bodkins Armentrout. Mary Armentrout was born on January 5, 1942, and is the granddaughter of Rose Lantz Armentrout Ogden and granddaughter of Charlie Lantz. Bill and Goldie Armentrout lived on Jay Montoney's farm between Glady and Beulah.

Rose Lantz Armentrout Ogden was postmistress and picked up and dropped off the US Mail to the passenger train at Glady Station. The store merchants' supplies were transported by railroad and unloaded at Glady Station.

As a young boy, I didn't quite understand the "swapping" and "bartering" between Bill and Uncle Doc Harris at the R.S. Harris Store in Glady. During the cold winter and heavy snows, Bill and Goldie would drive their unheated, four-wheel drive, canvas-covered Jeep from Jay Montoney's farm to Harris' Store in Glady. Mary was always dressed in a pink sweater set and wrapped in clean pink blankets. Mary's father Bill was said to have been the manufacturer of "spirits" that were good enough for the governor of West Virginia and which were furnished quietly to the governor's mansion on special occasions. I hear tell Bill's recipe may still be known.

When Beverly was the Randolph County seat, during one hot summer month, circuit court was recessed from the hot courtroom in Beverly and moved to the banks of Cheat at High Falls for circuit court of Randolph County to carry on the circuit court proceedings and business of the court. High Falls is the end of the Tygart Valley Special from Elkins and also the lower end ride for the Cheat Bridge "Salamander".

27

# Harper

Early historians debate the Shawnee and Seneca Indian Trail over Cheat Mountain - Cheat River to Beverly. One of the passages is said to have been the Harper Trail near Harper Water Tank and sidetrack across Fishing Hawk and Files Creek to Beverly.

Big John Mine was operated to mine Sewell coal by hand and horse-drawn mine cars. The Sewell coal was 3'6" thick and was across the river at an elevation of 3,210 feet. It closed because of "black damp" (poor ventilation) and a bad roof that caused death to miners. Several Italian immigrants worked at Big John Mine. I don't know if Jimmy Dean got the lyrics for Big Bad John from the Big John Mine on Shavers Fork, Cheat River, but it was most appropriate for timbering operations. It has a most applicable description for the early coal mine camp living and operations on the Cheat River Basin. The coalmines added to the traffic on the Cheat River Division. Other coalmines included, Clubhouse Mine, Whitemeadow, Lennan #1, Lennan #2, Deer Lick Mine and Farm Mine.

Walter Fansler, Owen Fansler's son and a brakeman for the railroad, was 1.3 miles from Bemis and the Campbell Creek seam walking the coal cars near Big John Mine when he was killed from falling from the moving coal car. Another brakeman, Winemiller, was killed at Greenbrier Junction. "Braking" was, by far, the most dangerous job on the entire operation. On December 18, 1923, another young brakeman, Frank Harris, was killed while making a coupling at the "square turn". He was caught between the engine and a car and squeezed to death. His father, Gerald "Buck" Harris, brother to Raphael Simeon Harris, was conductor on the same train. Frank was the grandson of Barnabus and Mary Crockett Kissinger Harris.

H.M. "Harl or Big Cub" Coberly stood about 6 feet 5 inches

and weighed about 260 pounds and spoke in such a low soft kind tone that all subordinates minded his demands without delay to please "Big Cub". "Big Cub" Coberly was promoted and transferred to Cumberland Maryland Junction, Maryland and took Charlie Triplett with him as a section gang hand. Charlie had two younger brothers, Ira William and Harry Jasper, to help support as well as his mother Lora Arbogast Triplett. Charlie caught typhoid fever in Maryland from swimming in the Potomac River and almost died.

Charlie earned the respect for his intellectual and leadership abilities from H.M. Coberly (father of Winifred, Herbert and Arward Coberly). When H.M. Coberly was appointed supervisor about 1927 by the Western Maryland Railroad from Elkins to Spruce and Durbin, "Cub" made Charlie Triplett the section gang foreman for the "Camp One," afterward named "Triplett" Section on the Western Maryland GC&E branch of the railroad. Charlie had about fifteen section gang hands and lived in primitive conditions. A three-room, tarpaper roof wood frame, uninsulated company house, with neither running water nor electricity, and a "path with a bath".

The railroad had to be prepared to transport heavy coal trains from the coal fields on Cheat and Elk river near Wester Springs through Elkins, Cumberland to Sparrow Point, Baltimore, Maryland, for both steel mills and foreign exportation of coal. Charlie accepted the challenge to improve the mountain industrial railroad to carry the coal trains.

On September 12, 1929, Charlie married his seventeen-year-old bride, Geneva Harris, "Queen of Willdell and Beulah 1928" and moved her to "Camp One," now "Triplett". Charlie achieved the challenge with Geneva's support and in 1934 received the promotion to section gang foreman at Cheat Bridge. Cheat Bridge had a public road, the "Staunton-Parkersburg Turnpike," currently US 250, where the "Salamander" operates downstream to both High Falls and upstream to Cheat Summit above Spruce.

## ℭ𝒪ugh 𝒪imes 𝒟on't 𝒮ast–ℭ𝒪ugh 𝒪eople 𝒟o

"Triplett" was the "starting," "boot camp" or "proving" ground for all new "gandy dancers" (section gang trackmen) and new section gang foremen until the modernization and consolidation of the Western Maryland Railroad with the Chessie System. The Western Maryland changed after WWII with the transition from Gene Williams, a West Virginian, as president to Arthur Grotz about the time that "Piggyback" freight transportation started. "Piggyback" were loaded trailers transported on flat railroad cars across country by train before the modern interstate highway system was started. They were unloaded and pulled by tractor to deliver the cargo's final destination. It was also the start of part-time employment for the "gandy dancers" section gang hands. Railroad management considered railroad track repair seasonal and started annual lay-offs during the winter months.

Probably, the only surviving Western Maryland "gandy dancers" or "section gang" men from "Triplett" are Lonnie Shifflett, "Punk" Bodkins, Leslie Bodkins, Charles "Red" Rhodes, Herman "Peck" Vance, Raymond Teter, Jack Adams, Earl Rhodes, Earl Bonnell and Bob Phares. Delbert Strawder, "Flick" Strawder, Jim Rhodes, Rich Nelson, Paul Nelson, Paul Hevener, Raymond Rhodes, Tom Thompson, Jim Harris and many more have passed away.

Elmer Davis, a trackwalker at Spruce and Cheat junction, was appointed section gang foreman at "Triplett" when Charlie Triplett was promoted to Cheat Bridge. Many other section foremen followed before the sections were consolidated under Arthur Groat. ( A trackwalker walked or rode a "Speeder" to check the railroad tracks ahead of freight trains to make sure the tracks were safe for the trains to travel).

One of Elmer's daughters, Anna Mae Davis Harris, a beautiful young, loving, chestnut red-haired, intelligent school teacher at Glady's two-room school married my uncle Ralph "Doc" Harris, a World War II veteran, after he returned from combat in the Pacific. "Doc" farmed and operated the family business at Glady. "Doc" Harris was a member of the May 12, 1942, largest group of Randolph County men inducted and accepted for combat from Elkins. "Doc" Harris didn't return from the Pacific until Japan surrendered in 1945 and the war was officially over.

"Doc" Harris had the reputation of a real trader. "Doc" could take a nickel and turn it into five dollars overnight. That has always been a "Celtic trait" to barter and trade. "An askin'" price and a "takin'" price.

From 1910–1960s the Raphael Harris Family operated a general mercantile business, saloon, farmed and lived in Glady. Their store, had storage buildings attached, included a large feed room, meat room, grocery, storage, retail store room, large glass cases, wooden counters on both sides of the retail area, a large pot-bellied stove, wooden-covered tobacco storage box, McCasky Register (to store charge accounts), cash register and a front porch possibly seventy feet long with wooden benches where the coal miners, railroad workers, logging and mill workers would congregate for their "toots".

Most every young boy in the Cheat River Basin carried a "Barlow" pocketknife purchased for him at one of the company stores. Most every mountain boy didn't feel "dressed" unless he had his pocketknife in his pocket.

### Helmick

Helmick is situate above Mile Post 12 (now 60.2). In the fall of 1954 there was a flash flood "gully-washer" Labor Day weekend after Charlie had allowed his entire crew to leave Cheat Mountain for their "holiday toot" or "doin's". I was home from college for

31

the weekend and we both worked tirelessly through the night by keeping the tracks clear of rocks and trees for four coal trains to travel through a mountain hill slide.

Several weeks later, I observed Charlie a "little put out" during a home visit from college. Charlie advised that a worker had "time carded" him for helping to get the train over the tracks during the flash flood through the Maintenance Way Brotherhood Union of Trackmen, Charlie told me, "Unions have been a great thing for the working man, but they may be going too far, which will eventually cause machinery to take over the working spots for men." No truer words were spoken concerning the mountains' complete transition the last fifty years. Charlie always taught, "You must give an employer a better day's work than you receive in pay or he can't afford to keep you working and stay in business."

Helmick is also a very good trout fishing area.

## McGee Run

Thanksgiving Day 1951 Glen Hamner had a group of bear hunters. I was a young fifteen-year old Green Bank High School student when we bagged a black bear in a hole. Bruno, a small shepherd-plot hound cross-breed dog, about one year old, found the bear holed up in a laurel thicket. When the bear was harvested, several of the hunters crawled through the laurel thicket and helped drag the bear out and carry it to the Cheat Mountain Road, US Government Road, at the head of Yokum Run. The McGee Run Laurel Thicket is a good place to find black bears in the fall season, if there are beechnuts and wild cherries.

## My Dog Slim

During the bear season of 1952 there was a twelve-month-old Norwegian - Airedale male, named "Slim," who chased a black bear, shot by Clyde Dotson of Doddridge County. Clyde got lost overnight after the bear kill. I was a Green Bank High School student and football player and stayed out all night hunting for Dotson. We found him the next morning. The high school principal, Virgil B. Harris, drove from Green Bank to Cheat Bridge to find me to play in the Friday afternoon football game. Mr. Harris related to Geneva, my mother, that I had ability and was wasting talent. Mr. Harris saw to it that I finished high school, played football and kept me overnight in his home when the weather was unsafe for me to travel from Green Bank to Cheat Bridge. Mr. Harris directed the faculty to deduct three percent for each day missed from my semester grades. Teachers didn't pay much attention and didn't deduct grades, as I had a decent average in the graduating class of 1953 at Green Bank High School.

After I left home to attend college, Slim always seemed to have the intuition that I was coming home for a visit and would liven up. Slim would go out on his own and harvest racoons near Cheat Bridge. Slim died of "coon dog fever" after being bitten by a raccoon.

## If You Dream It –You Can Achieve It

Bill Thompson was a high-profile West Virginia trial lawyer who served on the West Virginia University Board of Trustees in Morgantown, WV, and lived at Charlton Heights, Fayette County, near Montgomery, WV. Thompson accompanied several politicians to Helmick-McGee Run for a trout fishing vacation during the spring of 1940. I had a birch-cut fishing pole with a black line tied to the top and a #6 shank hook attached. Bill Thompson asked me what kind of rod, reel and fishing line I wanted. I replied that I wanted a line that didn't knot and tangle. I also told him I wanted a pole to fish rivers and creeks, meaning a steel telescope rod. Thompson responded that this was an intelligent answer and request. Thompson returned to Cheat Bridge a short time later with a telescope steel rod fishing pole, reel and fishing line for me. Thompson's kindness, generosity, friendly, caring, sincere personality caused me to always have a high opinion of lawyers because he was smart, well dressed, handsome, spoke well, drove a fine car, had a beautiful wife and could afford most everything he wanted. Bill Thompson was the kind of man, as a five-year old mountain boy, I wanted to grow up to be. Sheriff Jeff Whetsell, Virgil Hamrick, John Caplinger and others accompanied Bill Thompson on the 1940 fishing trip.

There was one seven-inch Rainbow Trout caught all week in the spring of 1940 before the outbreak of World War II across from McGee Run in the bottom of a "Laurel Thicket" of a very stiff guard railed curve.

I wrote a letter when I wanted to attend law school to a Judge Bill Thompson, Charleston, West Virginia. I was disappointed when I didn't get a response. However, I didn't realize my childhood idol was "Bill Thompson" from Montgomery, Fayette County. I saw Bill Thompson after I graduated from law school in 1962 and a few months before he died. He was a most distinguished man, with white wavy hair, a smoking jacket, black naugahide leather furniture in his study, black walnut beams, with all-wood interior finish, situate Charlton Heights just above Montgomery on the banks of Kanawha River. Bill was the same kind of man that I visualized during my young years.

As I talked to Bill Thompson in his home and related to him that he inspired me by his trip and gifts– "I knew that my goal to be a lawyer" was set on Cheat River in 1940 at the age of five years wasn't a mistake. I have, since childhood, heard there are too many lawyers and they're all starving to death. I have neither seen nor heard of a lawyer who actually starved to death. However, the successful practice of law requires dedication, hard work, "stick-to-itness" and the desire to serve your clients and appreciate the need for you to help solve their legal problems.

Mountain men practiced that you never ask a man to do a job you can't or wouldn't do yourself. That is why the various bosses and supervisors were such great leaders. They set the examples to follow.

## Lennan Mines (aka Lanan and Lanain)

There have been several different attempted coal-mining operations for Lennan Mines, but non were really highly productive.

Charlie Pyles operated Lennan Mines during WWII and Lloyd Rhodes operated the boardinghouse. Lloyd was like a "cat with nine lives," a real survivor and excellent hunter. His sister, Margie, who is still living, quit school and worked in the boardinghouse at Lennan Mines. There was a coal tipple, a bridge constructed across the river and two or three sidetracks to load the coal. The last operation for Lennan Mines was during the 1970s energy shortage when there was a high demand for coal.

## Lennan Section Camp

Glen Heflin was the first section gang foreman at Lennan Section Camp. He married Alice Jones from Glady. Alice was Tilberry Jones' sister. Judge Robert E. Maxwell now owns the Jones farm near Glady. Tilberry was quite a bear hunter. Glen Heflin later became section gang foreman at Slaty Fork or "Laurel Bank".

There were two houses that were twenty-four feet by twenty-four feet with kitchen, living room and two bedrooms (one for the parents and one for the children). There were also three railroad passenger cars with the wheels removed and mounted on a foundation, which provided housing for "gandy dancers" or section gang hands and their families at Lennan. The women would put blinds, pasteboard boxes or newspapers over the passenger car windows for privacy and raise their families. They also carried water from a mountain spring.

Lennan Section Gang Hands included, Orval Swecker, "Jack Hammer" Johnston, "Ground Hog" White, Jack Adams, "Punk" Bodkins, Phillip "Cowboy" Thorpe, Ernie Essex and Ira Vance, Jr., Dora Powers, John Hiner, Jesse Arbogast, Bernard Shifflett and Orville Shifflett, among many others.

There was a severe drought during 1931 that caused a mountain fire during the fall of 1931 that lasted until the spring of 1932. The Cheat Mountain section gang fought the fire in Lennan and Twin Bridges at Spruce instead of doing railroad track maintenance on the Shavers Mountain side of the railroad. The fire was caused by sparks from a steam locomotive. There was also a powered "weed burner" used during the summer months to burn the weeds and small vegetation growing on the railroad right of way that often caused "brush fires" that the section hands would have to fight. That always created excitement on the mountain.

Other Lennan section gang foremen were: Raymond Shelton, Lonnis "Pip" Fansler, Elmer Davis, Carl Kerns, Ike Vance, Doris Kerns and Delbert Strawder.

## Crouch Run

Crouch Run is across the river above Lennan and continues to hold Brook Trout.

## There Are No Secrets in Life

One very loud, cussin', yellin' logging teamster was Pat Tharpe. Pat lived at Beverly and his son Delmer was his grab driver. They

36

were working for "Bernie Walkup," a contract logger on the mountain near the Crouch Run and Whitemeadows area river face, the summer of 1954. I was driving grabs for Buck Barlow from the Summersville, West Virginia area. Buck and Pat had two different personalities. You could hear Pat a "cussin' and hollerin'" from the time he started with his load of logs all the way to the log landing. His son, Delmer, never followed Pat to the landing which was one of Delmer's designated job responsibilities.

One day it was rainy, wet and slick. I was "skipping the J-grabs" (removing them from the logs) at the landing with Buck Barlow. Pat was coming down the mountain as usual cussin' and hollerin' profanities at his team of horses. All of a sudden a couple hundred yards up the mountain on the skid trail Pat "screamed a death note". Buck and I ran to the site and found Pat Tharpe with both of his legs penned under a three feet in diameter Hemlock front log about a foot from a very large sandstone rock. Pat was squealing with pain. Fortunately, Pat's team "jayed off" and unhooked from the large Hemlock front log just before his legs would have been amputated from the pressure between the sandstone rock and the load of logs. I pulled Pat from under the Hemlock log after Buck hooked up the team to pull the log off of him. Pat finished the rest of the day a "little skittish." He didn't do a whole lot of "cussin' and hollerin'" at the horses for the remainder of that particular day.

Pat never forgot the "close call". FBI Agent Lenny Conley learned of the incident when I was being investigated to serve as an Assistant United States Attorney in the Northern District of West Virginia by appointment of the late Robert F. Kennedy, United States attorney general.

Cutting skid trails was a necessary procedure to skid the logs by horse. It was called "swamping". "Swamping" required a two-man crew each with a double-bitted ax. Arthur Townsend, who "swamped" all his life was about one hundred pounds soaking wet and could work any young man into the ground well into his seventies. Arthur died probably in his eighties.

On one occasion Arthur put Carl Tacy, former Marshall University and Wake Forest University basketball coach, and me down in about two hours, when we started out fast. Arthur was still moving at his same pace at 4:30 p.m., when Carl and I, who were college athletes, were worn out.

"Bernie" Walkup, an independent logger for Mower Lumber Company, had the contract to cut the "river face" of Crouch Run from 1954 through 1956. Crosscut saws and doubled-bitted axes were the tools used to prepare the logs that were pulled with two teams of draft horses. The teamsters were Pat Tharpe and "Buck" Barlow.

Some of the early log camp cooks below Cheat Bridge were John Kane (father of "Red" Kane and grandfather of Mark Kane, Durbin businessmen), Henry Cole, Lonnie Sager, Roy Griffith and many more. Each camp kept several teams of draft or work-horses. Possibly four to ten teams of horses, depending on the size of the log camp. Each team consisted of two horses with a teamster who drove the team, plus a "grab driver/skipper". The grab driver had a "grab maul" hammer on one side and a tool to remove the "J-grab" from the log. The grab hook made of heavy steel would be driven into the front end of the log and a short link chain on swivels would be driven in the side of the log. Another grab would then be driven into the front of a second log, and the procedure repeated until there were six to eight logs hooked to the team of horses, to pull the load of logs to the log landing to be loaded either by hand or a log loader on flat railroads cars to be transported to the Cass or Spruce mills.

I don't recall seeing Pat Tharpe without a chew of snuff. The evidence was brown coloring on both sides of his mouth.

The horse teamsters tended to their team of horses morning, noon and night. They fed and watered them, curried, brushed and combed their coats, covered them with horse blankets and doctored each of the horse's ailments. They saw to it they had proper fitting horseshoes and that no rocks or gravels were between their hooves and horseshoes to lame the horses. Horse teamsters were a most proud and necessary make-up of early logging and timbering operations.

Gordon Posten, a horse trader in Barbour County, sold many horses for the Cheat and Shavers mountains, upper Shavers Fork of Cheat River log woods work. He had a three-story barn at the current site of the Barbour County Fairgrounds that can be seen from US Rt. 250.

I accompanied my Dad, Charlie Triplett, Russell White, Parker Gragg and son Jack Gragg, Herman Greathouse, Arthur Cromer, Ralph "Doc" Harris, Emory "Red" Thompson, McClure Thompson, Bill Armentrout and Jay Montoney on weekends to trade or barter with Gordon Posten. It was entertainment in the late 1930s.

"Pratt Wye" - Glade Run - John's Run Area is approximately one mile upstream from Lennan where there was a Wye and sidetracks to turn 700 series steam locomotives. Sometimes there were 700 steam locomotives that would assist the steam-powered loaded freight trains up the mountain and stop at Pratt Wye and possibly return to Elkins or Bowden to wait to push the next loaded freight train up to Cheat Tunnel toward Elkins or return to Pratt Wye.

There were five "Wyes" from Elkins, at Bowden, Cheat Junction, Pratt, Cheat Bridge and Spruce. The "Y" shape allowed the locomotives to turn around from one direction to another on the tracks. There were also coal-mining operations on Shavers Mountain up John's Run during the Energy Crisis in the 1970s.

The Shavers Mountain Trail from Guadineer Fire Tower that ends on top of Glady Tunnel has a side Trail to Pratt Wye. Merle Rexrode, Jim Vandevander and myself mowed the Shavers Mountain Trail, which is sixteen miles long, for the US Division of Forestry the summer of 1953.

Mower Lumber Company had coal mining operations on John's Run during the 1970s energy crisis that were supervised by Ralph McDonald. Mower Lumber Company was indicted for "mine pollution". However, the criminal charges were dismissed when it was established that trout survived in the water one hundred yards from the spot that the state of West Virginia claimed the pollution occurred. The water continues to be monitored for improper drainage by government regulations.

## Mile Post 21 - Red Run

Below Red Run was the Lennan-Cheat Bridge Railroad section gang division of responsibility. There is a sharp guardrail curve as you approach the Red Run laurel and pine thicket bottoms. There was an extra rail and "ante creepers," small steel structures attached to the bottoms of the steel railroad rail to prevent the rail from moving when trains traveled around the sharp curve at old Mile Post 22.

Both extremely cold weather and hot weather caused the sharp curve to have problems. During the summer, the steel rails would expand and cause "sun kinks" that caused railroad cars to "derail" or wreck. That is the reason "ante creepers" were used and there were guardrail curves. There was a third inside rail to keep the rail cars on the tracks.

The Red Run Mine is across the river and 1 1/2 miles below Cheat Bridge at an elevation of 3,565 feet. Red Run contained a six foot total seam of Sewell coal, however, much of it was slaty. The mine was abandoned because of the low quality of coal.

Charlie gave me the nickname "Buddy" when I was born and that has stayed with me all my life among Mountain Celtic people. We were real buddies, as were most mountain fathers and sons. We worked together to survive.

I caught my first trout on the steel rod fishing pole given to me

40

by Bill Thompson in 1941, which was a nine in a half inch native Brook Trout a the mouth of the creek at the "Big Hole". The bait was a Cheat Mountain fish worm dug from Cromer's barnyard with a "grubbin' hoe". Charlie told me to wait for "three jerks" on the line before "you pull hard to set the hook". Charlie couldn't believe I was pulling a trout out of the water when he was still baiting his own hook. The ice jams on Cheat River were always most memorable and kept you awake at night with the flooding, crashing ice and high water during the spring thaws.

Charlie purchased me, at fourteen years old, a 12-gauge J.C. Higgins shotgun, three-shot bolt action with the front site missing. The wooden forearm was split and Charlie taped it. It had a loose slide safety on the right side of the barrel above the trigger that would release "to fire" going through a laurel thicket and cause it to discharge. The unsafe shotgun taught me early in life that no gun, loaded or unloaded, is safe and to treat any gun as "loaded and ready to discharge and kill". Norman Vance, a few years ago, let me have the shotgun back with the same tape Charlie wrapped around the cracked wooden stock about fifty-five years ago.

My mother Geneva, on one occasion had a wrap-around black line bamboo fishing pole. Geneva with chub tail bait caught a fourteen-inch Rainbow Trout in the deep riffles below the "Big Hole".

It's not uncommon to observe black bears crossing from the thickets on the railroad side of the "Big Hole" from the Guadineer Fire Tower area to White Top, Fort Milroy, which was General Robert Milroy's primary Cheat Mountain defensive position along the Staunton and Parkersburg Turnpike during the War Between the States, served to prevent the Confederate forces from entering the Tygart's Valley early in the war.

The Staunton-Parkersburg Turnpike was completed in 1845 from Richmond, Virginia, to Weston. Lemuel Chenoweth designed and constructed many of the wooden-covered bridges. After the road was completed, a number of taverns were built along the road, among them being Barton's Tavern at the foot of Cheat Mountain.

The Staunton-Parkersburg Turnpike, in a way, followed the old Indian Trails and is especially true of the section from Tygart River to the Greenbrier River. The road practically followed the old trail, and as early as 1805, this trail was used until 1824 when Randolph County built a good road to the Pocahontas County line.

The present U.S. 250 was rebuilt during the early 1930s. It replaced the original Staunton-Parkersburg Turnpike and "prior original" 1880s wooden-covered Cheat Bridge at Cheat Bridge where people board the "Salamander". The railroad crosses US 250 just below Cromer and downstream from Cheat Bridge near where US 250 crosses Shaver's Fork.

Cheat Summit "Fort Milroy" was a key fortification during the Civil War between General Robert E. Lee and General George McClellan. Union forces brought with them a small circular steam-powered saw; the first steam sawmill to operate in the Red Spruce forest of West Virginia.

### Winchester

The W.S. Dewing & Sons of Ashton, Michigan attempted to float logs down the Shaver's Fork River from a site near Cheat Bridge. A post office operated here for a short period during the 1880s. Between 1888 and 1896, Colonel Arthur H. Winchester built the "Cromer Swiss Chalet Home" and was in charge of cutting the timber and driving it to Point Marion, Pennsylvania.

# Cheat Bridge –
## A Million Dollar Childhood

Cheat Bridge had a post office and Sue Cromer was postmistress with a small store, service station (AMOCO), which was operated by a hand pump, with the gallon gauge at the glass top. There was mail service twice a day by Snowden Tracey who drove a 1934 Chevrolet car. Snowden would deliver not only the mail, but also supplies, medicines or small items for Cheat Bridge residents from Durbin.

Durbin had passenger train service from Ronceverte by the Chesapeake & Ohio Railroad (C&O RR) and Cumberland by way of Elkins to Durbin six days a week, which carried the US Mail and light freight on a separate car.

Two houses in the Cheat Bridge Community had "indoor" bathrooms and all the Western Maryland Company houses had running water. All Company houses were one-story and had three to four rooms.

The Cheat Bridge residents and families made their own entertainment, including: music, group singing, Wednesday night prayer meetings, maple syrup and apple-butter making, quilt making, canning, hog butchering, going after the milk cows, berry picking and daily visits to discuss current events "by word of mouth" and express their own personal opinions.

All children had assigned chores, such as, sawing and splitting fire wood, caring for the chickens, finding and gathering eggs, feeding the hogs, going after the milk cows (the cows all wore bells and foraged upon the vegetation along the railroad Whitetop and US 250), milking the cows, washing clothes on washboards, washing dishes, cleaning the kerosene lamps and lanterns, pouring out and cleaning the slop jars (or chamber pots), assisting in preparation of meals, sewing, patching, cleaning the house, and any other necessary jobs, to survive.

Cheat Bridge had Western Maryland Railroad telephone service from Elkins through Webster Springs with the dispatcher (operator) located at the then-existing Western Maryland Train Station in Elkins.

Railroad transportation was by handcar, motorcar or speeder. The "handcar" required two to four persons (one or two on the front and rear) to raise and lower the wide bars to propel the handcar in either direction, by means of a sprocket chain. There was also a "speeder" that one person could ride and pump like a bicycle that had four wheels. Sometimes "speeders" were used by "track walkers" to check the track for any broken rails or debris blocking the rails and endangering freight train travel.

All trains, handcars and motorcars operated on a schedule. All Western Maryland employees had to synchronize their watches as to the exact railroad times when getting orders from the dispatcher to operate the trains, motorcars, speeders and hand cars on the GC&E Railroad. All operators had to pass Bill Stanford or Oscar Williams' regular watch inspections at Stanford Jewelers in Elkins.

Dick Ayers and Truman Shaffer were the two men who kept the telephone lines operational from Webster Springs to Elkins. They traveled on an open motorcar with neither top nor cover in all kinds of weather conditions. Dick Ayers was a Western Maryland employee and Truman Shaffer was a Western Union Telegraph employee. Both were assigned to the Elkins Division of the Western Maryland Railroad.

"With the Dewing purchase, the West Virginia Pulp & Paper Company acquired an employee who was to prove invaluable in dealing with the mountain people in purchasing timber and obtaining rights-of-way as well as in cruising and surveying. This man was Harvey C. Cromer, a native of the Cheat Mountain area of

Pocahontas County. A self-taught man, Mr. Cromer was an excellent surveyor and knew practically every acre of timber and every boundary line in the Cheat Mountain country. He was described as a man of rugged character, honest to the core; a real woodsman, quiet, but diligent and thorough in his work. Although he was misunderstood by many people and often referred to as the "snake hunter," he was held in high esteem by the Lukes who owned WV P&P. It was people like Harvey Cromer who formed a loyal, devoted, and capable working force." (Taken from *On Beyond Leatherbark: The Cass Saga* by Roy B. Clarkson).

There were seven houses at Cheat Bridge, which included the Harvey Cromer, Sr. (large Swiss chalet style), with wood shingle roof, concrete spring water trough for refrigeration which ran the year round, an extra large kitchen and table that would seat twenty-five persons at a time, "indoor" bathroom, parlor (living room). "Granddad" Harvey Cromer's bedroom and study– "Grandma" Cromer's bedroom were all downstairs and two large bedrooms were in the loft upstairs.

"Granddad" Cromer kept a large floor model world globe, a pump organ, piano, a bronze bed stead, the highly-decorated "Aladdin" kerosene lamp, the most comfortable setting and rocking chairs, a large "pot-bellied" stove, coal box and wood box in the wall-papered room with several old black powder muskets in the corner near the front door of his room.

During the winter, ice covered the river. Cheat Bridge men would use a one-man, one-handled ice saw and cut huge slabs of ice and haul them by horse and sled to the log ice house. The ice slabs were buried in about three feet of sawdust as insulation for use in the hot summer months. Cheat Bridge and Glady hold the record for the lowest official temperature in Randolph County which was thirty-three degrees below zero on December 24, 1989.

Cromers also had a Delco Plant, to provide lights (kerosene powered electric generator), wash shed, wood shed, coal shed, cellar to store canned foods, corn crib, four-stall garage, blacksmith shop, small sawmill, playhouse for kids, trout pond, gas house (AMOCO) with hand pump, meat house, large chalet-style barn, chicken house, ice house and machine shed near the "now standing Old Cheat Bridge" serving the original Staunton-Parkersburg Turnpike. Harvey Cromer, Sr. had all the necessities needed to survive on Cheat Mountain.

Harvey Cromer, Sr. had 14 children and was said to have come from British Columbia to survey the real estate holdings, which was comprised of 98,500 acres with about 2,000 employees in Cass and Spruce and in the logging woods, for West Virginia Pulp & Paper Company of West Virginia and later Delaware in the 1880s. He was a "mountain of a man" who stood over 6 feet tall, had black rim glasses, long white hair and beard, wore either Ritchie or Duck back clothes the year round and walked with a cane. Harvey Cromer would frequently remain away from his home for several days, while fishing and hunting throughout the Cheat Mountain area. A visitor to Cheat Bridge on one occasion asked Mr. Cromer if he had ever been lost on Cheat Mountain. He responded, "No, but I have been badly confused for a few days at-a-time." He was a most kind and gentle man and was well learned and read. He passed away peacefully about 1944 at his home in Cheat Bridge with Charlie Triplett at his side.

A neighbor would always spend the last hours of an expectant death at the side of a neighbor instead of with a family member. People weren't taken to hospitals and nursing homes to pass on to another world. Often times the country doctor would show up to administer treatment to ease the pain during the last hours of the decedent. Funeral directors and embalmers came to the decedents home and performed the embalming of the body for services and burial. Funerals were sometimes held at the decedent's residence.

"Grandma" Cromer, Harvey, Sr.'s wife, always wore a bonnet

on her head, long dresses with sleeves and constantly cooked from early morning until late night and baked sugar cookies. Every youngster in Cheat Bridge would sit lined up each morning to receive one of Grandma Cromer's sugar cookies on the wood box with a lid 8x3x2 1/2 feet area between the back door to her kitchen and wood stove which had a hot water tank and warming closet above the stove fire box. None of the Cheat Bridge youngsters wanted "Grandma" Cromer to learn of any of their misbehaviors for fear they wouldn't get a sugar-coated cookie.

Pearl Cromer, their oldest son, was a "jack-of-all-trades" and was a financier in the Hopkins Mine operations about 1908-1914. Pearl also logged and operated a sawmill. During his life, Pearl walked with his hands behind his back carrying his gloves, dressed in a black wide brim felt hat, bibbed overalls and high top shoes. Pearl never married, but courted the same woman for many years, who eventually married the Durbin postmaster. She claimed she got tired of waiting on Pearl to ask her to marry him. Pearl built a house in Durbin and didn't last long enough to live in it.

Three of Harvey Cromer, Sr.'s sons, Charlie, Ott and George, were Shay engineers for West Virginia Pulp & Paper Company transporting log trains to the Cass Mill. Sue Cromer, their oldest daughter, never married and was postmistress at Cheat Bridge and sort of a secretary for Harvey "Granddad" Cromer, Sr.

Blanche Cromer Elbon was the youngest daughter and drove all the Cheat Bridge children who attended public school in a 1932 Chevrolet two-door car from Cheat Bridge, Randolph County, to Big Fill Barn, in Pocahontas County to catch a school bus. The students were hauled to Durbin Grade School (Grades 1-8) or Green Bank High School, twenty-three miles from Cheat Bridge. Children would leave Cheat Bridge about 6:15 a.m. for school and return about 5:45 p.m. All children would do their assigned chores, eat supper prepared on a wood-burning stove, prepare their lessons and go to bed. Most families would say "grace" before meals and read scripture from the *Bible* before

47

retiring for the night. The parents, if they had enough book learning or "book read," would help with the lessons, or if not, a neighbor who had gone to school would help.

Stark Wilmoth, superintendent of schools for Randolph County, and Mac Brooks, superintendent of schools for Pocahontas County, made an agreement between themselves to provide schooling for the Randolph County Cheat Bridge school children to attend Pocahontas County Public Schools.

Many of the children born at Cheat Bridge and Spruce were either delivered by George Hull, MD (University of Virginia School of Medicine), Eugene Burner, MD (University of Baltimore School of Medicine), or a midwife, if they couldn't get there from Durbin in time to make the delivery. Childbirth was a community celebration. The men would maintain a fire to heat the necessary water and "partake of spirits". The women were always complaining about the men not setting a good example for the newborn and being a bad influence on the new father.

Usually, the Cheat Bridge boys could slip around and pick up long hand-rolled cigarette butts made from "Buglar" or "Prince Albert" tobacco, "cuss" a little and maybe grab a drink of the "spirits" when the male adults weren't looking. On one occasion I recall a male friend about twelve years old being found by his mother "skidded" in the hog house with the hogs after the newborn arrived, severely impaired from "home brew" consumption.

Monday was the designated wash day and a few of the women would set a "batch" of "home brew" from "Red Top Malt" to work off the remainder of the week for the Saturday night "toot".

Some of the 1930s Cheat Bridge newborns were Donald Cromer, veterinarian, Staunton, VA; David Cromer, retired U.S. Air Force major; Patty Elbon Nottingham; Benjamin Elbon, large chain grocery store manager; George R. Triplett, attorney and former circuit court judge; Robert Vance, retired telescope operator, Green Bank Observatory; Kenneth Vance, retired Pocahontas County school principal and superintendent; Jack "Jig-

48

ger" Gragg, the son of Parker and Mamie Greathouse Gragg, who was Mower Lumber Company contract logger between Cheat Bridge and Cheat Club.

Jack Gragg was always an "A" student at Green Bank High School and Potomac State College (his ambition was to become a medical doctor); among many other successful and prominent citizens, in addition to several young ladies, Deloris Cromer, Marilyn, Jane, Louise, Carolyn, Vinnie, Patty Ann Phares, Avis Phares, Marilyn Davis, Jane Davis, Louise Davis, Carolyn Davis, Vinie Davis, Margaret Davis, who married, and have been most outstanding wives, mothers and businesswomen, and many others.

The West Virginia Pulp & Paper Company used the GC&E from Spruce to Triplett with numerous log camps at various locations with log railroad connecting to the GC&E. West Virginia Pulp & Paper and Mower Lumber Company had a carpenter gang, blacksmith shop, train shop, a "Wye" (to turn engines), a boardinghouse for workers, a coal tipple, a log dump with a coal-fired, steam-powered log loader on a flat railroad car to load logs from the log dump located at Cheat Bridge.

David Vachon, Hambleton, Tucker County, West Virginia was the blacksmith; Andy Sparks, Cass, West Virginia, was the carpenter gang foreman; Ray "Buzz" Sage was the log loader operator, Saul McNeely was the general superintendent and later Rocky Fisher and Clark Phillips, woods bosses; Bruce Crickard, Valley Head, West Virginia, was the surveyor; and Herbert Greathouse was the tong hooker. Harry Jasper Triplett was train superintendent for West Virginia Pulp & Paper Company and later Mower Lumber Company, after leaving Spruce as a section gang foreman. Pulpwood was transported to both Luke, Maryland and Covington, Virginia.

No Pain–No Gain
Tough Times Don't Last–Tough People Do!

49

December 7, 1941, Pearl Harbor Day, brought a real change to Cheat Bridge and Cheat River Basin.

I remember Carney "Dodger" Dugger, during the cold and stormy December 7, 1941, winter Sunday evening about dark, telling my daddy, Charlie Triplett, in my presence, (I was six years old and in the first grade at Durbin), "Charlie, the Japs bombed Pearl Harbor this morning. According to Roosevelt, it looks like many of us are going to be called to serve our country."

No truer words were ever spoken! Young men from the ages of fifteen to forty either volunteered or were drafted. Those who were underage, lied about their age and those underweight would eat a lot of bananas and drink a lot of water to weigh enough to be inducted. I know of some who served with one eye. Herb Coberly was with the "Lone Battalion," a paratrooper captured on the drop near Salerno, Italy, and survived seventeen months in a German Prisoner of War Camp. Herb was a former semi-professional football player prior to World War II. Herbert Coberly, who returned to Elkins after WWII, advised me Colonel Larry Spears, US Army pilot, was the pilot of the C-47 with an eight-inch hole shot in the cabin by ACK –ACK Gun ground fire when he was ordered to jump with his twenty-five paratroopers under his command near Salerno, seven miles from the "drop zone".

"Hub" Herb told me that he met Spears after WWII in Elkins and Spears thought he and Herb had played football against one another. Herb reminded Colonel Spears that he was the pilot who ordered Herb and his paratrooper platoon to bail out seven miles from the "drop zone" at Salerno, Italy, that led to Herb's capture by the German Army. Jay Spears, former state senator and Colonel Spears' widow, confirmed the eight-inch hole in the C-47 plane piloted by her deceased husband.

The hemophilia bleeder, U.S. Marine veteran from Davis High School, Harold Mosser, Marshall University basketball star, football and basketball coach at Green Bank High School was discovered by a dentist about to pull a tooth on a ship after the Battle of Guadalcanal headed for the next Pacific Island invasion he told the dentist of his affliction. The dentist wanted to immediately medically discharge Coach Mosser. Mosser refused to return to his hometown and be called a "Slacker" or "4-F" (4-F meaning physically unfit to serve). Coach Mosser was assigned to New Zealand for the remainder of World War II.

Lloyd "Dabney" Kisner, Jr. was shot down in Belgium and remained in seclusion for three years. When he returned home he constructed the Pocahontas Motel and was an avid bear hunter.

Every male was required to register with the Selective Service Board to be drafted to serve in the U.S. Military within thirty days of his eighteenth birthday. Many combat veterans returned from WWII with body parts missing, to find that a young attractive wife had deserted them, or they had "combat flashbacks," unable to sleep. The government really provided very little professional help for the WWII, Korean or Vietnam combat veterans.

We had three different first grade teachers at Durbin Grade School, Violet Hoover Arthur, Marguarite Kisner Widney and a Mrs. Collins, during the 1941-1942 school term because the young first grade teachers tried to follow their husbands called to defend our great democracy against the Nazi and Japanese aggression.

President Truman got the "G I Bill" passed and made it easier to achieve higher education after WWII. Truman made college available to children of woods laborers, railroaders, coal miners and farmers who served in the U.S. Armed Services who prior to WWII had no financial means to attend college.

Electricity arrived at Cheat Bridge about 1948 through President Roosevelt's Rural Electrification Act. Bruce Nottingham was known as the "electric" man and was based at Durbin by Monongahela Power Company. Bruce was the Cheat Mountain school bus driver the 1941 school term.

If a housewife had an electric bill to exceed one dollar ($1)

51

monthly, she was a very extravagant wasteful woman. A young man was taught to watch how any prospective bride peeled potatoes to determine whether or not she was worth marrying.

Rozzella Tacy Rosencrance registered all eligible voters at Cheat Bridge as either Democrats or Republicans. She lived on Becca's Creek, was Democratic in politics and raised four fine daughters. A picture of Christ, Franklin D. Roosevelt and John F. Kennedy hung on the wall of most homes during the 1960s.

## The Mountain People Had Pride and Earned Respect-- Respect Can't be Demanded

1930 through the 1940s Western Maryland Railway Cheat Bridge families included: Ted Irvine, Rich Hedrick, Brooks Hedrick, Russell and Edna Dugger White, Charlie and Geneva Harris Triplett, Carney and Irna Dugger, Richard and Vonda McCauley, Hansel and Cozzette Howell Phares, Robert and Grethal Wimer Cromer, Brooks and Freda Phares Davis, Harvey and Anna Greathouse Cromer, Pete and Blanche Elbon, Willie Bodkins, Irving White, Gus McGee (the fiddler), "Nig," Plummer, Clinton Taylor, Schraders, Gern and Lola Cooper Mullenax, Jim and Letha Vance Cromer, Ray and Erin Vance McDaniels, Mr. and Mrs. Henry Cole, Melvin and Cecelia Johnson, Raymond and Lillian Shelton, Mr. and Mrs. Franctz Deglar (Cheat Club House), Brooks "Chippy" and Mary Nelson Vance, Ira William and Bernice Bowers Triplett, Earle and Hazel Nelson Vance, Lake McGee, Bruce Bowers, Fred Kissinger, Roy Bowers and the many fine children born at Cheat Bridge.

The Cheat Bridge railroad section gang had a tool house near the location where passengers now board the "Salamander". The tool house stored two motorcars, a handcar and push truck, as well as the necessary hand tools and supplies to repair the railroad, railroad jacks, spiking hammers (which weighed twelve pounds), sledge hammers, lining bars (weighed twenty-eight pounds), "Pullin' Bar" (to pull spikes in ties), metal rail gauge, a level board, tie tongs, both double and single rail tongs and many other necessary hand tools. A rail jack weighed ninety pounds. A section gang hand carried two jacks at a time. Richard McCauley was a coalmine fatality in Monongalia County. Richard could raise two ninety-pound railroad jacks above his head and hold them up with his arms straight.

The motorcars carried a turntable set that could be set up between the tracks on the railroad to turn the direction of the motorcar which carried the section gang. The motorcar pulled a push truck with the equipment to repair and maintain the railroad tracks. There was also a storage yard of necessary supplies across from the tool house and a long sidetrack.

There were other specialty crews housed in camp cars that temporarily would stay at Cheat Bridge for the railroad repairs. The gangs included the carpenter gang, bridge gang, extra track gang, ditcher gang, work trains and also the wreck train gang.

Some of the specialty crewmembers were: Clee Reed, Hubert Armentrout, Slim Calain, Shorty Doerr, Aladine Reed, Pete Filler, Bud Filler, Punk Phares, Everett Wamsley, Marshall Phares, Jennings Doyle, Pete Cross, Emmett Cross, Henry Huffman and many others.

There was also a "Black Shanty" where the section hands would have shelter from the severe weather conditions, build a fire in a pot-bellied coal stove and possibly eat lunch. The "Black Shanty" was hidden in the "laurel thicket" from the railroad official when they came to inspect the Western Maryland Railroad from the Baltimore headquarters. The "Black Shanty" was against Western Maryland regulations.

The section gang foremen would also hide certain section hands from officials as they passed them working on the railroad tracks, to prevent the officials from seeing the poorly-dressed or poorly-groomed employees. Every foreman was proud and wanted to

53

make a "good showing" of his section to the railroad officials dressed in shirts and ties as they passed by inspecting the operations. Railroaders had great pride and strived to give the Western Maryland Railroad Company "a better day's work than they received in pay". At the outbreak of WWII, the West Virginia Pulp & Paper Company paid a higher hourly wage rate than both the Western Maryland Railroad and Union Coal Mines.

When an illegal deer was harvested, everyone at Cheat Bridge shared the venison with other families.

Observe the "bullet hole" on top of the sign at old Cheat Bridge where you board the Salamander. It's bullet hole from a sawed-off shotgun that state police troopers French Armstrong and Bill Steffick had me, a young college student, to shoot to test for accuracy. The discharge cut a laceration in my upper lip and left the scar I carry today. They later told me that were afraid to shoot the sawed-off shotgun themselves. I had returned during college Christmas vacation of 1954 after a plane crash near Crouch Knob that two VPI students survived and walked to Cheat Club in about two feet of snow for Russell White to call for help.

I have defended several mountain dwelling men in US District Court on criminal charges for mere possession of a similar illegal sawed-off shotgun. The state police troopers were issued, as standard equipment, the same type of sawed-off shotgun that they had me test for accuracy fifty yards away with a "slug cartridge".

Cheat Mountain and Cheat River people worked hard all week and had their Saturday night "toot" to Bemis and catch up on the news by word of mouth. The "toot" was going to town, Durbin, Glady, Mill Creek, Elkins, Valley Head, listening to the "Grand Ole' Opry," Gabriel Heater, Lowell Thomas, war newscasters for WMNN Fairmont or Wheeling on a battery-operated radio, having a square dance at Durbin Grade School or attending a double feature movie in Durbin, with at least one feature being a western.

Charlie Triplett always believed what goes around will come

around. It may take generations. If you do good, your family will be blessed. If you do bad things to people, you and your family will suffer the consequences. Always look for the good in people and try to overlook the bad.

## If You Can't Say Something Good About People Keep A To Yourself!

During the Depression most men were out of work. Section gang foremen and working trackmen saw to it that the unemployed families had the necessary food staples to survive. Everybody shared what they had with needy families. It was a self-sponsored independent welfare system created by the Mountain Celtic Culture to ensure survival of all the families on the mountain. The physically disabled or mentally impaired were kept in the community and cared for by the community and no one "tolerated" teasing or putting them down. You were taught, "If you can't say something good about a person, keep your mouth shut". You were also taught to "size up" a situation and neither panic nor rush into a crisis blindly. The same held true when a stranger came to town. Watch how he walks, looks and holds himself as he walks toward you.

Everyone wore "patches" and "hand-me-down clothing," including shoes. Some men wore burlap sacks wrapped around their feet and legs for overshoes in the wintertime to work in sub-zero temperatures. Mothers taught their sons that it was most important to keep your body and clothes clean instead of "fretin" about the patch on your britches that some young lady may see. Women washed the cloth (cotton) feed sacks and made pillowcases, bedclothes, curtains and clothes from them. One lady, now in her eighties, remembers the bottom of her underpants had a star and "Morning Star" printed in red on the seat. My cousin,

55

Wanda Powers Sharp, told me she was ten years old when she visited a friend in Bowden and saw her first pair of lady's pink silk panties. Wanda said she thought those were the prettiest pink things she had ever seen.

The women washed clothes by rubbing them on a washboard in a round metal washtub, or, if you were lucky, a Maytag square tub wringer washing machine, which was operated by a gasoline motor. Monday was "wash day".

People were taught to survive and the Green Bank High School motto, taught by Virgil B. Harris, Tweard Blackhurst, Minnie Parg, June Riley, Harold Mosser, Roy Clarkson and Allen Stewart was "United We Stand–Divided We Fall" –Meaning we must be One For All and All For One–Togetherness, otherwise it is "divide us and be conquered"–another Celtic culture trait.

The first year of integrated schools in 1955, an Afro-American named "Bo Jackson" from Frank was elected as president of the senior class. "Bo" was an All-State Class "B" football team member.

People sang to prevent depression as a self-taught treatment and returned "grace" before meals and family prayer prior to retiring at night in most homes. I remember being on my knees praying at the bedside with my mother and hearing the steam whistles blow, meaning the WWII with Germany was over in the spring of 1945.

The "Cheat Bridge" whistle stop sign stands at the entrance to our driveway in "Triplett Holler" with a small sign underneath that reads "Home Again". I remember when it was placed at the upper sidetrack at Cheat Bridge by Charlie Triplett and his crew about 1939-1940 as the "whistle sign" for oncoming steam locomotives.

Cheat Club was built in 1912. J. Wilmoth was the first proprietor and later established the Wilmoth Hotel in Durbin. Frantz Deglar and his wife, Carrie Greathouse Deglar were the second company caretakers. The Club is at Mile Post 25, one mile up Shavers Fork from Cheat Bridge. Many dignitaries such as Henry Ford I, Harvey Firestone, Sr. and Harvey Firestone, Jr., Thomas A. Edison, John Burroughs, among others, found peace, relaxation, inspiration, motivation and stimulation for thinking during their stay at Cheat Club for visits to Cheat Mountain during August 1921. The Cheat Club Registry is a most interesting handwritten book containing many comments from its "free-spirited" male and female guests.

Captain Dick Smith, former athletic director for Washington & Lee University and Clayton B. Williams, dean of Washington & Lee University Law School, among many others, made grouse hunting trips to Cheat Bridge during the 1940s–1950s.

The "Cheat Mountain Salamander" is a rare amphibian species and survives only on Shaver's Fork, Cheat River, Cheat and Shaver's Mountains.

Russell and Edna White became the caretakers of Cheat Club about 1948 for the second time. The Club hosted the Western Maryland Railroads officials who entertained potential customers or clients, such as, U.S. Steel, Bethlehem Steel, power companies, foreign exporters and politicians, who provided favorable business assistance or political help for the Western Maryland Railroad.

The Club House was furnished with hard maple furniture, bathrooms, a large clubroom, and a large dining room with a table that would seat forty to fifty people at one time. There were two trout ponds which was constructed in the early 1900s for brook trout breeding purposes. These were stocked well with large brook trout for the guests. The water source, which fed the ponds, came from Fish Hatchery Run. The Cheat Club was often threatened and damaged by the ice jams, spring thaws and spring flooding which continue in the 2000s.

Russell White and Edna, his wife, took great pride in maintaining a first class operation. Russell and Edna worked tirelessly seven days a week on a set salary. Their responsibilities included cooking, baking, cleaning, mowing, general custodial services, maintaining and grooming the entire successful Cheat Club operation. "Cleanliness is next to Godliness" was used as the Mountain Celtic people slogan.

The Cheat Club had a gasoline-powered generator in the event a storm knocked out the electricity. Russell was furnished a Ford or Mercury four-door Station Wagon to drive with the "Western Maryland Railroad" emblem painted on both sides of the vehicle's front doors. The emblem was red, gold and black with the words- "Western Maryland Fast Freight Line".

Cheat Club and its equipment were kept in excellent condition by Russell and Edna White. Russell was also aware of any and all activities and "goings on" up Shavers Fork. On one occasion, I came home for Christmas break from college and bagged a buck deer on the ridge above Fish Hatchery Run. I was dragging the deer (out of deer season) and saw large footprints in about a foot of snow. I carried my .32 Special Model 94 Winchester Carbine Rifle and buck deer on my back to a spot above the Cheat Club House road. When I returned after dark and took the buck deer home and was skinning it out with Dad, Russell White showed up and helped to skin the deer. Nothing was ever said to law enforcement. The meat was shared among Cheat Bridge residents.

The Deglers, in the early years, maintained a dairy herd, chickens, hogs, storage cellar, wood house, brook trout fish hatchery, coal house, a running spring house. Frantz Degler, was a self-taught "botanist," who kept his herbs, plants, and vegetation. The spring house refrigerated or cooled their perishable foods.

# Education is Accumulated Experience– You Can Learn Something From Every Person You Meet if You Are Interested In Learning

Frantz Degler and Harvey Cromer, Sr. lived at Cheat Bridge. Jack Darling, (a mountain hermit survival man), lived in a shanty at the top of Cheat Mountain at Hopkin's Mines. They were self-taught "book read" learned older men who frequently sat on the railroad tracks near the Cheat Bridge Post Office and discussed current events. They inspired, motivated and stimulated the minds of the Cheat Bridge children with their constant teaching and interrogations of the young inquisitive minds.

Jack Darling was said to have been a Philadelphia lawyer, who got fed up with the big city life, corporate law practice and came to Cheat Mountain in the 1920s. Jack survived on the bare essentials.

Neighbors were never afraid to correct a misbehaved child. Usually when a neighbor gave you "birch tea," (a whipping with a small birch tree branch) and a parent found out, you got another at home. The same held true if you got spanked at school. Kids were "skittish" to disclose being "whupped".

There were always tales told by Pearl Cromer, Sue Cromer, Blanche Elbon, Frantz Degler and Jack Darling about being followed by panther or mountain lions near Cheat Bridge. The last mountain lion killed on Shavers or Cheat Mountain was at Wheeler, below Bemis and Glady, in the early 1900s near the old Vandevander Place.

Bob Cromer, youngest son of Harvey Cromer, Sr., did harvest a wolf at Cheat Bridge. The wolves had attacked his milk cow and chickens during the night. Bob used his Model 12, Winchester pump, 12-gauge shotgun. That also brought many spectators and visitors to Cheat Bridge, including Dr. George Hull. I believe that was about 1939.

Bob Cromer built wooden bear pens and caught black bears. The Cromers' attempted to tame the bears that were sometimes chained or penned in Harvey Cromer, Sr.'s front yard. The entire Cromer yard had a well-constructed wooden panel fence and was gated. There was also a wooden board sidewalk to avoid tracking mud in the house.

## Fish Hatchery Run

Fish Hatchery Run got its name because the Cheat Club maintained a brook trout hatchery for its guests during the 1920s and it continues to spawn native brook trout.

The area from the trustle to the end of the sharp guardrail curve at Mile Post 26, and the wide, deep hole in the river, across from Lambert Run, is an area good for black bear crossings.

Lambert Run also had a log hauling railroad and trestle that connected to the GC&E and had a trestle across the river.

On November 30, 1950, Thanksgiving Day, a bear hunting party bagged four large black bears and had two bears to recover on Friday. There was a real Cheat Mountain "white-out" blizzard that resulted in about four feet of snow from Thursday through Saturday. That was the greatest snowstorm in Randolph County history. That ended the 1950 bear-hunting season. There was fifty-seven inches of snow in Pickens with that blizzard, making it the highest snowfall on record in Randolph County to date.

Unusual snow accumulations have been a problem for Cheat Mountain throughout its history. Several sources recorded the heavy snow, which occurred during the winter of 1855, along with the Trotter Brothers letter to the U.S. postmaster general.

Read the 1855 letter to the U.S. Postmaster General:

"Mr. Postmaster General,
Washington, D.C.

Sir:

If you knock the gable end out of Hell and back it up against Cheat Mountain and rain fire and brimstone on it for forty days and forty nights, it won't melt the snow enough to get your d--- mail through on time.

Yours truly,

Trotter Brothers
By: (s) James Trotter."

You piled all the "kivvers" you could find on your bed to stay warm in a house that was about the same temperature inside as it was outside. When you awakened in the morning there would be snow on the bed where the snow blew through the cracks of the doors and windows.

Both sides of the river have beech, black cherry, maple, red spruce and yellow birch timber growth to Spruce and the Big Cut called "the Summit". The log camps are seeded with apple trees along the GC&E Railroad through Cheat Summit. "Tweard" Blackhurst, a Green Bank High School teacher, always spoke of "Johnnie Appleseed" walking from Elkins to Spruce up the railroad scattering apple seeds. The truth was the apple tree grew from the seeds and peelings thrown out as leftovers from the log camps. The apple seeds were cast upon fertile ground and took root and grew into fruit bearing apple tree that still bear fruit today.

There were many log camps, including a camp at the 26 Mile Post across the river from Lambert Run.

There are also several fresh water springs that supplied water for the hard working railroad section gang hands and loggers along the railroad bed.

Pearl Cromer bagged a large seven-point buck deer in the late 1940s on Lambert Run and he had to make three trips to carry the venison out on his back to Cheat Bridge. There were only game trails and no vehicular routes.

Bonar, a young state police trooper stationed in Elkins, was a WWII U.S. Marine veteran. He followed seven escaped Huttonsville Correctional Center prison inmates across Becky's Creek, Crouch Knob, down Lambert Run and captured them without severely wounding any of them. Bonar marched them to Cheat Club where Russell White called the authorities for reinforcements to help Bonar. Bonar retired as the WV State Police superintendent.

There were always "groundhogs, woodchucks or whistlepigs" burrowed along the railroad bed. Young men would take a "grubbin' hoe," .22 caliber rifle and their hunting dog and harvest a ground hog or two during the summer months. The only thing wasted on a groundhog was its "whistle".

The riverbottoms were abundant with "ramps" that were dug. Everybody on the mountain had ramps (leeks) as the "spring tonic" for cleansing and purification. Dr. George Hull and Dr. Eugene Burner saw to it all kids were wormed by "Dr. Frye's" worm medicine each spring so they would grow.

The sugar maple trees were tapped for sugar water that was boiled over an open wood fire in copper kettles and made into maple syrup or sugar cakes. Dandelions and turnip greens, sassafras roots and birch-bark tea and other herbs were used as foods to survive.

A young hunter or fisherman carried a pack on his back with a small hatchet (ax), hunting knife, skillet, matches, cover, extra pair of socks, coat, cap, and gloves. He made a "lean to" wood hut for cover with spruce boughs to prevent him from taking a cold or getting pneumonia. He slept under the "lean to" with an open fire between a bed of sandstone rock, which radiated heat.

He would fry his fish or wild meat over the fire and possibly have a few Irish potatoes to roast.

Lice was another problem which was commonly brought into the schools by infected students. Parents would sometimes apply kerosene oil to the affected hairlines creating a severely burned area on the nape of the neck.

## Mile Post 27–28

Burnt Run and Rocky Run are across the river and have a heavy laurel thicket with real good trout fishing in the river. There was a log campsite in the riverbottom about half way between Mile Post 27–28. That was also a good black bear crossing.

That is the location where I led the plane crash search party, during the 1954 Christmas vacation, comprised of Charlie Triplett, Brooks Davis, Richard McCauley, state police troopers French Armstrong and Bill Steffick to the crash site that the two VPI students survived in about two feet of snow and walked out without snowshoes. We walked from Cheat Bridge to Crouch Knob and returned to Cheat Bridge.

There were no roads above the Cheat Club House until about 1964. All travel above Cheat Bridge to Spruce was by railroad or foot.

There is a big hole of water at Mile Post 28 that always seemed to keep a large rainbow or brown trout. White tail deer were rare during the 1930s in West Virginia. Charlie Triplett bagged a nine-point buck above Mile Post 28 across the river during deer season in November 1937 with a 30-40 Craig rifle. The buck was a real trophy at that time and people came from miles around to see the deer. There were no taxidermists in West Virginia and the buck deer had to be sent to Pennsylvania to be mounted.

There was a water tank approximately a quarter of a mile below the Hopkins trestle or bridge that replenished the water for the steam locomotives traveling up and down the GC&E Railroad. A log camp near the water tank was operated by Roy Griffith from Tucker County in the early 1940s when Water Tank Hollow was logged.

In the late 1930s B.I. Hudkins, MD, a well-known surgeon at St. Mary's Hospital, Clarksburg, WV, and many other professionals, leased land for a campsite from either Mower Lumber Company or West Virginia Pulp & Paper Company. They constructed "WAMPUS," a hunting-fishing camp for their relaxation at the mouth of Water Tank Hollow. The camp was approximately two hundred yards from the lower end of the Hopkins River Trestle.

There wasn't much alcohol consumption nor frolicking at the Hudkins' camp. The camp was burned to the ground at least three times and Dr. Hudkins always rebuilt the camp from his own savings.

Dr. Hudkins resided at Wolfe Summit, Harrison County. The Salem town officers, Dr. Ritter, MD, Salem, Dr. Hudkin's, son-in-law, Ora Stutler from Doddridge County was the cook and sometimes a preacher, and Reverend Freeman, would accompany Dr. Hudkins to the camp. Mr. A. R. McIntyre and the Stewart brothers also were guests. I believe one of the Stewart brothers lives in Barbour County and is retired from the coalmines.

You can see a large cliff of rocks above the trestle high on the mountain that provided a nest for "Golden Eagles" to hatch and raise their offspring. Harvey Cromer, Sr. had two mounted Golden Eagles at his home at Cheat Bridge. One of the Golden Eagles was harvested by Harvey Cromer, Sr. from the rock cleft overlooking the Hopkins railroad trestle. The "Fighting Golden Eagles" was the school mascot name for Green Bank High School.

# Cabin Fork

Across the river at Mile Post 29 above Hopkins trestle is the Cabin Fork (First Fork) Bottom. Cabin Fork had log camps and there were two sidetracks with a log railroad that connected to the GC&E. One of the most famous early log camps was "Camp No. 21". There was lower Hopkins Siding at the mouth of Cabin Fork. Upper Hopkins Siding had a phone box shed at the supper end of the sidetrack. Cabin Fork is a large tributary to Shavers Fork and was abundant with native Brook Trout and possibly was six miles to the headwaters, which started in Pocahontas County. The logging company constructed a logging railroad along Cabin Fork to near the headwaters and several log campsites were along the railroad during the early 1900s and which continued upstream from "Camp 21". There was a trestle crossing Shavers Fork near the lower Hopkins Siding.

The bottoms were swampy and steam shay locomotive engines were used to transport logs to Cass. The shay locomotive couldn't pull the full load of logs piled on the flat railroad cars across the swamp. The engine would hook a long, big, thick blacksmith-made linked chain to one car at a time and pull the loaded log car across the swamp on the railroad so the train wouldn't sink into the soft bottom because of the heavy weight. Each of my sons have about fifteen feet of the blacksmithed chain we found.

A brakeman, Ira Coberly, aged twenty, was seriously injured when he fell from the train between "Camp 38" and the main line and had his right leg cut off at the knee. Ira "Peg Leg" Coberly was the cook for the upper Hopkins Siding log camp located on the railroad side of Shavers Fork. "Peg Leg" Coberly later operated one of the best hotdog/beer joints in Elkins, after leaving the

Cheat Mountain logging operations. "Peg Leg's" son, Ira, is a retired U.S. Army colonel and served on the Randolph County Commission. Ira's daughter, Delia Coberly Loftis, is the administrative assistant to Randolph County Prosecuting Attorney Earl Maxwell, a sixth generation Maxwell family Randolph County attorney.

After the road was constructed to Cabin Fork headwaters by Mower Lumber Company in the 1970s, a couple of loggers, who lived in Durbin, were on a "Saturday night toot" and had heavily partaken of the "spirits". A couple of young state police troopers chased after them. The loggers were operating an old model four-wheel drive Willy's Jeep pickup with a wooden bed, and scattered gas cans, chainsaws, tools, etc. from Durbin to the headwaters of Cabin Fork. The loggers had several criminal charges filed by the Prosecuting Attorney James Cain against them in Randolph County. I was successful as their defense lawyer defending the loggers because the crime originated in Pocahontas County and ended in Pocahontas County, where they were arrested. However, the young arresting officers were unaware of the Randolph-Pocahontas County boundary lines. Proper venue and jurisdiction at that time for prosecution was Pocahontas County. The criminal charges were dismissed and couldn't be refiled because of double jeopardy.

Thanksgiving Day 1953, Charlie Triplett and I bagged two wild turkeys in about a foot of snow in Hopkins Bottom in the laurel thicket after crawling from lower Hopkins Siding along the bank of Shavers Fork mainly on hands and knees. At that time wild turkeys were as scarce as "hen's teeth" in West Virginia. Again, the Model 94 Winchester .32 Special Carbine was on target. Incidentally, turkey season may have just ended.

Wayne Bailey, a wild life biologist, was hired by the WV Conservation Commission to improve the turkey population in West Virginia about 1949. Gail Swecker, a hard-working West Virginian Conservation employee, walked, carried his tools, cleared the food plots, planted and fertilized the ground on Cheat Mountain and Shavers Mountain after WWII until his retirement to improve and enlarge the wildlife population on upper Cheat and Shavers mountain that all hunters still enjoy in the 2000s. Gail lives in Huttonsville with his wife Elizabeth Rosencrance Swecker. Their daughter, Betty, married Russell Linger, Jr. with about the sixth generation of Lingers working the Linger Dairy Farm. Elizabeth is the daughter of Rozzella Tacy Rosencrance.

## Mile Post 30

There is a deep, swift hole of water near Mile Post 30 with a cold, fresh creek flowing from a deep hollow that holds trout. Many trout have been caught from the rocks on the railroad side and opposite side of the deep hole. It's also a place where occasionally the Big Salamander, the "Water dog," an amphibian will get hooked on the "night crawler, chub tail or minnow bait". Such an experience to a young person is extremely intimidating and requires the cutting of your fish line rather than trying to remove the hook. The heavy tug feels as though your line is snagged before you pull the "ugly salamader" to the top to see that you have hooked a "water dog" instead of a big trout.

Many large deer, turkeys and black bears have been harvested up Mile Post 30 Hollow and across to Rocky Run that comes out under "Crouch Knob" between Mile Post 28 and 27 in the thick, heavy laurel thickets a distance below the water tank and Hopkins River Bridge Trestle. It is also good trout fishing from Mile Post 30 to the curve above Black Run, which is Mile Post 31.

# Black Run & Mile Post 31

Black Run empties into Shavers Fork before you reach Mile Post 31 and it is very "red rusty" colored, clean water, said to be caused by the heavy laurel thickets. There are two kinds of laurel, "Big" laurel and "Little" laurel. The West Virginia state flower is "Big Laurel," and has a beautiful pink flower during June each year.

There are always trout in the hole at the mouth of Black Run. There was a connecting log railroad to the GC&E, Western Maryland line from Black Run and log camps during the 1940s.

However, during the energy crisis of the late 1970s, Cheat Mountain had extensive strip coal mining operations from Lambert Run, Crouch Knob, Black Run, Buck Run and Snyders Knob. There were also many operations on Fish Hatchery Run through Water Tank Hollow on the Shavers Mountain side of the river. There were railroad sidetracks with a tipple that the coal was trucked to and dumped from coal trucks into railroad steel hoppers at the Black Run location. There was a tipple and two long sidetracks that are visible to the "Salamander" rider from Cheat Bridge to Spruce.

There was a large coal washing plant facility constructed in the 1970s at Cheat Bridge that operated twenty-four hours daily. Joe Ross was the cleaning plant supervisor that washed, cleaned and sorted the coal for shipment and use.

You will observe the area traveling to Spruce on your left at Cheat Bridge. The low gap at the head of Black Run is the headwaters of Stewart Run that flows into the Tygart River near Elkwater and is also near the headwaters of Conley Run.

The Cheat Bridge Western Maryland Section ended at Mile Post 31 and was ten miles long commencing at Mile Post 21 below Cheat Bridge. The Spruce Section started at Mile Post 31.

# Buck Run–Mile Post 32–Hopkins Mines

As you approach Buck Run and Mile Post 32, you pass Slide Hollow, Shavers Mountain side, across the river that also produced some big buck deer, as well as black bears. The fall deer season of 1967 produced a twelve-point, thirteen and a half year-old white tail buck deer with his tail cut off when stocked from Michigan, according to wildlife biologists who closely examined the buck when checked in at the old Thornwood "CC" Camp and currently the National Science Camp for Youth.

The fall deer season of 1957 caused a three hundred plus pounds black bear to be harvested on the knob just below Buck Run on the Cheat Mountain side. The front body parts were not completely removed from the harvested site. Other deer hunters who found the front quarter remains of the black bear, vowed, "It had to be the biggest buck deer ever harvest on the mountain". They didn't realize it had been an illegal bear kill. However, the Pocahontas County Commission offered a five dollar reward for every dead black bear because black bear were considered sheep killing varmints in Pocahontas County. Two of my brothers-in-law and nephew, John Ross, Leo Pase, Sr. and Leo Pase, Jr., accompanied me on that deer hunting experience. Charlie hauled us to Cheat Bridge after dark on the motorcar.

The black bear dog chases would sometimes start on Thorny Flats near Snowshoe or the "Big Cut" above Spruce at Cheat Summit and end in Cheat Bridge. The farmers from Slaty Fork, Big Springs, Mace, Valley Fork, Mingo, Valley Head, Cass and Stoney Bottom, southern Randolph and Pocahontas counties, would take all their dogs and run, walk and sometimes crawl through the laurel thickets and end up in Cheat Bridge at dark–tired, dry, exhausted, with their clothes torn and tattered–and the bear usually evaded the hunters, including "Ole Sluefoot". "Sluefoot" roamed Cheat and Shavers mountains from Buck Run, Tygart Valley, Big Run, Spruce, Slaty Fork and Thorny Flats.

To my knowledge "Ole Sluefoot" the black male bruin died from old age rather than a nimrod's bullet. There were about half the toes missing from his right front foot that showed up from his footprint track in mud and snow where he stepped. Many a tale has been told about "Ole Sluefoot".

## Climb Cheat Mountain and Look Down at the Beautiful Valley and Flowing Cheat River Below and it Will Help You Find Peace of Mind

### Hopkin's Mine

Hopkins Mine, was located east of Snyder's Knob, an elevation of 4,400 feet, between Buck Run and Beaver Creek and was operational between May 18, 1908 and June 30, 1914. Explorations showed a sizable seam of Gilbert Coal. Pearl Cromer was one of the persons who helped finance and operate the mine for the extraction of the Gilbert Coal.

There was an incline shuttle car line and tracks from the top of the mountain that ran on narrow gauge small railroad tracks with a cable line to both lower the loaded mine car to the railroad tipple at Hopkins Siding and pull an empty coal mine car to the top. The seam was five feet eight inches thick and had a ten-inch sandstone parting. Mules and horses pulled the two-ton hand-loaded mining cars from inside the deep mine to the top of the incline. Very little history is available about the mining operations.

Fred Pezzulli, an Italian immigrant, was a section gang foreman and contracted to dig and clear the cuts near Hopkins Mine for the railroad company. Fred and his wife, Loretta, had several children: Tony a podiatrist, Frank an administrator for Walter Reed Hospital, Fred, Jr., a medical doctor who practiced in New York City, and several daughters who were nurses, were all born

70

at Hopkin's Mine by a midwife delivery.

The Frank Family, another Italian immigrant family, had three sons, and moved to Detroit, Michigan. Andy was a supervisor for Chrysler, a second son was a lawyer and another son a dentist. All were born at Hopkin's Mine. They would return to Cheat Bridge when Mrs. Frank was in her seventies and attempted to walk to Hopkin's Mine on the railroad tracks. It was against Western Maryland Railroad regulations, but Charlie Triplett would ride the Frank Family to Hopkin's Mine on the motorcar. Mrs. Frank found her out-door oven where she baked bread and pastries for her family and boarders and the primitive slab shanty rock foundation where she gave birth to her sons.

## Almost Heaven–West Virginia

Until the extensive strip coal mining operations of the 1970s, there was an area to the left of the incline toward Beaver Creek on top of Cheat Mountain that was the most "peaceful setting" anywhere to be found. The peaceful area had big rocks, covered with heavy moss and extremely large virgin red Spruce trees that for some reason had been left untouched by the early timbering operations. It felt like "taking a walk in heaven" with the peace and serenity you experienced and the coldest pure spring water came out of the sandstone rocks among the moss for a cool drink on a warm summer day.

My son, George R. Triplett, Jr., a physician in Lexington, Virginia, and I found ice and snow under the big boulders during the 1970s in the late spring while taking a father-son walk together when we were on a spring gobbler hunting trip.

That was an area close to where Jack Darling had his "shanty". Jack was said to be the Philadelphia lawyer who got fed up with city high class Philadelphia living and became a "hermit mountain man" on Cheat in the 1920s to 1930s. Boocche Cussins remembers Jack having made himself a self-destruction death apparatus

71

"above his bed in the shanty to bring about his fast demise, if the pain became unbearable to Jack." Booche Cussins also remembers the following, "There was a man who used to come through Spruce that my mother said was a bum. I didn't know where he came from or where he was going, but I suspect he passed through on his way to Cass. I remember his shabby clothes; his very untidy look and that he needed a shave. My mother said his name was Jack. He would come to our back door to ask if he could get something to eat. My mother always gave him something until one day she saw him coming and closed the door. When Jack knocked, Mother yelled, ". . .ain't no one home." Jack slammed the screen door and stormed off the porch. My mother always laughed about that and how Jack never came back. Excerpt taken from *The Log Train*, Issue 53, Page 4, Devane W. Cussins-Spruce.

Jack's body was found in his shanty after he wasn't seen for a period of time.

*The landmark for Hopkin's Mine on the railroad is a large boulder in the river that usually has a large trout under the boulder.*

## Beaver Creek–Between Mile Posts 33 and 34

There were logging operations at the commencement of WWII and for the duration of WWII near the Beaver Creek area. Lonnie Sager was the camp cook. Lonnie always kept soda pop and candy available at his camp, which was different from all other log camps. Lonnie also made the best doughnuts.

The cooks would always save the table scraps, peelings and leftovers from meals and dumped them into a fifty-five gallon steel barrel. The section gang foreman would haul the fifty-five gallon barrels to Cheat Bridge where the contents were cooked over an open fire, mixed with "midlins" and fed to hogs that provided winter meat to the railroad track men's families.

The pork was salted with "Morton Salt," and sometimes smoked with hickory flavoring. The hide, which contained fat, was roasted in wood stove ovens to save the lard and pork rinds. Other parts of the butchered pork was ground into sausage or canned in quart or half-gallon glass jars. The salted hams, shoulder and sides were stored in meathouses or smoked over a hickory fire and stored in the meat sheds.

Roy Houchin and a Dr. Church, a dentist from Grafton, had a camp at Beaver Creek. It was an entirely different setting than Dr. B.I. Hudkins' Camp at Cabin Fork. Roy, Dr. Church and his medical doctor brother were well known to partake of the "home-made mountain spirits," moonshine and bourbon whiskey. They were good-hearted, fun-loving me, but you never knew in what kind of condition you may find them when visiting their Beaver Creek fishing hunting camp.

Roy Houchin would harvest more than a dozen turkeys, several deer and black bears in a year without the help of dogs. Roy had one eye. He lost the other eye in a Durbin fist and knife fight. Roy was probably one of the best tracking and stalking wild game hunters in the upper Cheat and upper Greenbrier River area. Roy and Isaac Moore were caught by the game warden in the early 1940s with over two hundred native trout in lard buckets. Roy Houchin's camp was burned to the ground in the early 1950s and was never rebuilt.

Rex Albright, Sr. and Rex Albright, Jr., Buck Howell and Artie Shaw from Elkins had a small camp at the mouth of Beaver Creek near the railroad. Beaver Creek got its name because there were several beaver dams up Beaver Creek and on Shavers Fork above and below Beaver Creek. My cousin, Wanda Powers Sharp, remembers her brother-in-law, Charlie Fansler, she and her sisters, Juanita, Okareta, camping out at Beaver Creek, tearing down the Sager log camp and carrying the lumber to the railroad to be hauled on a push truck pulled by a motorcar to help construct a new home for Charlie and Juanita in the late 1940s.

The Randolph–Pocahontas county boundary line crosses the railroad above Beaver Creek and near Mile Post 34. Canyon Point is a deep and sharp bend in the river. There is a small low bluff above the Canyon that will bear both wild cherries and beechnuts when freezing temperatures, frosts or blight kills the beech and cherry at other locations along Cheat Bridge.

## The Log Train

If you will listen a song I will sing
About my daddy who ran a log train
Way down in the southland of old Alabam
We lived in a place that they call Chapman Town

And late in the evening when the sun was low
Way off in the distance you could hear the train blow
The folks would come running and Mama would sing
"Get the supper on the table here comes the log train"

Every morning at the break of day
He'd grab his lunch bucket and be on his way
Winter or summer, sunshine or rain
Every morning he's run that old log train

A sweatin' and swearin' all day long
Shouting "Get up there oxen keep moving along
Load her up boys cause it looks like rain
I've got to get rolling this old log train"

This story happened a long time ago
The log train is silent God called Dad to go
But when I get to heaven to always remain
I'll listen for the whistle on the old log train.

# MILEPOST LOCATIONS

*(as taken or compiled from CSX, B&O, WM documents)*

| Mile | Location |
|---|---|
| 0.0 | Tygart Jct. "RA" |
| 0.2 | Tygart Siding (850') |
| 0.6 | Byer Mine |
| 1.0 | Hobo Rock, Keystone Mfg. |
| 2.0 | Old B&O Tygart Jct. Yard Limit |
| 2.9 | Adma |
| 3.7 | Ruthland Mine |
| 4.0 | Middle Fork |
| 5.0 | O'Brien |
| 5.6 | Black Joe Mine Bridge |
| 5.9 | Clements (former 46-car pass. siding) |
| 6.1 | Empire Mine |
| 7.4 | Wilmoth (Abbott) Falls |
| 8.1 | Wilmoth Mine |
| 8.2 | Jones Crossing/Wilmoth Ford (Weese Camp) |
| 10.6 | Wilmoth Mill |
| 10.8 | McLean Station (acRiver- Abbott, aka Lehigh/Arnold) |
| 11.4 | B&O Wye |
| 11.5 | Belington Freight Station "BN" |
| 11.7 | Belington Passenger Station |
| 11.8 | WVC Engine House* |
| 12.1 | Roberts* |
| 12.6 | Weaver Jct., aka Gahanhurst |
| 13.0 | Charco |
| 13.8 | Dartmoore |
| 15.3 | Junior Sta. (acR- West Junior) |
| 16.0 | Gage Platform |
| 17.1 | Coffman |
| 17.6 | (acR- Dan Foy) |
| 17.8 | Laurel |
| 18.0 | (acR- Skidmore) |
| 18.7 | (acR- Findley) |
| 19.4 | Nova Scotia |
| 19.9 | (acR- Lieter Jct.) |
| 20.1 | (acR- Lieter) |
| 20.4 | Harding (acR- Bentley Coal Co.) (acR- Monroe Yard) |
| 20.9 | Swamp Run |
| 21.8 | Norton Siding (1200') |
| 22.1 | Roaring Creek Jct. "RJ" (acR- Norton; Coalton Branch) |
| 24.1 | Aggregate |
| 25.1 | Pearson (MP 116.2 original WVC&P line) |
| 26.1 | (Buxton, MP 115.2 on original WVC&P line) |
| 26.5 | Homewood |
| 28.4 | Elkins "DS" |
| 28.5 | Huttonsville Jct. |
| 0.7 | Elkins Jct. |
| 2.0 | Yard Limit |
| 1.9 | Arnold Hill Summit |
| 2.8 | Arnold Hill |
| 3.3 | Arnold Hill Spur |
| 4.9 | Myles |
| 5.2 | Platform |
| 5.4 | Myles Lbr. Siding |
| 6.6 | Beverly Handle Co. |
| 6.7 | Beverly Sta. |
| 7.2 | Lacraft Siding |
| 8.3 | Bruce Hardwood Siding |
| 9.5 | Westvaco Siding |
| 9.7 | Dailey (Kenwood Siding) |

| WM Central | | Location |
|---|---|---|
| 9.9 | | Dailey Platform |
| 0.6 | 28.6 | WM-B&O Freight House (Davis Ave.) |
| 0.8 | 28.8 | Elkins Pail & Lbr. (Brown's Lbr.) |
| 2.9 | 30.9 | Canfield |
| | 31.6 | Isner Loop |
| 4.8 | 32.8 | Tunnel Siding (1200') |
| 4.8 | 33.2 | Tunnel No. 1 (1716.5') |
| 6.1 | 34.1 | Lumber/McCauley |
| 4.5 | 35.6 | Meadows |
| 7.7 | 36.7 | Raine |
| 9.4 | 37.4 | Faulkner |
| 9.6 | 37.6 | Nydegger Stone |
| 10.1 | 38.4 | Bowden (Team Track and stub siding) |
| 11.6 | 39.6 | Kight/Harper |
| 12.0 | 40.0 | Revelle |
| 13.1 | 41.1 | Weese Crossing/Logton |
| 14.8 | 42.6 | Woodrow (4200' siding) |
| 15.6 | 43.7 | Flint/Pond Lick |
| 16.2 | 44.2 | Montes |
| 16.9 | 44.7 | Walker |
| 18.8 | 46.8 | Bemis/Fishing Hawk |
| 15.3 | 47.3 | Carl |
| 20.8 | 48.3 | Elk River Jct.* Spring Switch |
| 1.1 | 49.1 | Greenbrier Jct.* |
| 1.7 | 49.7 | Point |
| 2.8 | 50.8 | High Falls |
| 3.4 | 51.4 | Deer Lick coal tipple |
| 5.9 | 53.9 | Harper Water Tank |
| 5.9 | 54.2 | Harper Siding |
| 7.4 | 55.4 | Big John mine |
| 8.1 | 56.2 | Triplett |
| 12.1 | 60.2 | Helmick |
| 15.7 | 62.9 | Linan |
| 16.6 | 64.8 | E. End Pratt wye (w.e. 65.5) |
| 24.0 | 72.0 | Cheat Bridge |
| 28.5 | 76.4 | River |
| 28.9 | 76.9 | Water tank |
| 28.9 | 76.9 | 3-span 151' bridge |
| 29.1 | 77.1 | Hopkins Siding (w.e. 77.5) |
| 29.3 | 78.5 | Hopkins Mine Siding |
| 30.7 | 78.7 | Black Run |
| 32 | 80.4 | coal tipple |
| 37.4 | 85.4 | Twin bridges (2nd bridge 85.5) |
| 38.7 | 87.0 | Spruce (4800' siding) |
| 40.8 | 88.8 | Summit Cut |

acR= across river "XX" B&O telegraph ID
*"long" mile created with CSX renumbering
*38.7* WM mp (italic)

75

| Train Order Offices | Station Numbers | STATIONS Thomas Subdivision | Miles from Cumberland | Miles Between Stations | Passing Siding Capacity in Cars | Coal—Water—Wyes—Turntables | Other Tracks |
|---|---|---|---|---|---|---|---|
| TO | 167 | CUMBERLAND | 0.0 | 0.0 | | W | Yard |
| | 168 | RAIS SBLT | 0.1 | 0.1 | | | Yard |
| | 166A | MARYLAND JCT | 1.3 | 0.6 | | WCTY | Yard |
| | | RIDGELY END OF MD. JCT. WYE | 1.5 | 0.2 | | | |
| TO | 154 | MY | 1.7 | 0.2 | | | Yard |
| | 153 | VIRGINIA AVE | 2.7 | 1.0 | | | 27 |
| | 155 | W. E. MD. JCT. WYE. KNOBMOUNT END TWO MAIN TRACKS | 1.7 / 1.0 / 3.5 | 1.9 | | | Yard |
| | 04 | SEYMOUR | 5.7 | 2.2 | 82 | | |
| | 06A | PINTO ALLEGANY PLANT SIDING | 8.4 | 2.7 | | | 50 |
| | 07 | PINTO STA. SDG | 8.4 | 0.0 | | | 6 |
| | 010 | RAWLINGS | 11.6 | 3.2 | 121 | | |
| | 010 | RAWLINGS STA. SDG | 11.9 | 0.3 | | | 3 |
| | 014 | BLACK OAK | 15.0 | 3.1 | 117 | | |
| | 017 | GREEN | 18.4 | 3.4 | 60 | | |
| | 021 | McCOOLE | 21.5 | 3.1 | | | 8 |
| | 023 | POLAND | 25.2 | 3.7 | 145 | W | |
| | 025 | WESTERNPORT | 26.8 | 1.6 | | | 118 |
| | 025A | FOUNDRY | 27.4 | 0.6 | | | 17 |
| | 026 | LUKE | 27.7 | 0.3 | | | 47 |
| TO | 027 | W. VA. C. JCT | 28.5 | 0.8 | E65 / W86 | Y | Yard |
| | 028 | HAMPSHIRE | 29.3 | 0.8 | | | 78 |
| | 031 | WARNOCKS | 32.5 | 3.2 | 88 | | |
| | 033 | BARNUM | 34.6 | 2.1 | | | 24 |
| TO | 036 | SHAW | 37.5 | 2.9 | 125 | W | 57 |
| | 036 | SHAW LUMBER | 37.6 | 0.1 | | | 15 |
| | 038 | NEFFS | 40.4 | 2.8 | 56 | | |
| | 040 | CHAFFEE | 41.4 | 1.0 | | | 47 |
| | 041A | HAMILL MINE | 43.9 | 2.5 | | | 79 |

| Train Order Offices | Station Numbers | STATIONS Thomas Subdivision | Miles from Cumberland | Miles Between Stations | Passing Siding Capacity in Cars | Coal—Water—Wyes—Turntables | Other Tracks |
|---|---|---|---|---|---|---|---|
| | 043 | BLAINE | 44.7 | 0.8 | | | 11 |
| | 044 | POTOMAC MANOR CROSSOVER | 45.3 | 0.6 | | | |
| | | POTOMAC MANOR | 45.6 | 0.3 | | | 54 |
| | | HARRISON CROSSOVER | 45.8 | 0.2 | | | |
| TO | 045 | HARRISON | 46.3 | 0.5 | | Y | |
| | 045C | WOLFDEN MINE | 47.1 | 0.8 | | | 25 |
| | 045A | WOLF DEN No. 3 | 47.3 | 0.2 | | | 10 |
| | 048 | HUBBARD | 49.3 | 2.2 | | W | 8 |
| | 050 | SCHELL | 51.5 | 2.2 | 77 | | 3 |
| | 054 | WALLMAN | 54.9 | 3.4 | 119 | | |
| | 056 | STEYER | 57.0 | 2.1 | | W | 6 |
| | 058 | GORMAN | 58.7 | 1.7 | 80 | | 12 |
| TO | 060 | BAYARD | 61.9 | 3.2 | 114 | | 147 |
| | 061 | ARMSTRONG | 63.0 | 1.1 | | | 161 |
| | 062 | WILSON | 63.9 | 2.0 | | | 9 |
| | 064 | DOBBIN | 65.1 | 1.2 | 62 | W | |
| | 065 | HENRY East End | 66.7 | 1.6 | 249 | | |
| | 065B | McKELVEY | 67.0 | 0.3 | | | 10 |
| | 066 | KEMPTON JCT | 68.1 | 1.1 | | | |
| | 066A | KEMPTON MINE | 70.1 | 2.0 | | | 124 |
| | 065 | HENRY West End | 68.6 | 2.5 | 249 | | |
| | 070 | BEECHWOOD | 71.0 | 2.4 | | | |

TT6 - 9/25/49

| Train Order Offices | Station Numbers | STATIONS Thomas Subdivision | Miles from Cumberland | Miles Between Stations | Passing Siding Capacity in Cars | Coal—Water—Wyes—Turntables |
|---|---|---|---|---|---|---|
| | 071 | FAIRFAX | 73.0 | 2.0 | | Y |
| | 071A | FAIRFAX MINE | 73.2 | 0.2 | | |
| | 074B | BAND RUN JCT | 73.3 | 2.1 | | |
| | 074B | PIERCE Nos. 39-40-43 | 75.9 | 0.6 | | |
| | 074D | FAIRFAX SAND | 77.3 | 1.4 | | |
| | 075B | THOMAS No. 23-34 | 76.8 | 2.5 | | |
| TO | 075 | THOMAS | 76.9 | 1.1 | | WC |
| | 13 | DAVIS No. 36 | 81.0 | 4.1 | | |
| | 14 | FRANCIS MINE No. 41 | 81.4 | 4.5 | | |
| | | RENBUSH | 77.4 | 0.5 | | Y |
| | 075D | BENBUSH No. 38 | 78.2 | 0.8 | | |
| | 076A | COKETON | 78.4 | 1.0 | | |
| | 076B | DOUGLAS MINE | 78.6 | 0.2 | | |
| | 077 | DOUGLAS | 78.7 | 0.1 | | |
| | 078 | MOUNTAIN SWITCH | 79.6 | 0.9 | | |
| | 082 | TUB RUN | 81.4 | 1.8 | | |
| | 083 | LIME ROCK | 84.8 | 3.4 | | |
| | 085 | HENDRICKS East End | 86.1 | 1.3 | | |
| TO | 086 | HENDRICKS West End | 87.1 | 1.0 | | WY |
| | 087 | HAMBLETON | 88.0 | 0.9 | | W |
| | 088 | PARSONS-EXCELSIOR | 89.8 | 1.8 | | |
| | 088 | GOULD—TANNERY | 89.8 | 0.0 | | |
| TO | 089 | PARSONS | 90.5 | 0.7 | 115 | Y |
| | 093 | MOORE | 94.1 | 3.6 | | |
| | 098 | HADDIX | 98.5 | 4.4 | 28 | |
| TO | 090 | MONTROSE | 100.7 | 2.2 | 121 | WY |
| | 0103 | KERENS | 104.5 | 3.8 | 49 | |
| TO | 0107 | GILMAN | 108.2 | 3.7 | | |
| | 0109 | LEADSVILLE | 110.6 | 2.4 | | |
| TO | 0110 | ELKINS | 112.1 | 1.5 | | WCTY |

| Train Order Offices | Station Numbers | STATIONS Emoryville Subdivision | Miles from Harrison | Miles Between Stations | Passing Siding Capacity in Cars | Coal—Water—Wyes—Turntables |
|---|---|---|---|---|---|---|
| TO | 045 | HARRISON | 0.0 | 0.0 | | Y |
| | 045 | NEW SIDING | 0.5 | 0.5 | | |
| | 045 | EDDY MINE | 0.6 | 0.0 | | |
| | 81A | OAKMONT | 1.2 | 0.6 | | |

| Train Order Offices | Station Numbers | STATIONS Belington Subdivision | Miles from Elkins | Miles Between Stations | Passing Siding Capacity in Cars | Coal—Water—Wyes—Turntables |
|---|---|---|---|---|---|---|
| TO | 0110 | ELKINS | 0.0 | 0.0 | | WCTY |
| | 0110 | C. & C. JCT | 0.4 | 0.4 | | |
| | 0114 | AGGREGATE | 4.4 | 4.0 | | |
| TO | 0118 | NORTON | 7.3 | 2.9 | | |
| | 0119 | HARDING | 8.1 | 0.8 | | |
| | 0123 | GAGE | 12.8 | 4.7 | | |
| | 0124 | JUNIOR | 13.7 | 0.9 | | |
| | 0125 | OLD DARTMOOR | 14.7 | 1.0 | | |
| TO | 0128 | BELINGTON | 17.6 | 2.9 | | WY |

B. & O. R. R. crews operating between Elkins, Norton and Belington, will be governed by W. M. Ry. Time-Table and Rules.

| Station Numbers | STATIONS Huttonsville Subdivision | Miles from Elkins | Miles Between Stations | Passing Siding Capacity in Cars | Coal—Water Wyes—Turntables | Other Tracks |
|---|---|---|---|---|---|---|
| o110 | ELKINS............ | 0.0 | 0.0 | | WCTY | Yard |
| o110A | ELKINS JCT......... | 1.2 | 1.2 | | | |
| o4 | ARNOLD HILL........ | 3.3 | 2.1 | | | 2 |
| o7 | BEVERLY............ | 6.7 | 3.4 | | | 27 |
| o10 | DAILEY............. | 10.1 | 3.4 | | | 45 |
| o10 | KENWOOD............ | 10.1 | 0.0 | | | 25 |

| Station Numbers | STATIONS Durbin Subdivision | Miles from Elkins | Miles Between Stations | Passing Siding Capacity in Cars | Coal—Water Wyes—Turntables | Other Tracks |
|---|---|---|---|---|---|---|
| 110 | ELKINS............. | 0.0 | 0.0 | | WCTY | Yard |
| 3 | CANFIELD........... | 2.9 | 2.9 | | | 10 |
| 5 | TUNNEL............. | 4.8 | 1.9 | 31 | | |
| 6 | LUMBER............. | 6.1 | 1.3 | | | 4 |
| 9A | FAULKNER........... | 9.4 | 3.3 | | W | 5 |
| 10A | NYDEGGER STONE... | 9.6 | 0.2 | | | 23 |
| 10 | BOWDEN............. | 10.1 | 0.5 | 41 | Y | 28 |
| 12 | REVELLE............ | 12.0 | 1.9 | | | 2 |
| 13A | WEESE CROSSING.... | 13.1 | 1.1 | | | 8 |
| 14 | WOODROW........... | 14.8 | 1.7 | 105 | | |
| 15 | FLINT.............. | 15.6 | 0.8 | | | 3 |
| 17 | WALKER............. | 16.9 | 1.3 | | | 36 |
| 19 | BEMIS.............. | 18.8 | 1.9 | | W | 12 |
| | ELK RIVER JCT...... | 20.8 | 2.0 | | | |
| 2 | CHEAT JCT.......... | 21.8 | 1.0 | | W | |
| 3 | HOLLAND............ | 23.2 | 1.4 | | | 17 |
| 4 | GLADY.............. | 24.5 | 1.3 | | | 15 |
| 8 | BEULAH............. | 27.8 | 3.3 | | | 9 |
| 0 | OXLEY.............. | 30.7 | 2.9 | | W | |
| 1 | WILDELL............ | 31.3 | 0.6 | | | 7 |
| 5 | MAY................ | 36.4 | 5.1 | 55 | | |
| | BRAUCHER........ .. | 41.4 | 5.0 | | | 8 |
| 6 | OLIVE.............. | 44.7 | 3.3 | | | 5 |
| 7 | DURBIN............. | 46.9 | 2.2 | | WY | Yard |

| Train Order Offices | Station Numbers | STATIONS G. C. & E. Subdivision | Miles from Elk River Jct. | Miles Between Stations | Passing Siding Capacity in Cars | Coal—Water Wyes—Turntables | Other Tracks |
|---|---|---|---|---|---|---|---|
| | M22 | ELK RIVER JCT....... | 0.0 | 0.0 | | | |
| | M22 | CHEAT JCT. YARD.. | 1.6 | 1.6 | | W | 35 |
| | M22 | GREENBRIER JCT.... | 1.1 | 1.1 | | | |
| | P1 | POINT.............. | 1.7 | 0.6 | | | 40 |
| | P6 | HARPER............. | 5.9 | 4.2 | | W | 12 |
| | P9 | TRIPLETT........... | 8.1 | 2.2 | | | 16 |
| | P12 | HELMICK............ | 12.1 | 4.0 | | | 27 |
| | P15 | LINAN.............. | 15.7 | 3.6 | | W | 9 |
| | P17 | PRATT East End..... | 16.6 | 0.9 | | Y | 6 |
| | P23 | CROMER............. | 23.9 | 7.3 | | | 13 |
| | P24 | CHEAT BRIDGE....... | 24.0 | 0.1 | | | 24 |
| | | RIVER............. | 28.5 | 4.5 | | W | |
| | P29 | HOPKINS............ | 29.3 | 0.8 | | | 17 |
| | P39 | SPRUCE............. | 38.7 | 9.4 | | CWY | Yard |
| | P41 | SUMMIT............. | 41.2 | 2.5 | | | 7 |
| | P46 | MT. AIRY........... | 45.2 | 4.0 | | | 12 |
| | P48 | DUNLAP............. | 47.1 | 1.9 | | | 7 |
| | P49 | WALNUT............. | 49.0 | 1.9 | | | 11 |
| TO | P53 | LAUREL BANK........ | 52.8 | 3.8 | 60 | WY | Yard |
| | P57 | ELK RIVER BRIDGE... | 56.7 | 3.9 | | | 10 |
| | P63 | HICKORY LICK....... | 63.2 | 6.5 | 92 | W | |
| | P63 | GOLDEN RIDGE No. 6 | 63.3 | 0.1 | | | 138 |
| | P69 | BYERS.............. | 67.5 | 4.2 | 37 | Y | |
| | P69 | MINE No. 4......... | 67.7 | 0.2 | | | 239 |
| | P71 | MINE No. 5......... | 69.9 | 2.2 | | | 93 |
| TO | P74 | BERGOO............. | 74.1 | 4.2 | | CWY | Yard |
| | P75 | MINE No. 3......... | 75.4 | 1.3 | | | 30 |
| | P80 | EAST BARTON........ | 80.3 | 4.9 | | | 80 |
| | P81 | BARTON............. | 80.8 | 0.5 | | | |
| | P81A | MINE No. 2......... | 81.2 | 0.4 | | | 166 |
| | P82 | DEEP RUN........... | 82.1 | 0.9 | | W | |
| TO | P86 | WEBSTER SPRINGS.... | 85.6 | 3.5 | | | Yard |
| | P86A | BACK FORK JCT...... | 85.9 | 0.3 | | | Yard |
| | P87 | BACK FORK.......... | 86.9 | 1.0 | | | Yard |

# $\mathcal{B}$ig $\mathcal{R}$un–$\mathcal{M}$ile $\mathcal{P}$ost 35–$\mathcal{T}$he $\mathcal{B}$ull of the $\mathcal{W}$oods

The mouth of Big Run is downstream approximately one third mile from the Mile Post 35 Trestle and is the area where the overhead log skidders operated by coal-steam power, mounted on two flat railroad cars. One flat car had the steam powered system engine with a coal storage big and the other flat car held the fifty to seventy-five feet perpendicular boom or tower that had many heavy cables tightly and securely anchored, bound and attached to heavy boulders, stumps or trees at their base. There was a circular revolving sort of wheel at the top of the tower that could turn in two directions with at least three cables attached to the top of the tower. One heavy cable was low to the ground and the top cable had fifteen to thirty smaller choker cables that were snared around the front end of the log and hooked to the larger cable to pull the logs to the skidder site railroad log dump.

The choker cables may be seven to ten feet in length. The only kind of weather that prevented overhead skidders from operating was two feet of snow. Neither wind, rain, heat nor twenty below temperatures would stop the skidders from full operation.

The skidder crew had the skidder boss, the operator, foreman and a couple men working the log pile at the landing where the logs were pulled in from the mountain to the railroad sidetrack where the skidder site was located. Woodrow Sharp was the skidder boss for "Skidder #5".

The choker gang was made up of the choker boss, bull hooker and two to three choker hookers, who hooked chokers and pulled slack on the cable, if the cable was too tight. All members of the choker gang wore calk shoes (shoes with a half inch to one calk tracks in the soles and heels in order not to slip when climbing the logs that may be twenty to forty feet high and one hundred feet in depth. The Skidder #5 choker gang boss was Pat Elza, who stood six feet five inches, skin stretched over bones with one top "snaggled tooth" in his mouth. Pat Elza could take six feet in one step when he got excited and was also the "steward" of the so-called Company union in the mid-1950s. Nevin Summerfield was the "bull hooker".

The rigging gang was made up of the real "bulls," strong men who could climb big trees to install and mount the cables. The rigger crewman had to be able to carry two rolls of cable, one on each shoulder through the heavy "slashings" treetops and limbs where the skidder path would drag the logs to the skidder site down to the railroad skidder site. The distance may be a half mile away. Each roll of cable would weigh fifty to one hundred pounds.

There was an anchored tail tree at the backside of the skidder trail and an anchored middle tree. The logs would be pulled from the tail tree to the middle tree and then pulled to the skidder site log landing.

Mose Peters, Cass, WV, was the head rigger and rigging crew boss for Skidder #5. Smokey Shreve, Mill Creek, WV, was a long-time rigging crewmember.

The "bell boy" had a battery-powered transmitter and line that connected the "choker gang" to the skidder operator that would signal the different procedures to pull the logs to the skidder site landing. "Pappy" Taylor was the bell boy for the #5 Skidder. The top compliment for a lumberjack was to be called "The Bull of the Woods" was the strongest, meanest, risk taking dominant man in the log camp.

The overhead skidder site would be located to provide an area of $360^0$ to drag the logs to the skidder site landing and was always selected by the Woods Superintendent Clark Phillips, Rocky Fisher, assistant superintendent, Bruce Crickard, the surveyor and the skidder boss. A skidder site may last for a year or more. It was a big operation to move the overhead skidder from one location to another. It usually required relocating the entire log camp operation.

79

Many men were killed or severely and permanently injured by cables breaking. If a cable broke, it took everything in its path and each person got as low to the ground among heavy rocks as he could, if he had enough time to save his body from death or injury. The rigging and choker gang crew earned a "little more" on their hourly wages because of the dangerous risk taking and extremely hard work.

The logging of Big Run Watershed started during WWII, about 1943. The logging wasn't completed when the Mower Lumber Company terminated the overhead skidder and logging camp operations during the late 1950s at the headwaters of Cabin Fork. The old log railroad from Cass ran up Leather Bark, toward Bald Knob and then followed the present U.S. Government Road to the drop off to the current Cabin Creek concrete bridge.

The 1950s brought enclosed old passenger railroad cars coupled together to house, feed and quarter about 100-150 Mower Lumber Company employees on a side track near the cutting, skidding and transportation to the big mill in Cass. Shay engines hauled the logs daily from the top of either Shavers or Cheat Mountain to the Cass Mill. I recall the Skidders # 4 and 5.

Elva June Phillips, a classmate and special friend in our forty-four member 1953 Green Bank High School graduating class, pressured her dad, Clark Phillips, to give me a job on the Mountain the summer of 1955. Clark Phillips first assigned me to hooking chokers on the choker gang with Pat Elza and later to the rigging gang with Mose Peters. I couldn't afford calk shoes. It was a very wet, rainy summer. I purchased a pair of six-inch top work shoes and six pairs of thin socks for five dollars from George Joseph, Dry Hoods Store in Elkins and didn't try the shoes on before purchasing them. I later learned the shoes had no inside lining. I rubbed twenty-three blisters on my feet at one time and used up all the first aid materials on the Mountain to treat my feet and worked every day. We also carried two rolls of wench line cable fifty to one hundred pounds on each shoulder through timber slashings as a member of the rigging gang.

At night, I felt like dirt was in my bed while asleep. I would wake up each morning with "red bites" all over my body. One day, while sitting beside Pat Elza, I felt something crawling on the back of my neck. I crushed the creature and blood smeared over my fingers. Immediately Pat Elza recognized it as a "bed bug". Pat took six-foot steps at a time to the camp to inspect my "top bunk bed" during our lunch break. Pat's inspection of my bed, which was over Kenneth Taylor, a timber cutter from Mill Creek, found "bed bugs" along the folded seam of the mattress filled with my blood. "Buck Chestnut," who was the "lobby hog" for the camp really caught Pat's "cussin" because it gave Pat the Company Union Stewart, a real issue against the Mower Lumber Company for poor working conditions on the mountain. The bed bugs didn't bother anybody in camp except me.

A few weeks later, the pre-season football camp started at Davis & Elkins College. I had been awarded a football scholarship at D&E . I left the Mountain under the ultimate choice given me by Clark Phillips, woods superintendent. Clark Phillips traveled to and from the Mountain daily by motorcar.

Workers arose from 4:30–5 a.m., breakfast was over by 6 a.m. and each worker started walking to the job site on "your own time" to arrive before 7 a.m. The skidder whistle blew at 7 a.m. and the entire woods operation started for the day. The lunch whistle blew at 12 noon and you walked to lunch and returned at 1 p.m. on your own time and started work when the whistle blew at 1 p.m. You worked until 5 p.m., when the skidder whistle blew to end the day's work. A workday was nine to ten hours and the extra hour was to pay for your board and room to Mower Lumber Company.

Most workers went home for the weekend. We walked at least three miles out the mountain top railroad and down Shavers

Mountain to Back Mountain Road, which runs from Durbin to Cass, a distance of fourteen miles.

The summer of 1954-1955, we walked to David Moore's residence on Back Mountain Road where several workers had vehicles parked. I rode with William O'Dell, Highland Park in Elkins, who worked as a tong hooker on the log loader, a crewmember and sometimes fired the skidder (shoveled coal and greased the skidder) on Skidder #5. O'Dell had seven to eight riders in the 1938 Dodge-Plymouth car that he drove to Elkins. Mother would make me take my clothes off and bathe in a "round metal wash tub" in the outhouse next to the back door each Friday evening when I came home from the Mower Lumber Company Log Camp at the head of Big Run.

## Over the Hill

When you were terminated from employment, it was termed "over the hill" or "git shed of". There was no "lollygaggin" in log camps. It had rained for several days on the mountain. The railroad tracks were filled with water and the woods were extremely slick. I had a cold, twenty-three blisters rubbed on my feet, was recovering from being "kivvered" with bed bug bites and was listening to the pouring rain from an all night rainstorm hitting the top of the railroad bunk car early one cold August morning.

None of the workers had "hit the track" to the woods. All of them told me to get out of bed. I told them it was "unfit for a dog" to be out in the weather, let alone us work in it. A few of the men agreed. Some said the mill needed our logs. All the workers had returned from breakfast; I hadn't gone to breakfast. Suddenly I heard chalk shoes from all the bunk cars and lobby cars hitting the track, splashing water and loud voices– "There comes the old SOB." That meant Clark Phillips had arrived on his motorcar from Cass and the crew hadn't "clum" the mountain in the heavy rain.

I remained in the top bunk in bed. Clark Phillips approached me fully attired in raincoat and rain hat. It was about 6:30 a.m. before the starting whistle from #5 Skidder blew at 7 a.m. Phillips gave me a few of his choice words, which I recall, after he inquired why I was still in bed and not on the hill.

I replied "Do you think I'm crazy? It's not fit for a dog to work in this weather."

Clark Phillips kinda smiled— "Get your ass on the hill or over the hill."

I responded, "Over the hill." I ate my breakfast, packed my bags and descended the log woods for my last time and walked home to Cheat Bridge.

The work experience made me realize I had better work hard, make good grades, save money and graduate from college; and that the Cheat Mountain lumberjacks, railroaders, gandy dancers and coal miners were better men than me.

George Shimer from Elkins was the cook at #5 Skidder site. There was neither refrigeration nor electricity. The longer the week went the more sugar, salt and lard you consumed from George Shimer's kitchen. The table was the full length of a passenger railroad car and was loaded with any kind of "vittles" you desired, except fresh fruits or fresh vegetables. Once in a while there may be a orange or apple from the Cass Company Store. You had three full meals a day. Pie, cake, salt side pork, gravy, coffee, homebaked bread, and a variety of beans and Irish potato dishes were served for breakfast, lunch and supper. All pastries were baked at the camp and each meal had beans and potatoes fixed many different ways. Coffee was served with canned milk. There was always plenty of "Arm & Hammer Baking Soda" for heartburn or indigestion that each worker usually experienced. The proper medical term today is "acid reflux".

The lobby car and bunk cars had the aroma of "Balsam Myrrh,"

Sloan's Liniment and Yeager's Liniment used to treat the aches and pains for muscle soreness and joint stiffness at night after a hard day's work.

I recall Russell Taylor, a most kind, gentle timber cutter accidentally cut his knee with a double-bitted ax one morning. We tracked his blood from the woods and on the cross ties to camp at noon. The cook, George Shimer and Buck Chestnut, our lobby hog, wrapped his knee with "bed sheets". Russell walked with a cane off the Mountain to David Moore's house, up Back Mountain Road to near Kisner's Motel at the Pocahontas–Randolph county line on U.S. Rt. 250 before he got a ride to Mill Creek for Dr. Spencer or Dr. Leggett to treat the deep cut across his knee joint. Russell Taylor caught "blood poison" in his knee and never returned to the "woods". Russell probably didn't have the benefit of good workers' compensation coverage at that time.

Timber cutting in the Cheat River Basin log camps was done by hand-powered two block or four block crosscut saws. A timber cutting crew consisted of two sawers and one "Knot Bumper" who trimmed the limbs and treetops with an ax. There were no gasoline powered chainsaws. Some of the timber cutters were Tom Yokum, Kenneth Taylor, Squire Kittle (still living and married a woman from New Zealand in WWII), Cecil Kittle and Charlie Tackett, Vance Howard and many others.

My former Green Bank High School teacher, Roy Clarkson, stated the injury to his back as a young man while stacking green lumber at Cass Mill is what prompted him to attend college and become a school teacher. Roy is retired from the biology department of West Virginia University.

The Mower Lumber Company Operations provided food, clothing and shelter for many families' survival in southern Randolph County and northern Pocahontas County. The overhead skidder operations started above Beaver Creek and extended to the headwaters of Shavers Fork, to the headwaters of Tygart River at the top of Mower Company Farm, Rock Run, Thorny Flats (now Snowshoe and Silver Creek Resorts).

The Cass Mill was closed July 1, 1960. Burned to the ground and, was never rebuilt and The Mower Lumber Company skidder operations ceased, as did the pride of the rugged workers and their families. The railroad workers, lumberjacks, coal miners and their families from Cheat River Basin headwaters, on to Spruce and Point Marion, PA, answered President Franklin D. Roosevelt's call "To Give a Better Day's Work For a Fair Day's Pay". They gave their full measure! They were the most dedicated, hardest working, honest, sincere, caring, sharing and considerate people I have every been blessed to have known.

We usually received two pairs of blue jeans, a couple new cotton flannel long-sleeved shirts, high-topped shoes and socks at the commencement of the school term. The trousers had "patches" sewed on the knees and seats by our mothers and grandmothers come spring. Trousers were referred to as "britches". Many walked a "right fur piece" to attend school. The girls wore skirts below their knees just above their ankles, brown and white saddle oxfords and white "Bobbi socks". Young, beautiful country girls could walk through the same mud holes as boys and remain unsoiled when they arrived at Green Bank High School. The boys would be mud from head to toe. I could really never understand the reason.

Most young ladies couldn't afford perfume and would place a "dab" of vanilla or lemon food flavoring from their mother's kitchen cupboard behind their ears to "smell good" for their dates or attending "the doin's". The young mountain ladies "made do with what they had" and were very beautiful. They often had a strong smell of Ivory or Lux soap. However, the young ladies kept their bodies immaculately clean although there was somewhat a lack of indoor plumbing and bathing facilities in the company wood frame uninsulated houses. We all had Saturday night baths in the round steel wash tubs and the girls usually got the first chance to get bathed. Summertime bathing was done by the entire family at the swimming hole. Many of the Mountain Celtic young ladies left our area in the 1950s, married and made their "lucky husbands" millionaires because of the traits instilled in them by their families and through the upbringing experienced in their mountain homes.

In the early 1900s the timbering and logging operations were performed by teams of draft horses and transported to the mills at Spruce and Cass by railroad as previously described from upper Cheat.

The summer of 1931 was dry; a real draught that caused a fire near the Twin Bridges above Big Run and below Spruce. The fire was started from the "sparks" of a steam locomotive and burned until the following spring. The fire damage was visible for the remainder of the 1930s through the 1950s. The area was covered with briers, rocks, moss and brush, but no trees. The fallen-over vegetation from the fire damage along the Shavers Mountain side of the railroad was more than a mile along the railroad to the top of Shavers Mountain and beyond.

There were a couple hunting camps at Big Run. A camp was constructed after 1955 by Larry Pnakovich son of Al Pnakovich of Valley Bend, WV while he was a student at Tygart Valley High School. Al was a three hundred pound, six foot five inches tall Hickory Lick coal miner, who raised his son on the Cheat Mountain. Larry was the probation officer for the late Judge Jack Nuzum, circuit court of Randolph County. Lee Sharp, "Bud" Sanders, "Bull Dog" Smith, Archie Beck and others had hunting and fishing camps near Big Run Trestle.

# Spruce

An earlier writer, Max Robin characterized the town of Spruce as. . ., "Often mentioned, but seldom explained." Certainly, anyone who ever heard of Spruce could not help but be fascinated. After all, communications on the Cass Scenic Railroad trains for years have pointed it out as a ghost town, a town that never had any roads, and the "highest and coldest town east of the Mississippi".

Devane "Booche" Wade Cussins has written an article, "A Childhood At Spruce" published in Issue 40 of *The Log Train* that fully describes what it was like to grow up at Spruce. Devane was born January 17, 1936, and lived at Spruce until he was about fifteen years old.

There was a two-room schoolhouse and one room was used as a classroom, while the other room was used as a "playroom" when the weather was too bad to go outside. There were eight grades.

There were about twenty houses in Spruce during the 1930s-1950. Some were single family and some were two family, but all were two story, except for a few shanties for the bachelors. Each house had its own outhouse with a path. All houses had cold running water, which usually froze in the winter. Each house had its own trash pile in the back. The kitchen sink sewage was piped to the lower end of each yard.

Most everyone had pet wild animals, such as, bear cubs, skunks, raccoons and groundhogs, as well as dogs and cats. The residents hunted wild game, fished, trapped and, in the springtime, dug ramps. The ramps were dug and then carried in burlap sacks or bushel baskets.

There were two Western Maryland water tanks for the 700 series steam locomotives, Trackman's Tool House, Log Pond from old Pulp Wood Peeling Mill, Jumbo's store building, hotel, two-room schoolhouse, Western Maryland Locomotive Repair Shop and the twenty residential dwelling houses, coal storage bin tippled and storage bin. The Western Maryland kept the large "Steel Snowplow Car" at Spruce mounted on the front of a railroad car and pushed in front of the steam locomotive to remove snow. There were four to seven 700 series Steam Locomotives kept at Spruce by the Western Maryland Railroad to help pull and shove the loaded coal trains up Cheat Mountain from Webster County through Slaty Fork, and Mace to the "Big Cut" or Cheat Summit above Spruce.

Winter was a fun time for Spruce kids. Groceries were purchased from Troy Mace at Mace and hauled on Lem Vance's motorcar and push truck to Spruce, except in real bad weather. In severe winter weather, Frank Imes would send a 700 series steam engine and caboose to Mace for the groceries. Cow's milk to drink was a luxury. Another way of getting groceries was to send the grocery list to the A&P Store in Elkins. They would ship or "fetch" the groceries to Spruce in a boxcar. The only vegetables grown in Spruce were green onions, lettuce, tomatoes, radishes and turnips because of both late spring and early fall frosts.

If you traveled by motorcar at night, a man would sit up front and hold the kerosene lantern to light up the tracks in front. The "big cut" was always bad for slides and falling rocks and often required a trackman/watchman. There were numerous cold water springs along the railroad tracks near Spruce.

There were three "dog houses" or "phone box houses" at Spruce where men loafed, spun their tales and "caught up on local current affairs." Each shack had a pot-bellied stove, a couple of benches, coal box, railroad spike kegs to sit on and a Western Maryland telephone. The telephone allowed the trainmen and "gandy dancers" to get their "line up" or orders and authorization to use the railroad tracks to travel to the desired destination from a railroad "dispatcher" in Elkins.

The swimming facilities were a swimming hole above Spruce where the old Shay logging tracks crossed the river and the other was at the Twin Bridges below Spruce. The coal heat was free along the Cheat River railroad communities. When the loaded coal train came to a stop, every healthy male would climb up the steel ladder on the side of the steel coal car and roll the lumps of coal onto the ground on each side of the tracks. Then the families would haul the coal in a wheelbarrow to the coal house. All houses had a small wood shed beside the coal house. Kindling wood was cut to start the fire and coal was added. All the railroad repair buildings had steam heat.

Most families had a Maytag square tub washing machine powered by a small Briggs and Stratton gasoline engine. They also had steel galvanized round washtubs and a washboard.

Some of the families and people I remember at Spruce were: **Cussins**-Sylvester, Edith, Albert (Bud), Devane (Booche), Nancy Sue; **Sharp**-Rosie, Johnny, Lee, Alice, Steral; **Powers**-Dorie, Dovie, Okareta, Wanda, Murl, Bernice, Arveda, Joyce and Jerry; **Nelson**-Jeff, Grace, Jack, Bob, Harper, Barbara Jane, Sondra; **Teter**-Carl, Dessie, Bud, Bernice, Mildred, Pauline; **Fansler**-Charlie, Juanita, Patty, Clarence, Rosalee, Millie, Junior, Jennnie, Gordon, Berry, Anita Fay and Danny; **Weese**-Bert, Edna, Leo and Jeanette; **Vance**-Lemuel (Lem), Mint; **Vance**-Nathan, Elaine, Deloris and Maurace Presseau; **Arbogast**-Herb and sons Bud and "Pig"; **Imes**-Frank, Mamie; **White**-Sheffie, Mattie Lou, Jasper, May and Dale; Charles Boyd; John Boye; Carl Dunham; **Rock**-Vernon, Mrs. Rock, Betty; Lonnie Sager (cook at log camp); Thad Higgins (lumberjack; Kelly-Woodrow, Pete, Earl; **Broughton**-Tom, Mrs. Broughton, Hershel, Virgil, Eddie, Betty, Carol, Mr. Mullinax; **Sanders**-Bud, Sherwood; **Calain**-Charlie, Mrs. Calain, Darlene, Melly, Odbert, Jimmy; school teachers-

Louise Brown, Mr. Clendenin, Miss. Ruth Blackhurst, Grace Nelson, Mr. Bell, Emma Gail Reynolds; Johnny Bolyard; Mary Champ, daughters Bonnie and Marge; Luther and Georgia Cross; Jennifer Hedrick; **Gainer**-John, Bob, Boyd; **Miller**-Bing, Omie Donnie, Bud and Kinney; **Morgan**-Jim, Flossie, Betty, Shirley, Wayne; **Oldecker**-Roy, wife and son Bobby; **Owens**- "Jumbo" Clyde, wife and son, Harvey; **Phillips**-Outen, Sylvia, Charlie; Charles "Red" Rhodes; Charlie Ratcliff; Earl Rosier; **Simmons**-Russ, Eve and Jenny; **Semones**-Russ, wife, Elmer and Arthur; John Young; Thurmand and Dessie Watson; Harry Jasper and Violet Triplett; **Kissinger**-Charlie, Fred.

There were double and triple sidetracks from lower Spruce Train Yard that would hold hundreds of freight railroad cars, steel car hoppers, boxcars and flat cars.

My high school teacher, Warren E. "Tweard" Blackhurst, at Green Bank would ask the question, "What is the only town that had a schoolhouse, store, post office and sawmill and train shop with residents that has never had an automobile driven to it?" The answer was "Spruce". W.E. Blackhurst is the author of *Riders Of The Flood* and other books about lumbering at Cass.

Spruce, during the early 1900s was made up of one hundred plus two-story wood-framed houses for mill workers, railroad workers and their families. Houses were on all sides of the hills and railroad tracks. My cousin, Wanda Powers Sharp, told me Spruce had one hundred families when the pulp peeling mill operated. The store was operated by an Italian immigrant, "Jumbo," who later had a small variety store in Durbin.

There were also "drummers or peddlers" who carried their merchandise or wares on their backs and walked from Elkins to Spruce to sell, trade or barter their merchandise. Three of the early peddlers who later opened businesses in Elkins were George Joseph, "Sol" Goldberg and Alex Goldberg.

There were several young women and men who commenced

their teaching careers in the two-room wood-frame schoolhouse of Spruce. They roomed and boarded with a Spruce working family. Several of the teachers roomed and boarded with my cousin Dora Powers and his family.

There were four to seven steam locomotives kept at the Spruce train ships by the Western Maryland Railroad. There were general locomotive mechanics and apprentices. A few living Western Maryland employees at Spruce include, Sherwood "Bud" Sanders, Patrick Dugan, Guy Mundell and Bert Weese, who was a locomotive engineer. Some other locomotive engineers were: Charlie Kissinger, Charlie Phillips, Charlie Kittle, Arthur Semones, Doris Pritt, Coy Lambert, David Bohon, Liedy Bohon, Elmer "Red" Warner and Sam Waugh, Jade Powers, Jeff Nelson, Herb Arbogast and Charlie Calain, Preston Triplett, Jack Triplett and Sylvester W. "Pappy" Cussins, Lawrence Kisner, and many others. Bert Weese and his wife were great companion hunters and their son Leo was born at Spruce and started the first grade at Spruce.

Transportation was by walking or riding a motorcar to Cass, Mace, Mount Airy or Cheat Bridge. Charlie Calain constructed railroad wheels on a Model "A" Ford, two-seated car and traveled to and from Spruce to Mt. Airy.

Several children were playing near the Frank Imes' house when Mrs. Imes came flying airborne from the house to the front yard exposing herself. She immediately got up, straightened up her clothing and stated– "Frank, you mustn't play so rough next time."

Frank Imes– "By God, I ain't playin' and you better straighten up!" Frank Imes was the trainmaster at Spruce and was most attentive and felt responsible for the railroad families' best interests and welfare.

Frank Imes would disperse Jim Morgan, by either motorcar or with a 700 series steam locomotive to Cheat Bridge in the sub-zero temperatures in heavy snow to meet and transport Dr. George

Hull or Dr. Eugene Burner from Cheat Bridge to Spruce in the cab of the 700 series coal-fired steam engine locomotive. Jim Morgan was a railroad trackman and "hostler" for the 700 series steam engines. He kept the steam engine's coal fire "stoked up and banked" and saw there was plenty of coal in the coal tender and water in the water storage tank. Frank Imes was killed stepping from a 700 series steam locomotive at Hickory Lick Tipple on Elk River to throw a switch at the Bethlehem Mine coal loading facility.

Dr. George Hull, M.D. was a complete opposite make-up than Eugene Burner, M.D. Both were cigar smokers and had cigar or cigarette holders to hold their lighted cigars or cigarettes.

Dr. George Hull was from Highland County, Virginia, and a University of Virginia Medical School graduate. Dr. Hull was known to sample the home-mountain manufactured spirits by many mountain people.

Both Dr. Hull and Dr. Burner wore either black Angus Hide or Black Bear Hide fur coats with a black fur hat and gloves on the cold winter train rides to Spruce to deliver the Weese, Broughton, Sharps, Powers, Teters, Morgans and other children born at Spruce. Betty or "Granny" Rock served as midwife, if the physician was unable to make it in time for the new delivery.

The early section gang foremen at Spruce were my Uncle Harry Jasper Triplett, Lemuel Vance, (father of Earl Vance, Letha Vance Cromer, Eva Vance McDaniel and Thelma Vance Burner). Lemuel was the grandfather of Carol "Sis" Vance, Robert "Bob," Beth Vance Beverage, Kenneth Vance and "Little Earl" Vance.

Lemuel was a very straight-laced, well-groomed exception. His shop cap was well starched, clean, with bibbed overalls pressed, clean work clothes and wore a good watch chain in his bibbed overalls. Lemuel usually had a "good chew of Mail Pouch or Beech Nut Tobacco" and had great pride.

Nathan, brother of Lemuel, was a section gang hand. Nathan

worked for Lemuel and was known to enjoy a "toot" on payday in Elkins and return to Spruce with a hangover for work on Mondays. Lemuel was a big 240 pounds plus and Nathan was about 140 pounds with "skin stretched" over bones. Dora Powers was a section gang hand and moved to Spruce about 1927 with his wife and family and was the last family to move from Spruce in 1950.

Late one hot summer afternoon in the sun, the Spruce section gang, after replacing crossties by hand were attempting to properly line up the steel rails with Lemuel directing and supervising the alignment to his pride and satisfaction. A steel lining bar weighed twenty-eight pounds and the section hands would spread out, and under the directions of the foreman, pull with thrusts either "toward" the river or "away" from the river a certain number of times on the signal "YOO-HE, YOO-HE". Nathan was dragging his lining bar across the new cross ties as the men walked back and forth from one location to another and Lemuel stated, "O' Nathan, pick up your bar and carry it like the rest of the men."

Nathan, ringing wet with perspiration and exhaustion answered, "I can't. I'm tired. You said you were going to quit an hour ago." Lemuel got the message and the crew returned to the Spruce Tool House to end the day's work.

There was always a shortage of beautiful, attractive women; actually not enough to go around for all the men. On one occasion a jealous husband who believed a sixteen-year-old male was attracted to his wife, immediately, fatally shot the boy. The circuit court of Pocahontas County sentenced him to the penitentiary, but he was released at his first appearance before the West Virginia Parole board.

Lee Sharp, a section gang hand who had two or three fingers missing from a blasting cap explosion, was a real hunter and fisherman. When I was about six years old, I saw my first twenty-five inch rainbow trout and a twenty-six inch brown trout caught by

Lee on Elk River. Lee Sharp was continuously catching "black bears" in wooden bear pen traps and taming them to lead on a leash.

There is an old railroad grade from the River Bridge on Spruce that was the Mower or West Virginia Pulp & Paper Company railroad that connects with the Bald Knob railroad line leading down "Leather Bark" to the old Cass Mill Site. The current road travels up Black Run to Snowshoe Resort, which is near the Western Maryland and West Virginia Pulp & Paper Company Junction.

### Big Cut–Cheat Summit
*(see cover photo)*

For many years the Woods Family were always the caretakers of the four thousand acres plus Mower Company Farms that were sold to Bill and Claude Hylton, owners of Friendship Stockyards, near Baltimore, Maryland, during the early 1960s. Norval Woods, then his sons Clarence Woods and Wilson Woods, were the farm managers.

During the 1950s when Saul McNeely was woods superintendent, the food got so bad, and the bed bugs were "eating the men alive" in the camps so bad, the beds and mattresses were worn out, which led to a "revolt or strike" by the workers. They all left the Mountain until Saul McNeely and Fred Weber, general superintendent at Cass and Rocky Fisher provided new bedsteads, new springs, mattresses and better "grub". The old bedsteads and springs can still be observed on the old railroad grade on the Tygart Valley side of the Cheat Summit or Big Cut near Mile Post 88.8. The old logging railroad ran along the mountaintop down to the head of Rock Run across the Mountain from the Company Farm caretaker's house at the headwaters of the Tygart River.

## "The Bedrock Foundation"
## What is a Home Without a Mother?
## "The Mountain Woman"

This book focuses primarily on the mountain men who worked in logging, coal mining, timbering and railroading. What goes unrecognized is the support by their families, primarily, their wives. Unquestionably, the wife was the backbone and foundation for survival.

## The Hand That Rocks the Cradle Rules the World

A mountain woman is a most special person. A successful mountain family had the caring, giving, loving, hard-working, considerate, saving, solid woman who shouldered the ultimate burdens. She always had a warm smile, hug and kiss for her family. She provided words of encouragement to her family when times were bad.

The women always "breed out" a little better than the men. They have natural beauty and love with a solid strength and sense of quietness that controls "the man of the house" with a most positive influence without his knowing it. She requires her husband's attention, love, support and staying the course through good times and bad times. Mountain women "give all" of themselves for their men and families.

A mountain woman usually has a small "stash" of cash unknown to the rest of the family hidden in a drawer, can, apron, under a rug or in the fruit cellar for a family emergency. Women were held in "high esteem". If a man mistreated his woman the whole community and family "got down on him." The normal expression for a lazy man or abusive man was "he ain't worth takin' out and killin'."

Young men were taught by their daddies the kind of woman to

look for. Charlie commenced his teaching with me in the wood yard on the end of a "crosscut or buck saw". I didn't think Charlie knew much when I was fifteen to twenty-five. However, now at the age of sixty-eight, I realize that Charlie was the smartest and greatest man I ever knew!

How many of you young women can pass Charlie's 1953 advice to me? "Son, you are going to be leaving this mountain before long and you will be fixin' to find yourself a woman. You got to watch you don't get stung bad.

"Find yourself a woman who knows how to cook, sew, patch, can, raise a garden, is smart, kind, savin', good lookin' and not lazy; that she is clean, will keep a clean house, is healthy and doesn't wear a lot of make-up. A woman who knows how to take care of children. One that doesn't wear expensive clothes, because you won't be able to afford an expensive woman. A woman that doesn't complain. Get over to her house and see what her family looks like. Get there unexpectedly early one morning before she gets a chance to clean up, because that's the way you are going to see her when you get her. Take a good look at her mother, because that's what she may look like in later years. Try to get one that is smart and educated. Don't have sex with a woman you won't marry because the child is both your responsibilities."

# $\mathscr{P}$art II

O. NORMAN SIMPKINS, chairman of the Department of Sociology and Anthropology of Marshall University, has been a leader in bringing the distinctive culture of Appalachian America to the attention of the scholarly world, as well as a prime contributor to the development of pride in their heritage among Appalchians themselves.

One writer has said that his family is "100-proof Appalachian, being Scotch-Irish who came to West Virginia by way of Kentucky." Dr. Simpkins was born and raised in Wayne County and began his higher education at Berea College in Kentucky. He served as a combat photographer in World War II, and returned home to earn his AB and MA degrees at Marshall University. While earning his PhD degree from the University of North Carolina, he taught at North Carolina Central University, and later at Bowling Green State University in Ohio.

From 1957 to 1960 Dr. Simpkins was a member of the faculty of the School of Public Health of the University of North Carolina, doing field research among the Pueblo Indians of New Mexico. He then returned to Marshall University as a member of the Department of Sociology and Anthropology which he has headed since 1966.

In addition to his work in establishing the academic importance of Appalachian culture, Dr. Simpkins has engaged in many research, community development and action programs aimed at his main goal: helping the people of Appalachia develop the pride in themselves, their background and their accomplishments, which he sees as essential to rebuilding the strength of the region. He is currently engaged in writing a formal statement of his theory of social change, a major development of his past decade of thought. 97

# AN INFORMAL INCOMPLETE INTRODUCTION
## TO APPALACHIAN CULTURE

I'm going to try to give you some of the background of Appalachia from the cultural point of view rather than the historical point of view. I'm not going to be so much concerned with dates and names as I am with patterns of behavior.

Now there isn't a great deal published in this area available to you. The most accessible source is a paperback book available from the University of Kentucky called "Yesterday's People" by Jack Weller. Some of you probably have it. It's mostly about Boone County, West Virginia. However, it presents enough of the picture that you can understand something of the cultural characteristics of the people of rural Appalachia.

## CULTURAL BASIS

There are four basic reasons why Appalachian people are the way they are.

### Rural Farm

We've always been *rural farm oriented.* I'm talking about the people that came in and settled the area and not necessarily the people of today.

### Isolation

We've always been *isolated - physically, socially* and *culturally* isolated from the rest of the country, and whenever a group of any kind is isolated it tends to change less rapidly than the rest of society.

### Subsistence Economy

I used to say it's always been poor, but I don't do that any more since the war on poverty; what I'm saying now is that it's always been *under-capitalized.* I mean that in several senses. Unlike most of the rest of the country not as much capital has been invested in the region as in most sections of the country, so it is an underfinanced region of the country.

### Celtic Roots

The fourth reason why we are the way we are is, to me, the most interesting. Though there is some controversy about it, I think I have the facts fairly straight. The *culture* of this region *is basically Celtic.* Now this doesn't mean that only Celts came into this area to settle because there were a number of Englishmen, a number of Dutchmen, many of them were really Germans. We know them as the Pennsylvania Dutch. Some French Huguenots—the French Protestants who got pushed out of France, even a few Portuguese, a few Indians, and some blacks. All these went to make up the early population. Later, whenever the coal mines began to open up in the

98

1880's and '90's, there were Italians, Greeks, Hungarians, Austrians, Polish, and even Russians who came into the coal mining regions of Appalachia. By the time they came, the culture had already been set in its pattern and that's what I want to talk about because the way we act and think today is determined in a large part by who we were, where we came from, and the conditions under which we originally came here.

Now in more technical terms, the Celts who came in here were known as the Scotch-Irish. They weren't exactly Scotsmen and they weren't exactly Irishmen; that's why they're known today as the Scotch-Irish. My tall tale consists of telling you (a) how they got over here, (b) why they got over here, (c) what happened to them before they came, and (d) some little something about their cultural patterns, so that you can probably look at your next door neighbor and recognize something in him as having been around for a long time. I could go back to about 900 B.C. but I'm going to start at the time the Romans conquered England.

The time the Romans invaded what is now England was something like 55 B.C. The people who lived there were of Celtic origin. There were the Britons in what's now England, there were the Irish in Ireland, and there were the Scots in Scotland.

The Celtic peoples were prone to hard fighting, hard drinking, feasting for days on end, and just plain enjoying life. They were incapable of concerted action and thus no match for the Roman Legions. They loved music and many forms of oral literary competition. They were great believers in magic and the occult. Their priests, the Druids, were believed to possess special powers.

The Romans did not conquer either Scotland or Ireland; they conquered only the English part of it, what later came to be known as the Anglo-Saxon area. Now the Britons were pushed back into the hills, into Wales, into southwest England and northern England. The Romans stayed in England for about 400 years. The Romans were a city-dwelling people; they didn't get out in the country much. They built a lot of magnificent towns and cities, and eventually even built a wall across the northern part of England known today as Hadrian's Wall to try to keep those wild Scots from coming down and raiding the towns and cities. Hadrian's Wall still stands today.

When Rome got into trouble around the fourth century A.D., they pulled all their troops out of England which very quickly reverted back to the countryside. The towns went back to the forests and so on, and the Britons had it all over again. That left a vacuum, which was filled promptly by the Angles, the Saxons and the Jutes. These were Teutonic or Germanic people who came in and conquered what is now England. They spoke what later came to be the English language. That's where we get the word English, from the Angles. Whereas the Celtic people spoke Gaelic.

Then along about the seventh and eighth century A.D. the Vikings started coming in and raiding the coasts. Ireland by this time had developed its own brand of Christianity, and Ireland missionized England and the larger part of Germany. I won't go into the story of Saint Patrick but you know there's a rumor going around that Saint Pat wasn't an Irishman but may have been an English Protestant.

The Vikings, after raiding the coastline, virtually destroyed Irish civilization and Christianity because it was built along the coast around the cathedral towns. After they raided all around the coasts of the British Isles, and after they had been raiding for twenty or thirty years, they began to settle down. So all along the sea coast you have people descended from the Vikings. They had their own language, but they gave it up and adopted Gaelic or Anglo-Saxon depending on the area they happened to settle in. So the population of the Scots, the Irish, and even the English today has a high percentage of Viking ancestry. These are the people who came from Denmark and Norway mostly. These same Vikings you know settled over in Normandy in France and became known as the Northmen or Normans. Later on they came over into England and we'll have another part of the story. The Anglo-Saxons finally conquered all of what is now England. They didn't conquer Ireland; they didn't conquer Scotland.

Then in 1066 came the famous Norman invasion. These were Vikings who had only lived about eighty or ninety years in France, but in that length of time they had already given up their original language and had adopted French and had become thoroughly Frenchified, if I can create a word. They brought the feudal system with them. Now the Anglo-Saxons had always been a minority in England because you know when a conquering army comes in they are really very few though they control the area, and you speak their language if you're going to talk to them. The Normans came in and did the same thing to the Anglo-Saxons. These Anglo-Saxons had already converted much of England to speak English or what later came to be English--Old English, we call it. The Normans conquered England and required everybody to speak French. And they introduced the feudal system.

Things began to settle down, and in the twelfth century, actually 1155, something happened that started another whole chain of events (this is really probably where I should have started, but I had to set the stage). King Henry II was on the throne of England and was having trouble with those wild Irish over across the sea. They were trading and trafficking with the Spanish, and you know the English and the Spanish never got along. King Henry was afraid the Spanish might, with the help of the Irish, attack England from the back door. And he couldn't have that so he had to do something. He appealed to the Pope. Back in those days Popes were extremely powerful; they had a habit of giving land all over the world to whomever they wanted. Well the Pope had been trying to figure out what to do with those Irishmen because they were deviating from Roman Christianity. They had developed their own brand of Celtic Christianity. The ceremonies were not quite the same, and

100

they didn't listen to Rome too well. So Hadrian IV, the reigning Pope in 1155 gave Ireland to the King of England. In effect he said "You go over there and civilize those uncivilized Irish and bring them back into the true church". At the same time the English government was trying to conquer the Scots who had been causing trouble up in the North of England ever since Roman times. By the twelfth century the English had managed to conquer Lowland Scotland but not Highland Scotland. So from about the thirteenth century on, Lowland Scotland had been speaking English. Of course, after the Normans came in, their French combined with the old Anglo-Saxon resulting eventually in our present day English language.

Now, the English tried to subdue the Irish with the feudal system. The King would give a big grant of land in Ireland to some lord or noble or somebody that had helped him in battle or something and in effect make him the duke of that area. He was required to go over there and build a castle, subdue the local people, and provide the king with so many knights in armor, so many foot soldiers, so many spears, so many bows, so many crossbows, and so many horses whenever the king had to go fight. These dutiful Englishmen, many of them were really Normans who had learned to speak English, would go over and as very loyal Englishmen, try to subdue the local Irishmen. In about two generations they would become Irish themselves and were fighting the English.

This is a characteristic of Celtic culture and it still holds today. They absorb strangers and make Celts out of them whatever their biological ancestry. Only you don't see this in the history books because so many people from Ireland and from Scotland have been labeled in the history books as English. You have to get beneath the surface to get at it. George Bernard Shaw was one of these Irishmen who was really an Englishman who was really a Norseman. His family was one of those who had been sent over to Ireland and given a grant of land. So too, the famous Irish family of Burke's were originally Normans.

Well this went on from the twelfth century up into the fifteenth century. The English King would give grants of land to these loyal Englishmen and in two generations they had become Irish.

Then in the fifteenth century some of the native Irish chieftains in Northern Ireland, known as Ulster, committed treason. Some of them were former Englishmen who had become Irishmen. They absconded: left their estates, and escaped to France. So suddenly now the king had a problem. He had a whole hunk of land in Ulster and he couldn't let the Irish take it back over. So the British government, this was in the time of Queen Elizabeth, conceived the idea of moving all the Irish out, advertising for good solid English yeomen to come over and settle in Northern Ireland or Ulster. They promised them the land, and after they had been there five years they'd get a title to their land. Well, the English farmers weren't too happy to do

101

this; they weren't in any great trouble; they had plenty of land. The Lowland Scots, however, were being foreclosed off their land because of the Enclosure Acts. (England and especially Scotland was beginning to bring in sheep to raise, forbidding the peasants from raising their crops, and turning the land over to the lords to raise sheep). This was the merchantile period in which the theory was the way a country got rich was to sell something you've got to some other country and bring the gold in, and the more gold you had the healthier the country was thought to be. The English were selling wool to Holland because the best weavers were there. So instead of English yeomen coming in and taking advantage, it was the Lowland Scots farmers who seized this chance to get their own farm land. They already spoke English. Roughly a hundred thousand Lowland Scots farmers and twenty thousand English farmers took this new opportunity to get land and move over into Northern Ireland, into Ulster.

They were such good animal raisers they soon were running the market for horses and cattle and sheep in England. The English farmers began to protest. So the British government began to levy taxes on these Ulstermen to import their products into England. The Ulstermen simply planted their rows a little closer together and worked on the horses a little bit more and they still had the best horses and livestock.

So England finally adopted the practice of what's known as "rack renting". First the English reneged on their promise to give them the land after they had lived there five years, and required them to bid in their farm every year and they could make only one bid. If they didn't have the high bid, they didn't get any land to tend. And of course this broke them up since they often had to pay as high as 75 to 80 percent of what they raised to their landlord with all this rent money going to England.

So these Scotch-Irish got fed up with it. From about 1700 to 1776 over a half million of these northern Irishmen who were Protestants, who were Lowland Scots, (that's how they got to be known as Scotch-Irish) left the area and most of them came to the United States. They settled in the "out-back" country because they didn't have enough money to buy land along the seacoast where the colonies were. This was before the United States had declared its independence. The colonies were glad to get them because they wanted to use them as buffers between the colonies and the Indians. The Scotch-Irish moved into the "out-back" country of Vermont, New Hampshire, upstate New York, western Pennsylvania, (the Germans were already in eastern Pennsylvania) the Shenandoah Valley, and the Piedmont Area of Virginia and the Carolina's because that was the frontier then. They formed a buffer zone between the colonies and the Indians.

They came in with a horse, a cow, a sack of corn, an iron pot and a wife and several children, an ax and a long rifle. Now the highly accurate long rifle had been developed by the Pennsylvania Germans. It was a rifle rather than

102

smooth bore musket. To this day the governor of Kentucky and the governor of Pennsylvania quarrel over whether it's a Kentucky rifle or a Pennsylvania rifle.

These Scotch-Irish settled largely in the western part of Pennsylvania, the Piedmont area of Virginia, and the Carolina's. They filtered down the Shenandoah Valley along with some of the Germans that had settled in eastern Pennsylvania and into the mountains. Some came down the Ohio river and virtually eliminated the French who had earlier come down and settled a few places such as Marietta. The Scotch-Irish were English speaking when they came. Therefore you'll find very few evidences of the old Gaelic language. There's one or two places in West Virginia where it was spoken up until fairly recently. And they gradually moved over into the Yadkin, and through the Cumberland Gap into Kentucky and down the New River over into the Kanawha, into West Virginia; down the Ohio River into Ohio and Kentucky. This is how they got into Appalachia.

Daniel Boone is a prime example of the Scotch-Irish pattern of migration. Born in western Pennsylvania, he moved down the Shenandoah Valley into Western North Carolina, then over the Cumberland Gap into Kentucky and so on. Andrew Jackson was born in America six months after his parents came from Ulster. And the same kind of people incidentally later on moved out into the Ozarks. They have basically the same culture. They also moved out into the great plains area and are the people who started the cattle culture. I'm talkin about the real old cowboy West not the Hollywood kind. They were Celts, too. You look at the names of places out there and the names of families that started the early ranches and nearly all of them were Scotch-Irish. The history books call them English, but they were Scotch-Irish. For example, the Chisholm Trail is probably the most famous and Chisholm is about as Scotch as you can get.

## CULTURAL CHARACTERISTICS
### Livelihood

*Live On The Land*

The Anglo-Saxons, who are the English, were town dwellers. The Scotch-Irish were not. They were rural or country dwellers. And if you look at the settlement patterns in New England and the settlement patterns when you get into the Alleghenies, you'll see the difference. The Puritans, the English Pilgrims, were largely Anglo-Saxon in descent. They settled in towns and farmed the land roundabout. As a matter of fact for a long time up until after we became a nation, many of the towns in New England (and you know a town in New England is different from the towns in this area in terms of political structure) had laws requiring the people to build their houses within a half-mile or a mile (different towns had different distances) of the church. You

103

couldn't live out on your farm, you had to live in town within a mile of the church. As the town got larger they had to expand the distances slightly.

We've got our history all twisted around; we give them all the honor when actually there were other people settled in Virginia long before the English settled. Harry Caudill in his *Night Comes to the Cumberlands* says the people in Appalachia were descended from the scum of London. Now that's a lot of hooey. If the scum of London had gotten over here in the mountains fighting the Indians, they'd all been killed off. Most of the names in the region that were originally here are of the Scotch-Irish name pattern rather than the cockney London pattern of naming. The Scotch-Irish lived on the land. The Celtic pattern is, if you have land you live on it.

So, they built their houses on their land; it's what technically in sociology is called "open settlements" or dispersed farmsteads. There are several names for it, and this established the pattern of settlement from here on through. Of course when they got over into Ohio the government came along and surveyed the land out in squares. But in this area they used the old "metes and bounds" system. And if you had land you put your house on it. You didn't live in town and drive out to it. And this means you're isolated and you had to be a jack-of-all-trades. And that's why they needed their neighbors to come and help whenever the rain was going to get the hay, or something, and when there's more work to be done than you possibly can get done, you swapped work. They didn't have much money so they swapped work.

*Animal Raisers*

The Scotch-Irish or Celts were animal raisers primarily, while the Anglo-Saxons were crop growers basically. This results in a different way of life. For 2,000 years the Celts had been pushed up into the hills where they don't like authority, where they're always tryin' to be taxed, and that's the reason why they're animal raisers. They could always take a flock of sheep or cattle or pigs and run them over across the valley behind the next ridge and hide them from the tax assessor. If you have a field of wheat or corn or potatoes you can't do that very easily. The pigs run wild in the mountains anyhow and out of this comes an interesting aspect of the Hatfield-McCoy feud. If you remember—it originally started over a pig and whether the notches on the ears meant it belonged to one family or the other.

Going back to the old country, stop and think, most of the standard breeds of horses, cattle, dogs and sheep have Scots names or Gaelic names or Irish. They were developed either in Scotland or Ireland. The biggest horse and the smallest horse, the Clydesdale and the Shetland pony, they're both Scots. Outside of the Brown Swiss cow and the Holstein cow most of the others--the Angus, the Hereford, the Jersey and the Guernsey--were developed by the Celts, and I don't know how many breeds of dogs except the English Bulldog, the Anglo-Saxons bred that one. The pattern persists even when the people have to go to Detroit where they can't keep cows and horses and so on. They'll have some kind of animals around the place. A good sign of a Celtic home is a bunch of cats and dogs and if they can't have anything else, a parakeet or canary.

## Swapping

They did not have a money economy; they had a barter economy. Around here it's called "swapping". The pattern is still with us you know. This is one of the reasons why you see abandoned cars along the side of many houses in Appalachia. They originally swapped horses and cows and dogs. They transferred that pattern to automobiles and up until the 30's when the state passed a law requiring a use tax, they would sometimes swap cars two and three times a week. They'd just sign over the title to somebody else. I've seen a title back in the thirties that had eight or nine people who had signed the title and that was accepted. Finally one of them would turn it in and get license for it. Back then the license ran from January to December and so in the wintertime with no paved roads they'd just jack them up and not buy a license 'til after the first quarter had expired and that way they got them for three fourths price. The State changed the law, that's why the State changed it, to make it the first of July to the first of July so to make them pay twelve months for license tags. So every time they'd turn around, these people have been pushed around by government, by authority. They merely wanted to be left alone and live their life the way they wanted to live it.

## "Toot" Work Pattern

There is a characteristic in Appalachia of working very hard for a time and then doing something else to relieve tensions or redevelop equilibrium. There are various terms you can use. So they tend to go on a "toot" every month or six weeks. The workers in Detroit do the same thing. Supervisors up there know the Appalachians as people who will suddenly, without any reason whatever, from their point of view, take off and go home to visit. They'd take the whole family. The cowboy did this when he got paid; he went to town and shot it up at the end of the month. You find this pattern somewhat in your religion. You don't find it as much today as you used to in the rural areas. It's kind of a backsliding pattern. They get religion at a revival meeting and hang on to it for awhile; the preacher doesn't come around very often; they try religiously to live a new life and they hold on for a month or six weeks and they backslide. And they go up next year when the revival comes around again. 'Course they had two revival seasons you know in the region, originally, in the Spring and in the Fall. So a guy could stay pretty religious most of the time if they had enough revivals. I'm being a little facetious here but I think this will make you remember this pattern a little bit more. You

105

may have this pattern in schools. I've noticed it somewhat in some students at Marshall; they'll work very hard for a month or six weeks and then suddenly they'll just start cutting, start being absent for three, four or five days and then come back and work real hard again. The Army has encountered this with Appalachians; as a matter of fact, some areas of the Army, the infantry particularly, make allowances for this. If they're from the hills, eastern Kentucky or West Virginia or Tennessee, they expect them to go AWOL and they don't punish them too severely; they know they're going to come back.

### Easy Going Pace

Appalachians get their easy going way of life from the Scotch-Irish influence. An Appalachian can sit on his porch and rock all day without getting an ulcer over it. Most Americans have to be up and about doing something all the time.

## Personality

### Open Faced Outlook

A personality characteristic of Appalachian people that tends to get them into trouble in the big cities and sometimes in our consolidated school systems, is their "open-faced" outlook on life and acceptance of strangers once they get over their initial suspicions. They're too ready to accept them as "home folks". They haven't learned to build up a "front" to protect their ego. The smaller a kid is, the more likely he is to do this. He'll tell things on himself, or he'll say things that will give you insight into his behavior that will damage his ego, and he's not aware of this because he hasn't built up, as urban people have, this front of protection.

Now the reason for this is they come from an area where they know practically everybody; they don't meet many strangers and everybody knows you. So you can't build up a front if everybody knows your inner most thoughts. After they go to the city it takes time for them to develop this. Some of the older ones never develop this. That's one reason why they're not satisfied in Detroit and Cleveland and so on. You might watch for this, they do not have this -- I don't have a good word for it, I never have found a good word for building up of a front to protect their ego with strangers. Some of you may have a better name for it than I have. I haven't been able to develop a good name for it or find one in the literature that is satisfactory. If you see this kind of thing, they tend to hurt themselves by what they say and what they do, because they're not aware that they can be used by other people.

### Person Oriented

And if anything I say is of any value, this next statement is probably it. *They see other people as whole individuals.* Unlike the city person who tends

106

to see other people as objects. Now to see persons as wholes means that you do not see them in roles. A city person has to meet a lot of strangers in specific roles and tends to see them only in a narrow section of their life. He sees the clerk in the store, the official in the office, he sees the policeman in his role. The Appalachian does not; he sees the whole person. He does not see roles and this gives him difficulties in a bureaucratic situation. They go down to the Welfare office or the Employment office and they can't understand why the first person they meet can't solve their whole problem whatever it is. You know in a bureaucracy that person is only an intake clerk that merely sees that they fill out all the words properly on this form and then refers them to somebody else. And whenever the mountaineer is told to go over here to line number so and so, desk number so and so, they get hot under the collar about it because they think they're abused, or that she's got something personal against me, or she'd have taken care of it. I've stood at the complaint counter at some of the stores and I've seen this same thing happen. They can't understand why. Well, I get the same feeling. When something happens at school like no chalk available or something, I can't see why the person I approach can't solve that chalk problem even though they're not the ones that are supposed to provide chalk. I can't understand it myself. I get a little hot under the collar about it and I mutter about the bureaucracy at Marshall. Some of you probably had this kind of situation, or I come in and somebody's moved half my chairs out and put them in another room. Well I assume that the janitor has charge of this so I go to him. He hasn't any responsibility for this, he's supposed to sweep the floors. I can't understand why he couldn't have been there and kept those chairs from being moved out.

### Lack Conversation Ritual

Living in an area that is hard to get to, where they want to be left alone, they interact at a high rate with each other whom they know very well, but they don't interact with outsiders because there's few outsiders. And this has developed certain character traits. They're somewhat suspicious of strangers; "foreigners" from the next county. "Foreigner" in this area doesn't mean from France or somewhere; it means in the next county or over the hill on the next ridge or something like that. Now their patterns of interaction are the kind that develop in rural situations anywhere in the world where you have people who don't meet strangers very often. They're not necessarily uniquely Celtic. If you know all about the people you meet and you know all the skeletons in their closets, you don't have to have the usual ritual for getting the interaction started and then cutting it off. So here's a characteristic you find true today among kids in school from this rural background. And if you have them from town, they're only one generation in most cases removed from a rural background, so we still have much of it. The Appalachian has no need of a ritual for getting interaction started and then cutting it off, so it takes

107

him a long time to get started and it takes forever for him to cut it off and break away and get away from it. I've seen people when they go visiting and they're leaving, go out to the car, get the car started while the host comes out to say goodbye and the guest lets the clutch out on the car and moves down the road and the host is right along beside it and moves a quarter of a mile down the road trying to break away. They just don't know how to say good-bye and do it. They don't know how to start a conversation and they don't know how to end it. The more rural you get the more you're likely to see this.

Another thing, Appalachians have difficulty saying thank you and have difficulty accepting thanks. It hurts them; it's actually agonizing.

*Staring Impolite*

The urban-middle-class society and, of course, our school system teaches upper-middle-class values. Appalachian values are not upper-middle-class urban, they are rural. They're not necessarily lower-class, although if they get out of the mountains, they're classified as lower-class in many cases. But in the upper-middle-class urban society you have a belief that whenever you talk to somebody you look them in the eye, that shows you're honest and you've got nothing to hide. Not so in Appalachia; we have been taught that if you looked people in the eye that's staring, and staring is impolite. And so your hillbillys don't face each other and talk like this, they stand this way. And if you look them in the eye their eyes will shift off. And you get the suspicion that they're shifty or dishonest and that's not true. They're just trying to be polite in the only way they know how. It's impolite to stare. This stems from a time when strangers were suspect because they were likely to be a witch, and witches had the evil eye. And if somebody looked at you long, hard, and intensely, they'd give you the evil eye and make you get sick, or your cow's milk would dry up, or the milk get bloody, or somethin' like that. So Appalachians stand this way. Try this sometime. I have watched this at Marshall in the hallways where kids are talking to each other and the kids never stand this way, they stand this way. You walk up and start talking to one of them this way and you look him in the eye and he'll back off and turn this way and you come around this way. I've run them around in circles. They don't know they're doing it, but they do it never-the-less. This is simply because it's their value system, and just as it's impolite to point, it's impolite to stare. And they define staring as looking somebody in the eye. You watch a rural Appalachian, he will not look you in the eye. There is a time when he will; whenever he's lost his temper and he has become aggressive or hostile. He'll look you in the eye when he's coming at you, so watch yourself. So when you see a rural person in this region who looks you in the eye, it means they have already become anatagonistic and they're aggresive. You've already breached the bounds of common courtesy.

108

## Word of Mouth

The primary means of passing news among Appalachians is by word of mouth. While they may read about an incident in the paper, they don't really believe it until they get it first hand from someone else. Gossip and rumor are rife - and often times quite effective - and fast - and embellished. The word gets around the community that so and so's been all cut to pieces in a fight and carted off to the hospital. You rush over to the hospital thinking you're going to get to say howdy to him at his dying breath and find there's a three-stitch cut on the back of his hand! I've seen it happen more than once. You hear somebody's just cut all to pieces and you go over and all that's wrong with him is he's just mad - that's hillbilly for angry.

## Proud People

Another characteristic of the Appalachian is his reputation of having a high temper. They carry a chip on their shoulders; they're a proud people. Unfortunately, however, they're the one ethnic group that has lost their heritage in terms of knowing who they were, and who they are, largely because they were the first large ethnic group to come in who were not Anglo-Saxon. They settled in the frontier where they didn't interact with very many people and by the time the Frontier moved on, many of them moved on with the Frontier. They're scattered all the way clear to the west coast.

## Family, Kin, and Home

### Equal Inheritance

Their family system was one in which all the children inherited equally including the girls, and this was highly unusual in most parts of the world at the time the Celts had this pattern. This is largely responsible for the pattern that has developed in Appalachia since. When a couple gets married, the son gets his inheritance right then; the daughter likewise, and that's how they set up housekeeping. Each time the farm moves through the generations it gets split up into smaller farms and so you have a characteristic in this region of many farms too small to raise a family on simply because of this pattern. Now the Anglo-Saxon pattern was the eldest inherited and the others had to do something else. That's a device for keeping the farm, the land, together. The Scotch-Irish who came, came wanting land. Many of them squatted on some of William Penn's land that he'd set aside for his own family and he finally let them keep it without cost.

### Equality of Women

Another of the characteristics of the family pattern in Appalachia, and it's Celtic, is that women have as high a status as the man. The women are inde-

109

pendent and the couples choose each other; the parents had little or no voice in choosing who the kids married and it's still the pattern to this day.

They didn't have the honeymoon pattern which is now a prominent one; they had the "shivaree" if you've ever heard of the "shivaree" or "bell crowd", some of you know it as the "bell crowd". And the kind of humor that the Celts had in this region is exhibited in this. Of course the "bell crowd" was one in which neighbors got together and located where the couple was the first night they were married so everybody came with all the noise makers they could to keep them awake all night long and keep them from going to bed. The expected pattern was the young husband had to come out and bribe them to get them to go home and leave him alone if he had the money, and of course he knew this was coming so he'd better have some resources. His pattern was to try to not be there, and the joke on everybody was whenever they'd "bell" a house for hours and finally go in and get him and his bride and they'd not be there because they'd left and hid somewhere else. This exhibits the kind of humor you have in this area; it's a practical joking kind of humor that you still find in the region, particularly in the rural areas.

*Love of Homeplace*

They have a strong attachment to the land and the old "homeplace". They love the hills and every holiday is marked by the number of cars with out-of-state license plates back in the community returning to visit home and kin. They just get lonesome for home. They gotta go back and see the old "homeplace". They seem to be tied to the hills long after they leave the area. I used to tell my students at Marshall that many of them had to leave in the last twenty years but they always want to come back, and they're like most of the immigrants who came to this country who wanted to come here and making a "killing" and go back. Most of them never get back because there's no jobs here. So they come back every chance they get and visit. And whenever they die they want to be buried back here. If you don't believe me just stand on the 6th Street bridge at Huntington and watch. Watch the hearses come over. You'll find there's a much bigger traffic of hearses coming to West Virginia on the 6th street bridge than there is going the other way. If they can't die here they want to be buried here. You watch the newspaper and you'll know they're people from far off and they bring them back here to bury them. Cause they've got some kind of love for these hills. They don't boast about it and make a big noise about it, it's just there. And this is characteristic of so much of the culture. They are not selfconscious about it as many other groups are because they've never been aware that they are an ethnic group until they get outside the area.

110

*Clan System*

The Celts still had a clan system while the Anglo-Saxons had long since lost the clan system. Incidentally the Irish had it up until about 400 years ago. The Highland Scots had it up until 1745 when it was outlawed by the English. The clan still exists in Appalachia, they don't call it that but it's still here. I've got proof of it. It determines what kinship system you marry into, what church you go to, who you swap work with, who you get drunk with, who you help in times of crisis and so on, so the clan still exists, they just call it "set". Have you ever heard that term? When somebody dies they sit up with the body until burial, though they don't use the word "wake". They depend very heavily on kinsmen and neighbors, the "kith and kin". Kith incidentally is an old English word, I think it's English, meaning neighbors. And "kin", of course, is kinfolk.

Self-Government

*Independent*

Their attitude toward civil authority dates back to the days when the Anglo-Saxons pushed the Celtic peoples back into the rough mountain country of Western England and Lowland Scotland. For two thousand years these people have been set upon by tax collectors who always want to tell them what to do and how to do it. They have developed an attitude towards law, towards authority, which you find still in this region today, more so than practically any other area of the country.

They were rather disgusted with the British Crown when they came to this country. And so most of George Washington's troops who stayed with him were Scotch-Irish. At one time, and I won't give you the exact quote because I can't, he made a statement about give me men such as these and let me stay in the hills of West Augusta, and in effect he said I can fight the British off till hell freezes over. West Augusta was Washington's name for West Virginia. That wasn't his expression because he wasn't supposed to curse you know. They hated the British and so they fought very hard against the British in the revolutionary war. As a matter of fact the first declaration of independence or the first independent constitution—the Mecklenberg declaration in North Carolina—was developed by the Scotch-Irish. The state of Franklin in Tennessee, an abortive attempt to set off a new state, was developed largely by the Scotch-Irish. And of course many of them got land in the Appalachian area and eastern Kentucky particularly, for fighting in the revolutionary war. That was the "G I Bill" of those days. So if you look into some of the family histories of the region particularly over in eastern Kentucky, you'll find they first got a grant of land shortly after the revolution in eastern Kentucky for services in the Revolutionary War.

111

## Personal Politics

They take their politics personally. A bureaucratic city politician doesn't have a chance in the mountains. That's why nearly every politician in Appalachia publicizes the families he is kin to.

## Community Action

They developed an unofficial, an informal, I guess is the best word, means of getting together in groups. Whenever a problem came up the people in the community got together and solved the problem. And did it themselves. They didn't wait for the government to do it. The Anglo-Saxons would go to the mayor of the town. They always had official government. Celtic government was informal, virtually nothing, and they settled disputes by physical means. If you got in a quarrel with somebody, you fought it out.

## Fightin', Feudin', Fussin'

Another pattern in Appalachia is, you settle disputes by fighting it out. If you'd get in a quarrel with another family and one fight didn't settle it - of course whoever got licked would go home and get some recruits and he'd come back. So this is why you'd have the fightin', feudin', fussin' pattern in the region that died out in the late 1880's or thereabouts. You have that in mountainous areas all over the world where there's little law enforcement. You still have somethin' of this same pattern in the area. They don't actually go at each other with guns and whole families get involved, but you do get into disputes and incidentally, they like to use knives on each other. Every good Appalachian just like every Celt (incidentally the word Celt comes from the kind of weapons they used), you know, the Scotsman whenever he was dressed up, always had a knife, a Dirk, that's what they called it, stuck in his sock. So every good Appalachian carries a Barlow, when you get in a fight, you use your trusty Barlow.

## Food And Drink

## Ovenless Bread

Another difference between the Anglo-Saxons and the Celts was the Anglo-Saxons made bread in ovens; they baked bread in ovens and they used yeast and the Germans did too and so did the people around the Mediterranean. The Celts didn't. If you'll notice, all the standard Appalachian breads are all made in such a way that you can make them on top of the stove because they were not an oven using people until some time after the Civil War. From the Pennsylvania Dutch, who were really German, the Appalachians took over the Dutch oven. They were Deutsch or low German which meant they were from the northern part of Germany and in their dialect their names of themselves was Deutsch. You take any English-speaking

112

person and he's met some Deutschman and he comes home and tells his neighbors I met a Deutschman today what's he going to call him? He's going to say a Dutchman. Deutsch is not a word in English. It sounds odd, it doesn't sound like it's English or something. That's how they got the name, ''Pennsylvania Dutch''. The Appalachian people got the Dutch oven, that was their first oven, from the Pennsylvania Dutch. They cooked in the open fireplace until they discovered the Dutch oven.

*Milk Drinking Men*

Another characteristic of the Celts is they were one of the few people that grown men can drink fresh milk because fresh milk was one of their basic foodstuffs. And that's the reason why many American men today can drink fresh milk without being called a sissy. Most parts of the world men don't drink milk and there are parts of this country where no Scotch-Irish settled and the men there don't drink milk either, it's for kids and sissies. Now they never had any preserved kinds of meats like the Germans and Anglo-Saxons did. The Celts invented bacon, that's the only one they really had, along with fresh pork sausage which you can't keep very long. They did not develop any cheese, they drank their milk fresh or they used it in their cooking. The Germans and the Anglo-Saxons, they made cheese out of their milk, they didn't drink it raw. They took their meat and they preserved it, and if you'll notice most of the names of sausages and cheeses are from Germany or Northern France. The Appalachians even got cottage cheese from the Pennsylvania Dutch. The only sausage of any kind that they really developed, outside of fresh pork sausage which is not really preserved, was souse or head cheese. They eat their meat fresh, they drink their milk fresh or clabbered.

*Hearty Thirst*

Now there's another characteristic of Celtic culture that mention should be made of. The basic drink (you know practically every culture has a basic drink - alcoholic if they can figure out a way to get it) of the Celts originally was cider because wherever in Europe you find crab apples growing that's the area the Celts settled, and the people that live there today are basically of Celtic ancestry. Of course from apples, you get cider. Now it wasn't the cider that you know as cider, it was what we know as hard cider, but they had a way of making it even harder. They put it out in shallow pans in the winter time since they lived in a temperate zone, and they'd let it freeze, and you know water freezes in a pure form; so they'd let it freeze and they'd lift that thin sheet of ice off and that left a double strength cider, hard cider about 20 percent alcohol or 40 proof. I've tried it and it works. You'll notice the stress on apples in the region. Apples is one of their favorite foods and still is to this day. Apple pie, applesauce, and all that sort of thing, and incidentally, Johnny Appleseed was a Scotch-Irishman. His name was Chapman.

113

While in Ireland, the Scotch-Irish picked up a drink. They learned to make Irish Whiskey. The Irish had picked it up from the Arabs in North Africa and Spain when Spain was Moslem. It was made out of rye, and when they got to the new world they kept on making their rye. In the early days of the frontier, the early days of the history of the Ohio River and the Southern area, the most famous drink was Monongahela rye. It was rye whiskey made by the Scotch-Irish in western Pennsylvania; and after the United States was founded, they're the only ethnic group that ever rebelled against the United States Government. That was the Whiskey Rebellion. When the government needed some money to pay off the Revolutionary War debt, they levied taxes on whiskey. The Scotch-Irish weren't going to pay it and George Washington had to send out ten thousand troops into the area to calm things down. Well, by the time they got down into Kentucky they discovered that rye doesn't grow too well in this area, not like it does in Scotland or Ireland. It's too wet here, or too dry, or too cold, or something. They gradually slacked off growing rye.

Then somebody discovered (and there's an argument over where it was discovered, some say in North Carolina, some say in Bourbon County, Kentucky) they could make whiskey out of Indian corn, maize. And you know to this day, American whiskey made with corn is known as bourbon—it's different from Scotch.

## Religious Faith

### Calvinistic Creed

Now the Presbyterian church is a church that has always insisted on an educated ministry. So when these people came into the mountains the Presbyterian church did not follow them. First of all there were no seminaries in the mountains and the educated ministry didn't want to come in—they were townspeople. So they had to develop their own religion and the pattern largely developed in the great revival period in the last century. And they developed into the Baptists and the Methodists and the Holiness. Of course, the Methodist Church was really founded in England, but when it came to this country it readily adapted to the frontier. And if you'll look today at the creed or ideology, whatever you want to term it, of the Baptist and Methodist and the Holiness, it's all based on a Presbyterian pattern - a Calvinistic pattern, not on a Puritan pattern, in this region. The Scotch-Irish also were very instrumental in getting the Congregational Church started up in New England. They moved into the "out back" country of New England, in New Hampshire, Vermont, in that area. The Puritans didn't like them; they didn't welcome the Scotch-Irish. That's one of the reasons why they moved in the "out-back" country.

114

Cultural Absorption

Scotch-Irish ancestry and its tradition can usually be found in anywhere from 60 to 85 percent of the folks in any gathering in the region. That doesn't necessarily mean a person is of Scotch-Irish descent. It's a characteristic of Celtic culture to absorb other people and make them Celts culturally, not biologically. West Virginia is like this. The Dutch people, and some of you probably have names that are derived from Dutch, are just as hillbilly as some of the Celts are. The English became hillbilly because they had to in order to live here. Up in Raleigh county there is a group of Spanish people who speak with a hillbilly accent and they think like a hillbilly and act like a hillbilly because they are hillbilly, yet they're Spanish. In some of the coal mining areas where a number of the blacks settled, they have a hillbilly accent not a southern black accent. So the important thing I'm stressing here is the culture not the biological ancestry. The biological ancestry of one is just as good as another. But the pattern was set by the Scotch-Irish and many of the characteristics of Appalachia today are due to this characteristic along with being in a remote isolated area, and being farmers. And they will keep this pattern for two or three generations after they move to a city. And here's the reason.

You develop the kind of personality you have through the way you're reared, and you get your personality pretty much set by the time you get to school. Now what the new government policy of getting the kids into kindergarten and even getting them into the early childhood education is going to do this I don't know. But by the time you get these kids in school their personality is set and remember you tend to raise your children the way you were raised, not the way Dr. Spock said for you to do it. And this is why it will carry on for two - three generations before it gradually weakens and Spock begins to have some influence, if he's still around by that time.

## CONCLUSION

Over the years, the blending of many cultural strains, Celtic, Anglo-Saxon, Germanic, Southern European, African and others in this mountain environment have combined to produce a rich heritage of which every native son and daughter can be justly proud - a cultural endowment well fitted to answer every man's question as posed by John Steinbeck ''How do we know its us without our past?''

With the inroads of mass media upon isolation, highway networks opening up the back hollows, spreading urbanizing influences, and a rising level of living, the cultural heritage is rapidly fading into the past and in danger of being lost. It has much to say to the needs of man today. By careful study, to develop understanding and recapture something of its love of life, wisdom and ingenuity, and independent spirit to shed light on the present and the future,

115

it could well be that the desired rise in level of living may not be at the cost of man's humanity, but enrich and deepen insights into the Wonder of Life for all.

Adapted from Dr. Simpkins'
address at the Huntington Galleries
Mountain Heritage Week June 19-24, 1972
by B. B. Maurer

# Part III

'Tis a Blue Bird thought
I am thinking today
For you, my pupil and friend;
May the deeds which were wrought
And the lessons here taught
Your life to new energies bend.

117

FAULKNER SCHOOL, DISTRICT NO. 6

Beverly Dist., Randolph Co., W. Va.

April 2, 1920

Teacher, MARY VAN SCOY

Trustee, W. H. TRIPLETT

## PUPILS

| | |
|---|---|
| Charlie Triplett | Lorenza Calain |
| Edward Bonnell | George Calain |
| Denzell Bonnell | Norman Wright |
| Wilbert Arbogast | Ira Triplett |
| Archie Coberly | Jesse Coberly |
| Grant Kimble | Hugh Flint |
| Preston Triplett | Roy Engler |
| Robert Wooden | Harold Revelle |
| John Summerfield | Mary Triplett |
| Helen Triplett | Nellie Kimble |
| Mabel Calain | Janet Tingler |
| Golda Calain | Silvie Arbogast |
| Flora Wyatt | Estie Tingler |
| Flossia Summerfield | Florice Bonnell |
| Bessie Coberly | Kathleen Coberly |
| Odrey Kimble | Golda Arbogast |
| Dovie Howell | |

118

A-FIXIN' — Getting ready "We're a-fixin' to go to the store."

PEAKED — Pale or sick lookin' "He's lookin' mighty peaked today."

ASKEERED OF — Frightened or afraid of "He's askeered of his shadow."

DOIN'S — A function "Are you goin to the church doin's tonight?"

DAST — Dare "Don't you dast ask Zeke to the doin's."

HOLLER — A small valley "She comes from over in the holler."

FETCH — To bring "Go fetch the doctor."

VITTLES — Food or victuals "I hope ma's got the vittles on when I git home."

PUT OUT — Angry, annoyed "He shore was put out 'bout the meetin'."

SMART — To hurt "It shore smarts where I got hit."

YOU'NS — You or you all "You'ns ain't gonna git no vittles."

AIM — To intend or to plan "I aim to buy some land."

CUTTIN' UP — Acting a fool "Maud shore was cuttin' up last night."

BOOK READ — Educated or well informed "We aim to git little Flossie to git book read someday."

FUR PIECE — A great distance "He lives a fur piece from his kin folks."

GULLY-WASHER — A hard rain "We shore had a gully-washer last night."

HESH UP — Become quiet "Make Jamie hesh up."

HET — To become heated or upset "Don't let that get you all het up."

LOLLYGAG — To loaf or loiter "Why's Clem always lollygagin around?"

PIZEN — Poison "I seen lotsa pizen snakes in these parts."

AWFUL POORLY — Very ill "He's been lookin' awful poorly."

CRICK — A stiffness "Marvin has a crick in the neck."

AIRISH — Breezy or drafty "Shet your window. It's too airish."

BIGGETY — Stuck up or acting big "She's been actin' awful biggety these days."

CLUM — Climbed "I clum thet hill for the last time."

PLUMB — Completely "I'm plumb upset with her lollygagin' around."

KIVVER — Covered "Them young-uns is kivvered with the pox."

SHED OF — Get rid of or unload "You got to get shed of that old mule."

SMACK-DAB — On the dot, exactly "I shot him smack-dab thru his heart."

POKE — Paper bag "He put the chicken in a poke."

RED — To clean or tidy up "Red up your room before you fetch Grandma."

WHUPPED — Whipped or spanked "Pa shore whupped me when I fibbed to the widder woman."

SKITTISH — Nervous "Them mules git kinda skittish when his dogs howl."

ET — Eaten "Have they et?"

GANDER — To look at "Take a gander at her new outfit."

NAW — No "Naw, I never fetched the syrup."

PARTS — Area or neighborhood "What's he doin' in these parts?"

119

W.E. "Tweard" Blackhurst.

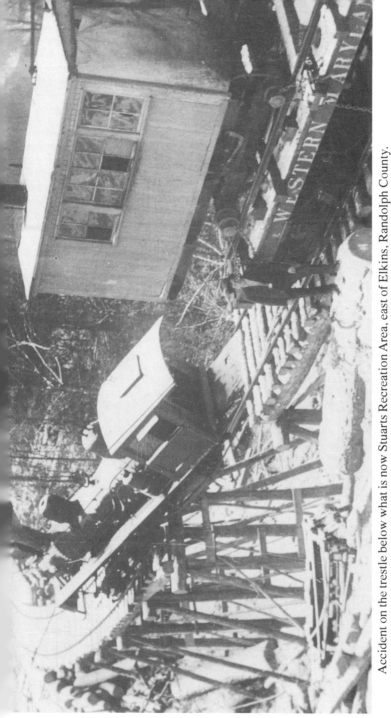

Accident on the trestle below what is now Stuarts Recreation Area, east of Elkins, Randolph County. This accident was caused by a workman carelessly rolling a log off the landing. The log rolled down the hill and knocked the trestle from under the locomotive. *Courtesy West Virginia University Library, D.D. Brown Collection.*

Pick up and drop off for Tygart Flyer Train South Davis Avenue-old freight station. *Courtesy of Clair E. Metheny.*

Durbin and Belington passengers at Elkins station 1925. *Left to right*: Hamond Schoonover, Charles Phillips and nephew from engines 51 and 52 with "cow catcher" on front of engine.

rch 30, 1950 Spruce extra coal train wreck from Isner Creek loop to west side of #1 "S" Tunnel. *Courtesy of Clair E. Metheny.*

August 7, 1953, Elkins Yard Track Gang, *left to right*: Bruce Bowers, Ben Arbogast, Hub Bodkins, BlakeWhite, Ira Triplett, Don Pritt, Doris Kerns and Clyde Keller.

Elkins round house locomotive repair crew, 1954, *left to right:* Luther Gross, O.R. "Bull Dog" Smith, Carl Haller, Pete Boxwell, W.J. Currence, Asa Galloson, Ted Poling, Clair Metheny, Jim Poling, Jim Riffle, Ed Poe, Granville Hess and Rudy Zirbs.

Elkins Yard Track Gang, *left to right*: Jay White, _____, "Bing" Clarence Miller, Wye Pritt, Ira Triplett, Raymond Teter and Charles Vance ca. 1938.

High Falls, Cheat River on GC &E.

"The Hermit," Jack Darling on GC&E near Hopkins Mine ca. 1930s. He was a former Philadelphia lawyer who found "peace of mind" on Cheat Mountain.

Typical Woodhick with "chalk (steel tacks) in soles and heals, high tops, rolled-up pants and felt hat smoking "corn cob" pipe in front of shanty bunk house. *Courtesy Mrs. George Evans.*

Men of Camp 15, on Cheat Mountain, 1915. Identified men are *left to right first row.* 1. Winters Ford. 2. Cleve Hunt. 5. Everett Sharp, 8. Harvey Craddock. *Second row.* 6. Floyd Branscomb, 8. Ezra Bennett, 9. Guy Ralston. *Third row,* 4. Wilson Darnell. 7. Lawrence Ralston. 12. Charlie Haglund. *Fourth row,* 10. Harry Osborne, 12. Ira Robertson. Fifth row, 1. Charles Propst, 3. John Osborne, 7. Lenny Dean. *Courtesy Connell Gillespie.*

Teamsters from Camp 30, Cheat Mountain, Pocahontas County, 1914. Horses names are: front row *left to right*, Prince and Fred, Scott and Harry, Frank and John, Tom and Jom, Tom and Paul, Pete and Lee; back row, Rock and Rowdy, Beech and Birch, Mike and Dick, Fly and Nell. *Courtesy Connell Gillespie.*

Men of one of the lumber camps on Cheat Mountain. This photo was taken on Sunday while the men were relaxing. Two men at the left front are sharpening an axe on a grindstone. *Photograph by J.A. Gardner. Courtesy H.E. Matics.*

Shay No. 3 of the West Virginia Pulp and Paper Co. in Cheat Mountain near Spruce, Pocahontas County. *Courtesy Pocahontas County Historical Society.*

Shay No. 5 plowing through the snow on Cheat Mountain near Spruce, Pocahontas County. West Virginia Pulp and Paper Co., Cass. *Courtesy Ivan O. Clarkson.*

Steam skidder on Cheat Mountain near Spruce. The intricate rigging is clearly seen as is the daredevil standing on top the tower. *Courtesy Ivan O. Clarkson.*

133

One of the five steam skidders to operate on Cheat Mountain from 1922 to 1960. *Courtesy of H.E. Matics.*

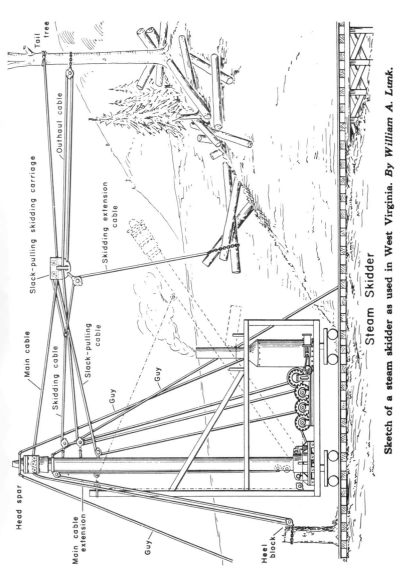

Head spar

Main cable

Skidding cable

Slack-pulling cable

Slack-pulling skidding carriage

Outhaul cable

Skidding extension cable

Tail tree

Main cable extension

Guy

Guy

Guy

Heel block

## Steam Skidder

**Sketch of a steam skidder as used in West Virginia.** *By William A. Lunk.*

The middle tree is incorrectly designated as tail tree and tail tree is at far end of skid trail.

135

Skidder on the right hand prong of Red Creek, Tucker County, 1913. The logs dangling in the air at the upper right are attached to the high-line and are being taken to the landing at the skidder in the distance. *Courtesy W.H. Sayger.*

Aerial view taken in 1957 showing scars left by steam skidders many years ago. Cheat Mountain, near Cass, Pocahontas County. *Courtesy U.S. Dept. of Agriculture.*

137

Fred Tyree, cook on Cheat Mountain. Food was cooked in wash boilers, lard buckets, and large pans on a Burton stove (Burton Range Company, Cincinnati, Ohio). The twenty loaves of bread shown at the left would be eaten in one supper. *From the Kyle J. Neighbors Collection.*

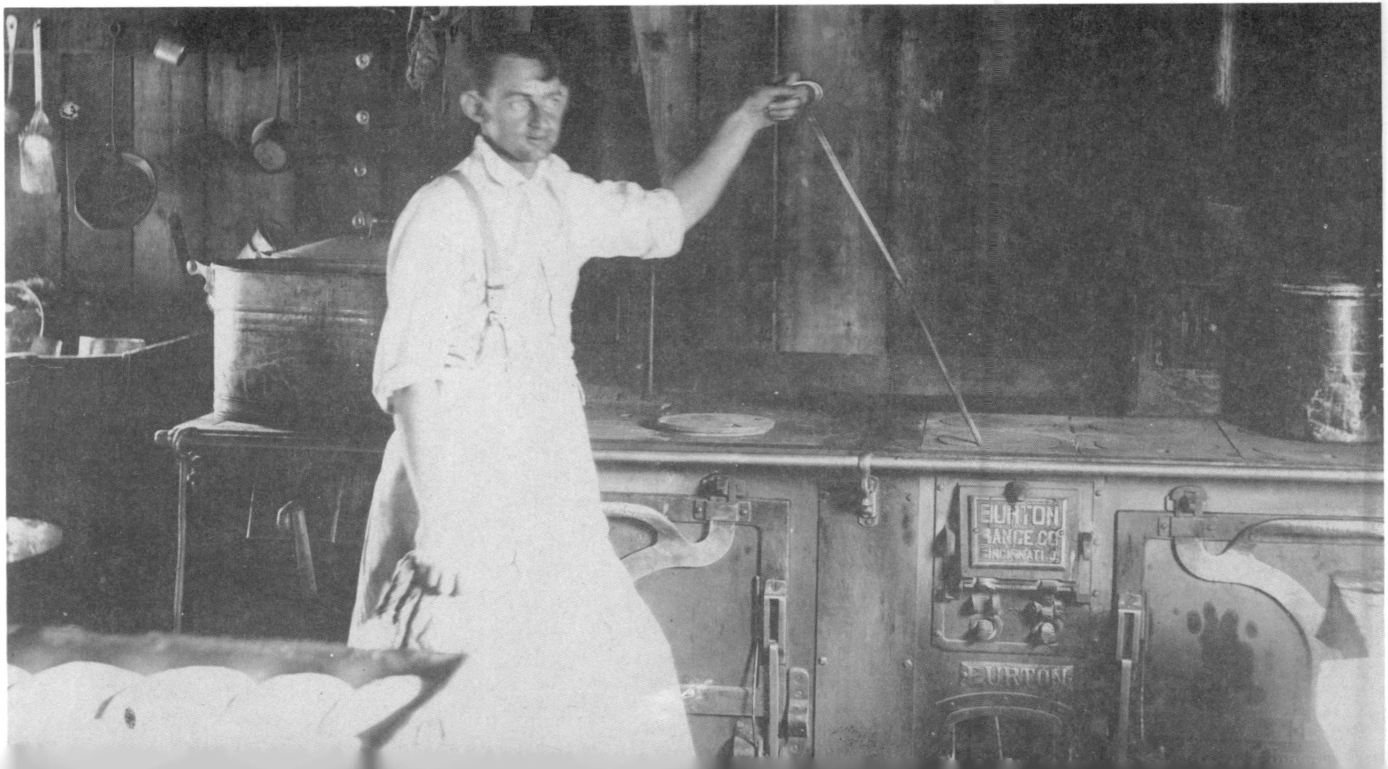

138

Looking from the kitchen into the dining room at a logging camp on Cheat Mountain. The cook and cookees worked seven days a week. The cook was paid $3.00 a day, the cookees $1.50 plus board and room in each case. *Courtesy Katherine Campion.*

Huge coffee pots, bowls of food, hot rolls, plates and cups on a table prepared for hungry loggers on Red Creek, Tucker County, 1910. Parsons Pulp and Lumber Co., Laneville. *Courtesy Frank Harr.*

Coal-fed steam log loader at Cheat Mountain usually operated by Ray "Buzz" Sage or his son Ray Sage, Jr., mounted on railroad flatcar with narrow gauge rails to change positions.

Lumber camp and crew on Cheat Mountain, Pocahontas County. West Virginia Pulp and Paper Co., Cass. Camp #21 at Cabin Fork. *Courtesy Eugene Burner.*

Red spruce trees dwarf the lumberjacks who are soon to cut them. Cheat Mountain, Pocahontas County on lands of the West Virginia Pulp and Paper Co., 1910. *Courtesy Mrs. Emory P. Shaffer.*

Log landing on Cheat Mountain. Logs were brought to the left side of the landing by teams of horses. Grabs holding the trail of logs together were knocked loose and the logs were rolled across the landing to be loaded on railroad log cars on the right or floated and driven down river. A log slide is next to the teams. *Courtesy Lacy Byrd.*

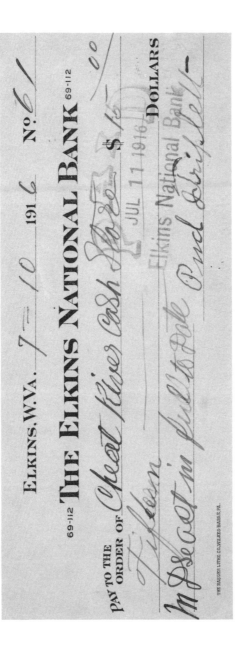

ELKINS, W.VA. 7—10 191 6 No. 61

69-112 **THE ELKINS NATIONAL BANK** 69-112

PAY TO THE
ORDER OF Cheat River Cash Store $15 00

Fifteen DOLLARS

JUL 11 1916
Elkins National Bank

M. J. Scott in full to date Paul Stripling

Creed Isner family. Faulkner ca. 1900 with children. *Front row, left to right:* Howard, Creed, George, and wife, Alice. *Back row:* Jeff, Shirley, May Kimble, Harry and Isaac.

Annotations on photograph: Jeff, Howard, breed Shirley, George, maykimble, Harry, Alice, later sold to Geo triplett

Jasper, Eliza and "Pud" Triplett at Triplett homeplace, Faulkner, WV built about 1800. Travelers stayed overnight at Triplett homeplace.

148

Wreck at Bowden, October 21, 1945, at Wye, turning for locomotives, included all section gangs from Elkins to Cheat Bridge. Engines 787 and 784.

Bowden, WV, showing stores and section gang toolhouse.

Railroad handcar at Revelle.

Pud Triplett's logging horses ca. 1910 near Weese on Cheat River at log camp barn. *In middle*, Pud with Charlie and Ira.

Skidding Harness

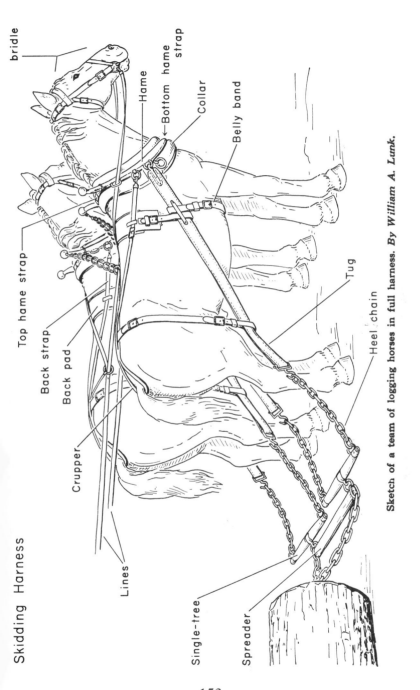

bridle

Top hame strap

Hame

Bottom hame strap

Collar

Belly band

Back strap

Back pad

Crupper

Lines

Tug

Heel chain

Single-tree

Spreader

Sketch of a team of logging horses in full harness. *By William A. Lunk.*

153

Ernest Smith with team of horses pulling logs to log landing early 1900s.

Summerfield Blacksmith Shop. (Pud Triplett *standing by horse*) near Weese. See "Arm and Hammer" signs to treat heartburn, indigestion or 2000 term "acid reflux" from consumption of grease, fat, salt and sugar. Also note "Liberty Bell Tobacco" sign above door, "Tags worth 1/2 cent each. Save your tags for 1/2 cent on next purchase."

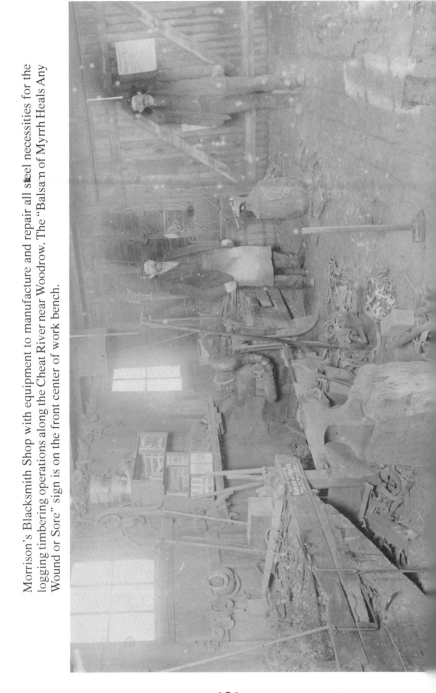

Morrison's Blacksmith Shop with equipment to manufacture and repair all steel necessities for the logging timbering operations along the Cheat River near Woodrow. The "Balsam of Myrrh Heals Any Wound or Sore" sign is on the front center of work bench.

*Left to right*, Robert Summerfield, Pud Triplett, Bob Flint on horse drawn wagon near Weese-Woodrow on Cheat River.

Log loader at Kline siding on Western Maryland railroad above Weese Siding and Woodrow.

Calvin H. Shiflett at ten with his puppies that could do no wrong,
Bemis, West Virginia.

Jerry Smith, 1975. Morning after state police lost their
hats at Shifflett's Store, Bemis, WV.

David and Doug
Shifflett. Morning
after state police
lost their hats at
Shifflett's Store,
Bemis, WV, 1975.

Old man Swopes, hermit who lived under rock cliff above Bemis, now known as Swopes, 1916. *Calvin Shifflett Collection.*

Walker Coal Co., tipple two miles north of Bemis, mid-1930s. *Calvin Shifflett collection.*

*Front row:* Clyde Humphrey, Dennis Davis, Leon (Hezzy) Wilt, Don Hinkle, Bill Davis. *Back row:* Ronald (Bruz) Cave, Ronald (Tuck) Shifflett, Aubrey Daniels, Ray Roach, Lamoyne Liller, Jim Liller, Raymond (Froggy) Dawson. Taken Bemis Ball Diamond 1939. Cross denotes "deceased". *Calvin Shifflett Collection.*

Bemis High School, 1939

1. Neal Humphrey, 2. Arnold Hinkle
3. Cha,s Phillips, 4. Paul Phillip
5. Don Hinkle, 6. Leon Wilt,
7. Kyle Liller, 8. Stan Waybright

9. Pat Phares, 10. Frances Hedrick
11. RosaLee Taylor, Lynette Phares
13. Naomi Lambert, 14. Joann Weese
15. Ruth Wimer, 16. Hazel Killian
17. Catherine Davis, 18. Alice Harris
19. Joe Shifflett, 20. Skeets Humphr-
ies, 21. ?, 22. ?, 23. ?. *Calvin Shifflett Collection.*

1939

162

BEMIS 1910

*Calvin Shifflett Collection.*

163

Bemis Lumber Co. Moving Camps on Cheat Mt. near Bemis 191C. *Calvin Shifflett Collection.*

164

*Left to right:* Jack Hayes, a Mr. Anderson, a Mr. Tingler, Arthur Lantz and Cap Rineard. *Calvin Shifflett Collection.*

Raphael and Lena Bowers Harris' daughters. *Left to right*: Alice, Jeannette, Greta, Mabel and Geneva.

Raphael Simeon Harris holding one of his horses at Glady, WV.

166

The old Flint family log homestead was located near the union of the East Fork and West Fork of Glady Fork River prior to the construction of the pictured sawmill and workers' homes at Glady.

Camp of Glady Fork Lumber Co. above Glady, WV.
*Courtesy of Clair E. Metheny.*

167

*Back row*: Sam Harris, ___ Cassity, Emory Thompson; *f*... *row*: Raph Harris in front of o*... nal Harris Store, Glady, WV.

Lora Triplett, Charlie, Ira and Harry, Glady, WV, ca. 1927.

Tom Thumb first steam engine with narrow guage track used in logging operations near Glady in early 1900s.

Glady Mill.

Believed to be Mr. Judy's team of oxen at Wheeler near Glady, WV.

170

Nancy Harris Booth and Anna Mae Harris
at Harris Store, Glady, 1949.

William Owen Triplett family, *left to right:* William Owen, Willis Lavenia
Triplett, Lester, Elma Isner Triplett, Marcella Triplett Channell, Glady Road,
1890. The house still exists between Alpena and Glady.

171

Glady Presbyterian Church Sunday School.
Mable Harris Payne is standing by post on *left front row*; other persons unknown.

Sunday Picnic Train Wheller Lumber Co., Whites Run, Glady, 1905, with local residents.

Successful bear hunt near Glady, WV, early 1900s. Tillberry Jones' friends. *Calvin Shifflett Collection.*

Glady Tunnel WV

C & I R.R. Tunnell near Glady, W.V. shortly after completion early 1900s. The railroad tracks to Durbin from Cheat Juntion were discontinued and pulled up during the 1980s. *Calvin Shifflett Collection.*

175

The Oxley Store near Glady was a famous social gathering place for the male population to "learn the truth from the horse's mouth." *Calvin Shifflet Collection.*

Piling and arranging the logs for skidding to Cheat Run for either the log drive to Point Marion, PA, or to load on railroad flatcars to be transported to Cass Mill. *Courtesy of Clair E. Metheny.*

Grand View Hotel at Glady, WV. Destroyed by fire 1907.
*Courtesy of Clair E. Metheny.*

Grandview Hotel at Glady was a first class lodging establishment that burned to the ground in 1907 ... the "boom town" started its decline. *Calvin Shifflett Collection.*

*Calvin Shifflett Collection.*

179

Head on three miles East of Glady, WV, on C&I, August 23, 1911, between freight train and passenger train. *Courtesy of Clair E. Metheny.*

Ben Stewart, engineer; Father of Arthur, Sam, Harper, and Clifford. Glady Fork Lumber Co., Glady, WV.

180

Lora Susan Triplett with brother.

"Doc" Harris and Pauline White, teacher, at Glady, WV, 1930.

One of the first Shay locomotives built used by Rumbarger Lumber Company at Bemis, WV, around 1900. *Left to right*: Ardie Fuller, Bill Miller and Bill Shockey. The Rumberger Lumber Co. at Harper siding 1907 or 1908. *Courtesy of Clair E. Metheny.*

181

Glady Western Maryland Section Gang circa 1946-1947. *Left to right*: Ora Strawder, Elmer Davis (Foreman), Rich Nelson, Carl Kerens, Herman (Peck) Vance, *kneeling* Earl Bonnell. *Calvin Shifflett Collection.*

*Front row, left to right*: Ernie Essex, Chester Rennix, Lester (Skinny) Rennix, Tom Rennix, Lee Cave. *Back row*: Mike Cassidy, Ralph Taylor, Emery (Red) Thompson, Delbert Reinard, Clarence Bowers. Glady Baseball Team 1918 Parsons Tannery bottom. *Calvin Shifflett Collection.*

Wreck of Spruce Ext., at Helmick on G&E, March 21, 1934, showing "wreck train crane." *Courtesy of Clair E. Metheny.*

# Cheat Bridge Was Town With Bridge

C HEAT BRIDGE exists in name only now. It is located approximately 1/2 mile South of U.S. 250 and W. Va. 92. Located on the old Staunton and Parkersburg Turnpike, between Huttonsville and Durbin, West Virginia. Built by Colonel Claude Crozet, a French engineer, who had fought with Napolean Bonaparte after the Revolutionary War.

Cheat Bridge was a booming town in the 1890's and up until the 1920's. The main industry was cutting timber, logging, getting the lumber to sawmills, then to market everywhere.

The road through Cheat Bridge, was used by both the North and South during the Civil War 1861-1865. Railroads were built through Cheat Bridge, Spruce, Cass, Durbin and Elk River, West Virginia. The stagecoach was also running between Staunton, Virginia, and Beverly, West Virginia. Mail was carried by horseback.

The 100 ft. span bridge shown in the picture was built by Francis O'Neale, contractor, in 1841, and demolished in 1910, for $3,160.00. The above picture was made in 1890.

## Post Office Was In A Home

The Cheat Mountain post office was located in Alfred Hutton's home from February 21, 1870, to February 2, 1881. The building which housed Uncle Sam's mail business was built in 1840, and burned to the ground one February day in 1881, but not before it got its picture struck. Pictured here` are: Caroline Hutton (with son, Napolean B. Hutton); Charles S. Hutton (boy on fence); Mosella Hutton Woodford (in front of post, left of porch); Elihu Moore (in front of gate); Alfred Hutton (Postmaster) (right of tree); 5th from right – man unknown; Eugene E. Hutton (on banis-

184

Slim–George's bear dog and loyal
friend before his wife, Frances.

Cheat Bridge.

Charlie Triplett and Harry Huffman, 1949, where passengers board the "Salamander" at Cheat Bridge in front of "track men" tool house, with garage and three-room company house in background after electricity arrived at Cheat Bridge.

Cheat Bridge with sign that 1954 bullet hole from sawed-off shotgun on old original Staunton-Parkersburg Turnpike where passengers board "Salamander". George Triplett was requested by two West Virginia State Police officers to see if the sawed-off shotgun was accurate. He didn't know until later in life that the troopers were afraid to shoot the gun they were issued. *Courtesy of Lars Byrne.*

Hole on Cheat Bridge sign, 1954. Sawed-off shotgun slug hole on Cheat Bridge sign that was caused by two West Virginia State Police officers who wanted to see if the shotgun was safe to discharge. Persons in possession of such a weapon in this century can be Federally prosecuted and imprisoned

Frank Campion, famous old-time foreman directs work at Cheat Bridge, Randolph County in 1890. *Courtesy his daughter, Katherine Campion.*

Harvey Cromer, standing in front of Cromer "Swiss Chalet" home, Cheat Bridge.

Record snow fall, Thanksgiving, November 30, 1950. Brooks "Choppy" Vance and Charlie Triplett resting after shoveling snow from the record snowfall where passengers board the "Salamander".

190

Cheat Bridge Section Gang 1953. *Left to right*: Brooks Vance, Charlie Triplett, Brooks Davis and Nathen Vance in front of motor car.

November 1937. Charlie and Buddy Triplett at Cheat Bridge with Charlie's 9-point buck that was a rare "trophy" in 1937 and which had to be sent to Pennsylvania to a taxidermist. Note Charlie's worn-out pants knees and no curtains in the windows of the house.

191

George Triplett, Robert Charles Triplett and Bill Cole
with two 5 x 5 bull elks and a 5 x 5 red stag.

Geneva Triplett and Buddy, Cheat Bridge, ca. 1939. "Goin' huntin'." Geneva is polishing shoes on bench at back door of company house. Note kerosine lantern hanging beside back door, the "railroaders" cap pinned to fit Buddy with a safety pin and his double-barrel pop shotgun.

George Andrew Triplett, three, landing
his first trout April 1, 2003.

192

Frantz Albert Degler, Carrie C. Degler, Owen Lutz, Manard Degler,
\_\_\_\_\_, at Cheat Mountain Club, late 1930s.

Cheat Mountain Club, Cheat Bridge, WV.

193

Cheat Club being built 1912 with baby. Carrie Degler, Frantz Albert Degler with four sons, Pete. Carl. Dick and Ed.

Geneva Harris Triplett 1930.

Edna and Russell
White, caretakers for
Western Maryland
Railway,
Cheat Club ca. 1950.

195

This fish hatchery was built and maintained by the Cheat Mountain Club on nearby Hatchery Run to propogate trout for stocking in the upper Shaver's Fork River ca. 1914.

The large Cheat Mountain Club House had been recently completed when this photo was made in 1912. Sportsmen from West Virginia and nearby states were guests here while hunting and fishing on the vast tract of land controlled by the Allegheny Sportsmen Club.

Western Maryland Railway company house at Cheat Bridge torn down ca. 1970 where Charlie and Geneva Triplett lived after 1934 with various other Cheat Bridge families.

Charlie "Zip" Triplett standing in front of Cheat Junction water tank circa 1928, the largest water tank on the Western Maryland. *Courtesy of Clair E. Metheny.*

Jack Gragg and George "Buddy" Triplett at Cheat Mountain Club, 1954.

Lower Cheat River. Isner, Triplett and Vanscoy Picnic (along with other Lower Cheat River families) 1930s, near Cheat River Inn.

Western Maryland track. Supervisors in "Big Cars" taken at Canyon Point above Cheat Junction. Charlie Triplett *far right* with shop cap at car #6.

Anna Mae Davis Harris,
Elkins High School graduation 1946,
at Cheat Junction when sister
Evelyn Bell was born.

Canyon Point
above Cheat Junc-
tion. Shows deep,
treacherous can-
yon where Cheat
River log drives
were made to Point
Marion, PA.

201

Shay No. 3 and loaded train on a wooden bridge across Cheat River near Big Run. Early engineers

Camp 15 from across Cheat River, 1910. Notice the hogs at the end of the bridge. The stable is the low, long building at the left. The other large building contains the kitchen, dining room and lobby downstairs, and sleeping quarters upstairs. *Photograph by Herman Work. Courtesy H.E. Matics.*

River drivers on Cheat River near Trowbridge, 1887.
*Courtesy Edgar Whetsell.*

Arks tied in the Greenbrier River below Marlinton, Pocahontas County, ca 1895. *Courtesy Pocahontas County Historical Society.*

205

Arks tied in the Greenbrier River near the present location of Cass. Pocahontas County, 1898. From *Riders of the Flood* by W.E. Blackhurst.

Arks tied in the Greenbrier River near the present location of Cass, Pocahontas County, 1898. From *Riders of the Flood* by W.E. Blackhurst.

Creed Isner. Faulkner-Cash Store.
Cheat River Cash Store and local Faulkner-Bowden residents about 1900.

Cheat River Store script 25 cent piece.

Charlie Triplett and Alice Harris
Antolini. Camp One on GC&E,
now Triplett ca. 1930.

Wreck of Spruce Ext., at Triplett on GC&E, June 15, 1935.
*Courtesy Clair E. Metheny.*

Motorcar, 1930s, on GC&E near Cheat Junction, H.M. Calain (Slim), Jasper White, Mrs. Lora Triplett, Charlie and Geneva Triplett with section hands returning to Triplett after a weekend.

Charlie and Geneva Triplett
at Triplett, 1929.

Jim Harris and
Charlie's dog,
"Spot," at
Triplett ca. 1930.

Charlie and Harry Triplett ca. 1928 on "hand car" that was
hand pumped by riders near Harper Siding.

1954-The coal dock and water tank in the Elkins yards of the Western Maryland Railroad served the steam engines for many years.

Spruce residents, left to right: Tom Broughton, engineer; Clair Metheny, locomotive repairman, and Kelly machinist. *Courtesy of Clair E. Metheny.*

Spruce Hotel. Spruce, Pocahontas County, 1910. Connell Gillespie, time-keeper and Walter Kohler, harness-maker, are sparring at the left of the entrance. Notice the female companionship for the lone-some lumberjacks on the front porch roof. *Courtesy Connell Gillespie*

View of the town of Spruce, Pocahontas County, 1910, taken from the mill. *Courtesy Roy Cook.*

Sawmill and planing mill of the West Virginia Spruce Lumber Company. These mills were built in 1901.
Courtesy of Mrs. Ica Sharps. From the Pocahontas

Pulpwood peeling mill and woodyard at Spruce. *Courtesy of P.E. Percy.*

The pulpwood peeling mill and the town of Spruce, 1919. The peeling mill was constructed in 1904 and the town of Spruce was built to house millworkers. *Courtesy of Mertie V. Clarkson.*

View of the town of Spruce, Pocahontas County, 1920 showing the pulp-peeling mill of the West Virginia Pulp and Paper Co., Cass. *Courtesy Mertie V. Clarkson.*

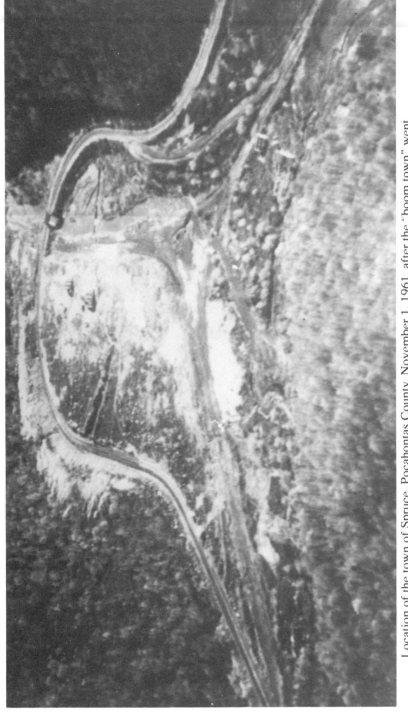

Location of the town of Spruce, Pocahontas County, November 1, 1961, after the 'boom town" went bust. The "Salamander" stops for a lunch break at top of curve before proceeding to the Cheat Moun-

Main Street, Spruce, West Virginia. There was no need for a roadway since there was no highway into the town and no automobiles. Built in 1904, the town of Spruce flourished until the pulpwood peeling mill was closed in 1925, then rapidly declined until by 1960, it was completely gone. The small houses in the street were coal houses, so located as to be near the railroad which ran on the left just out of the picture. *Left to right*, in the early 1920s, the homes of "Denny" Flynn, train conductor; George Clinebell, mill superintendent; Elmer L. Duncan, train dispatcher; and Ellet C. Smith, store manager and postmaster. This picture was taken in the early 1900s. *Courtesy of H.E. Matics. Information from Harry "Shorty" Duncan.*

221

Lee Sharp with bear early to mid-1940s at Spruce. Bear cage is made of poles. Lee was a train section gang worker, avid hunter and fisherman.

Devane W. Cussins at Spruce
on one of Mower Lumber Company's log train cars.

223

Photograph of metal number tags worn by Italian workers on the Greenbrier, Cheat, and Elk Railroad and the Spruce, Pocahontas County, 1915. Immigrants couldn't speak English and they had "numbers" for identification as railroad workers, railroad workers or coal miners on the Cheat River Basin. *Courtesy Ivan O. Clarkson.*

224

Three Shays and a Heisler lined up for night photography at the water tank at Cass. May 19, 1979. *Left to right*, Shay No. 5, Shay No. 4, Heisler No. 6 and Shay No. 2 or 3. *Courtesy of Terry E. Arbogast.*

Out for a Sunday ride on speeders at Spruce. Dr. U.H. Hannah is on the front speeder. Mrs. E.P. Shaffer and Joe Hannah on the second. (Speeders were basically four-wheeled bicycles powered by pumping peddles with a sprocket chain.) *From the Phil Bagdon Collection.*

Interior of the Pocahontas Supply Company Store, Cass. One of the largest company stores ever owned by a lumber company, it carried supplies for the town and the surrounding farmers as well as for the one thousand or more men working in the woods. The post office was located, at this time, in the store and is shown on the left. *Photograph by Underwood and Underwood. Courtesy of H.E. Matics.* Inset: Script was minted for use at Cass but as far as can be determined was never used. *From Nodie Bascomb. Courtesy of Harold Lee.*

227

Shay No. 4 setting in empty dump cars beside the Marion steam shovel during construction of Big Cut Cheat Summit above Spruce. The front cover photograph is long after the photograph now taken, 1910-1914. *Courtesy Mrs. E.P. Shaffer. From the Pocahontas County Historical Society.*

The 100-ton Marion steam shovel working on the Big Cut between 1910-1914. The engineer was George Crawford. *Courtesy Robert Dean. From the Kyle J. Neighbors Collection.*

Shay No. 4 giving the Marion steam shovel water while working on the Big Cut one mile west of Spruce. The Big Cut was nearly two thousand feet long and almost one hundred feet deep. It was the largest single engineering feat accomplished by the company and probably by any lumber company in the East. *From the Kyle J. Neighbors Collection.*

American Railroad Ditcher coal fired, steam powered, with crew on Cheat Mountain. Ditchers were used for grading, cleaning up slides, cleaning ditches, etc. Ditchers were modified log loaders mounted on a modified car with one set of trucks. The ditcher was marked on a railroad flat car with rails to change positions. *From the Kyle J. Neighbors Collection.*

*Left to right:* Jack Harris, Jerry Powers, Mack Teter, Perry "Fuzzy" Phillips, Bee Jordan, Mary Champ, Berylon Ferguson, Pappy Cussins, Forrest Judy, D.D. Saffel, Laurel Bank Western Maryland with 773

Italians, Austrians and Hungarians constructed all the railroad grades with picks, mattocks, and shovels until steam shovels and ditchers took over in the early teens. The man in the right front row is Harry Caddock. *Courtesy of Connell Gillespie. Inset:* Metal number tags were worn by the workers for identification.

Steam-powered American Log Loader Model C of the Spruce Lumber Company on Cheat Mountain, 1915. *Courtesy H.E. Matics.*

Shay No. 11 and crew at the Spruce water tank, 1916. *First man on left, Page McCloud, second from right, "Piney" Williams, engineer. From the Kyle J. Neighbors Collection.*

Shay No. 8 weighed 120 tons and was the first "big" Shay purchased at Cass. It was built in 1912 with cylinders fifteen inches in diameter and a 17-inch stroke and 40-inch drivers. This Shay was used mostly on the Cass Hill. The engineer was Sam Waugh. Shown here at the Cass Yard, 1916. *From the Kyle J. Neighbors Collection.*

Shay No. 5 near Spruce. Shays were ideal engines in snow. They could plow through snowdrifts almost as high as the headlight. Such conditions were frequent on Cheat Mountain. *Courtesy Ivan O. Clarkson.*

On November 1, 1905, Shay No. 5 was added to the company roster. No. 5 weighed ninety tons and was the heaviest engine to that date. Engineers were George and Charlie Cromer. Shown here on Cheat Mountain in 1910. *Courtesy Lurlie Curry.*

Shay No. 3 at a log landing on Cheat Mountain, 1904. This 70-ton engine was built in 1903 and was used at Cass until it was retired in the late 1920s. The engineer shown here is Cal Bradley. *From the Kyle J. Neighbors Collection.*

Four Shay engines at Spruce, Pocahontas County. West Virginia Pulp and Paper Co., Cass. *Courtesy Connell Gillespie.*

"Little Jim," first locomotive in Pocahontas County, hauled from Ronceverte, WV, to Marlinton, WV, by horse and wagon. Engineer "Big" Jim Watson weighed 286 pounds was known to woodsmen as "Big" Jim and locomotive was known as "Little" Jim. *Courtesy of Clair E. Metheny.*

#12 King of the Shays-weighed 308,000 pounds. West Virginia Pulp and Paper that hauled logs on GC&E to Cass Mill, George Cromer, engineer, wrecked at Spruce in collision with Western Maryland 700 series. *Courtesy of Clair E. Metheny.*

School kids behind schoolhouse at Spruce circa 1940s. *Back row*: Okie Powers, Milley Calain, Booch Cussins, Anita Fansler, Arveda Powers, Darleau Calain, A ice Sharp. *Second row*: Harper Nelson, Pauline Teter, Wanda Powers, Jean Fansler, Jannett Weese, Mildred Teter, Bob Nelson. *Front row*: Junior Fansler, Jimmy Calain.

242

Main Street at Spruce with the Western Maryland snow plow.

Devance W. Cussins, whose father was "Pappy Cussins" an engineer. Devance is standing with his toy "steam locomotive" in front of a Western Maryland Railway car on the sidewalk leading to the back door of his house at Spruce, 1939-1940.

700 series steam locomotive, Western Maryland.
*Courtesy of Clair E. Metheny.*

Spruce water tank with double spouts, locomotive shop, coal bin and sand bin for 700 series steam locomotives showing mill pond dam.

244

Durbin buses waiting at loading point in front of Durbin mercantile probably 1936-1937. Drivers were Russ Colaw, Bruce Nottingham and Kent Galford. The Cheat Bridge school children left home about 6:15 am and returned home around 6 p.m. from the 23 mile travel from Cheat Bridge to Greenbank High School. *Photo by E. Burner.*

View of west end of Durbin 1914.

Durbin Band.

246

Martin Van Buren Arbogast, Lemuel Arbogast's father.

Jake Currence, 105 years old, born, raised at High Germany, Randolph County. Never owned a vehicle, smoked nor consumed alcohol. Splits his own firewood and lives alone and is a direct descendent of William Currence, the Indian fighter and father of twelve children.

Emedio Rossi and Agatha Saccoccia Rossi,
parents of Frances Rossi Triplett.

J. Herman Isner, grandson of Creed Isner, son of Jefferson and
Icie Triplett Isner, on his horse, Blaze.

249

First row: Harold Mosser (Coach), Bobby Bennett, Kenneth Shears, William Sutton, Paul Tenney, and Marlin Shears; second row: Donald Grogg, Donald Gum, Sam Falgord, Bruce Bosley, Grey Cassell, Ivan Sutton, Eugene Teter, (Manager); The Golden Eagles enjoyed one of their greatest seasons in basketball, winning 27 in a row before dropping a 42-40 game to Fairview for the state B championship. William Sutton and Bruce Bosley were placed on the all-state tournament team. The team traveled over 2,300 miles and visited in 15 state counties

*First row*: Danny Nicely, Ray Galford, Paul Tenney, Ivan Sutton, Grey Cassell, Marlin Shears, Kenneth Shears, Henry Dickenson; *second row*: Mr. Mosser, (Coach), Bruce Bosley, Lloyd Nicely, William Sutton, Harold Lambert, Kenneth Cassell, Charles Bryant, Junior Vandevender, Jerry Crist, Bobbie Bennett, Eugene Teter (Manager); *third row*: Ray Sage, Thomas Tenney, George Triplett, Sam Galford, Howard Slaven, Merlin White, Billy Gainer, Bobby Dill, John Harris, Kirk Kerr. The Golden Eagles enjoyed a successful football season by winning the Northern Greenbrier Valley Championship. They dropped the conference game to Alderson by a 19-18 score. When another season rolled around the familiar faces of Paul Tenney, Grey Cassell, Donald McLaughlin, William Sutton, Marlin Shears, John Hevener, Kenneth Cassell and Lloyd Nicely were missed.

*Left to right*: Harry Jasper Triplett, Charles Robert Triplett, and Ira William Triplett dressed for their weekend "toot". *Courtesy Mrs. E.P. Shaffer.*

Pud Triplett just prior to his demise taken at his home in Faulkner with Isom Vance.

Jerome Barnabas Harris, 1836-1900.

Gail Harris, grandson of Gaylord Harris, played first base for the old "New York" Giants 1948-1950 and later the Detroit Tigers. Gail was the great-grandson of Jerome Barnabas Harris and Mary Crockett Harris and was raised in Abington, VA.

Raphael Simeon Harris after his stroke and near his demise.

Allen Nelson Harris' Dog Tags were the only items that Allen had from the Invasion of Guadal Canal thru Okinawa Invasion that stayed with him as U. S. Infantry Machine Gunner and recipient of the "Silver Star" and three Bronze Stars.

Allen Scott Harris, a three-time bronze star recipient and World War II veteran. He received the Silver Star, the American Philippine Liberation and Asiatic Pacific theatre ribbons for his heroic actions. In addition, Harris was awarded the WWII Victory Medal, the Good Conduct Award and a letter of appreciation from President Harry S. Truman.

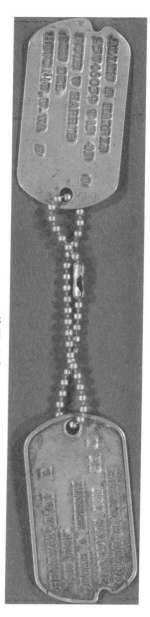

255

Lora Susan Arbogast Triplett with her long hair that at one time touched the floor while standing.

George Washington "Pud" Triplett.

Lora Triplett.

Arbogast Family.

1. Ira Triplett. 2. Charlie Robert Triplett. 3. Sam Peters. 4. Lou Peters. 5. Goldie Arbogast. 8. Sylvia Arbogast. 9. Webb Arbogast. 10. Christina Powers. 11. Ida Jane Arbogast. 12. Ira Vance. 13. Martha Ellen Vance. 15. Barbara Rexrode Arbogast. 16. Lemuel J. Arbogast. 17. James William Arbogast. 18. Lora Susan Triplett. 19. Anna Peters Queen. 20. Etta Arbogast Summerfield. 21. John Summerfield. 22. George Hobert Arbogast. 23. Jade Powers. 24. Lemuel Earl Arbogast. 25. Mary Howell Arbogast. 27. Amanda Saccs Arbogast. 28. Benjamin Arbogast. 29. William Bink Fansler. 30. Jennie Arbogast Fansler. 33. Opal Fansler Rosier.

259

*Left to right:* John Peters and Sam, Earl and Fred Arbogast, Etta and John Summerfield, Lemuel Arbogast, Lora Triplett, Charlie, Ira and Henry, Mary Arbogast and Daisy.

*Left to right* the Lemuel Arbogast Family: Anna and Sam Peters, Perry Arbogast, Ida Arbogast *sitting*, Lora and Charlie Triplett *sitting*, Mary Arbogast and Jenny Fansler.

Lemuel Arbogast's house at Revelle. *Left to right:* Bink Fansler, Pud Triplett, Lora Triplett, Ellen Arbogast and Lemuel Arbogast.

"Jake" Bowers and Ed Johnson having a "nip of the recipe" after a hard days work, as section gang hands seated on the motor car that, fortunately, had canvas flaps to partially protect them from bad weather including below zero temperatures.

Western Maryland Railroad Union picnic, 1948, for "track men, Stuarts Park, Cheat River below Lumber. Raymond Teter is about the only hardworking, "gandy dancer" still living.

George Triplett and Johnnie Rossi, 1957, Buck Run 350 pound black bear. Hunters thought hind quarters left in woods was biggest buck deer ever killed on Cheat Mountain.

Lena Bowers Harris and Raphael Harris, Glady.

B.I. Hudkins, M.D. Wompus Camp, Mouth of Cabin Fork above Cheat Bridge. Well known surgeon at St. Marys Hospital, Clarksburg, WV and resided at Wolf Summit.

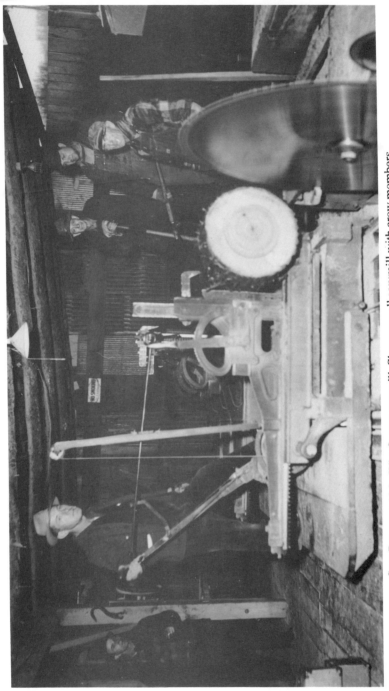

Sam Peters and Mr. Wirt Queen sawmill. Shows small sawmill with crew members.

Joyce Powers Maize, Wanda Powers Sharp and Okareta Powers Blake at Cheat Bridge waiting to ride the "Salamander".

Aunt Mary Hanes Crockett Harris Wamsley in front yard at Beverly, WV.

## BRUCE BOSLEY • Center, 49'ers

HT: 6'2" WT: 244 AGE: 35 YEARS PRO: 14 COLLEGE: W. VIRGINIA

**157**

A veteran of many campaigns, Bruce is considered one of the three centers in all of professional football. He originally broke in as a defensive end and was later switched to the guard position before taking over at center in 1964. For the past two seasons, was selected as the 49ers' team captain.

TO PRO BOWL!

BRUCE PLAYED IN THE PRO BOWL GAME 4 TIMES.

©T.C.G.

PRTD. IN U.S.A.

**Bruce**
# BOSLEY
SAN FRANCISCO 49ERS • CENTER

Dr. G.F. Hull

Allen Eugene Burner, M.D., Durbin, 1876-195

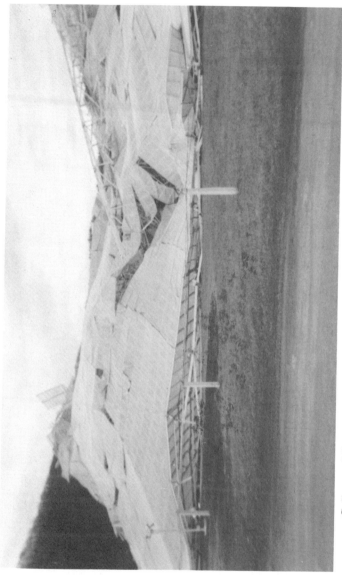

Collapse of Greenbank Observatory Telescope, Tuesday, November 15, 1988.

Green Bank High School, probably 1953.

Ralph "Doc" Harris and Anna Mae Davis Harris at Laurel Fork Picnic.

Charlie Clark, nationally known evangelist and singer who during a tent revival, inspired Charlie Triplett to have a religious change of lifestyle and contribute ten percent of his earnings to his place of worship the remainder of his life.

Geneva Triplett at Cheat Bridge ca. 1955.

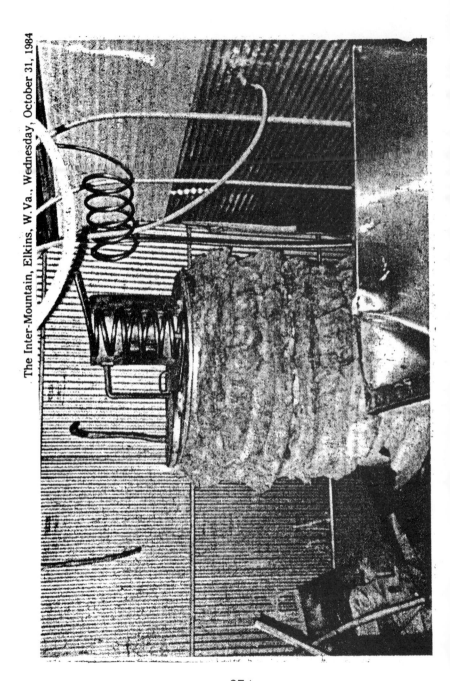

# WARRANT FOR ARREST

Case No. _____

STATE OF WEST VIRGINIA, _____ Randolph _____ COUNTY, to-wit:

To Any Law Enforcement Officer:

WHEREAS, _____ Tpr. W. D. Kershner _____ has this day made complaint

and information on oath before me _____ W. I. Heckel _____, a Magistrate in

said County, that ████████████

_____, Defendant

did commit a _____ Felony _____, in     that the said Defendant

on the _____ day of _____, 19 8 4, and prior to the issuance of

this warrant, in said County did unlawfully _____

Own, operate, or maintain a plant for the manufacture of distilled x spirits, or

aid or abet in the operation of said plant.

(60-6-10)

_____ against the peace and dignity of the State

Therefore, we command you in the name of the State of West Virginia, forthwith to apprehend the said

████████████, and bring that person before me

before some other magistrate in said County, to answer said complaint, and to be further dealt with in relation

thereto according to law.

Given under my hand this ___29___ day of _____ Oct. _____, 19 8 4

_William I Heckel_
Magistrate

Executed By: _Cpl. F. E. Sanchez_ In _Randolph_ County

Date: _10/29/84_

Arrest Fee _____ Jail Fee _____ Mileage Fee _____

# SEARCH WARRANT

STATE OF WEST VIRGINIA,

COUNTY OF __Randolph_____, TO-WIT:

TO THE SHERIFF OR ANY DEPUTY SHERIFF OF THE COUNTY, TO ANY MEMBER OF THE DEPARTMENT OF PUBLIC SAF OR TO ANY POLICE OFFICER AUTHORIZED BY LAW TO EXECUTE SEARCH WARRANTS.

Whereas, __Trooper W. D. Kershner_____, has this day made complaint on oath before

undersigned, Magistrate of said County, that on the __26__ day of __October_____, 19_8

and prior to the issuance of this warrant, in the said County of __Randolph_____,

_____ did unlawfully *(and feloniously) __manufacture, possess, and sell illegal__

__liquor (commonly known as moonshine).__
(State the Offense)
__own, operate, or maintain a plant for the manufacture of distilled__

__spirits.__        __(60-6-10)__

and that the complainant has cause to believe and does believe that property,

*a) ⊠⊠⊠⊠⊠⊠⊠⊠⊠⊠⊠⊠⊠⊠⊠⊠⊠⊠⊠⊠⊠⊠⊠⊠⊠⊠⊠⊠⊠⊠⊠⊠⊠

*b) (Designed and intended for use) (which is and has been used) as a means of committing such criminal offe

*c) (Manufactured) (sold) (kept) (concealed) (possessed) (controlled) (designed and intended for use) (which is a has been used in violation of the criminal laws of the state

*d) (Evidence of a crime)

Namely, __a moonshine still, parts thereof, corn, sugar, moonshine whiskey and other__
(State property to be seized)
__materials used in the manufacture of illegal liquor.__

is concealed in __a metal outbuilding located in a wooded area behind the sawmill on▋__
(Describe premises)
▋▋▋▋▋ __property along State Secondary Route 45 approximately four miles south of t▋__
__intersection of State Secondary Routes 45 and 46 at Helvetia, West Virginia.__

and that the grounds for probable cause for the issuance of this warrant are as follows: _____

__See attached affidavit.__
(State facts for belief)

that the name of the person whose affidavit has been taken in support of the issuance of this warrant

__Trooper W. D. Kershner__
(Type name on the line)

You are therefore, commanded in the name of the State of West Virginia to search forthwith the premises above scribed and all appurtenances appertaining thereto for the property above specified, to seize such property and bring same before me to be dealt with according to law.

Given under my hand this the __26__ day of __Oct.__, 18

*Strike out inapplicable words.

_William D. Hecht_
Magistrate

NOTE: W. Va. Code §62-1A-4 provides specifically that a warrant may be executed and returned **only within 10 days after its date.**

SCA-M2B
1st copy    Returned
2nd copy    Defendant

# WARRANT FOR ARREST

Case No. _____

STATE OF WEST VIRGINIA, _____ Randolph _____ . _____ COUNTY, to-wit:

To Any Law Enforcement Officer:

WHEREAS, _____ Tpr. W. D. Kershner _____ has this day made complaint
and information on oath before me _____ W. I. Heckel _____ , a Magistrate in
said County, that ████████████████

_____, Defendant

did commit a _____ Misd. _____ , in    that the said Defendant
on the __2__ day of _____ May _____ , 198 4 , and prior to the issuance of
this warrant, in said County did unlawfully _____

   Sell alcoholic liquor in this State without a licence.

   (60-6-7)

*Pleaded Nolle Contendere 10/29/84 or fine $50*

_____ against the peace and dignity of the State

   Therefore, we command you in the name of the State of West Virginia, forthwith to apprehend the said
████████████████████ , and bring that person before me
or before some other magistrate in said County, to answer said complaint, and to be further dealt with in relation
thereto according to law.

   Given under my hand this __29__ day of _____ Oct. _____ , 19 84

William I. Heckel
Magistrate

Executed By: Tpr. W D Kersh _____ In _____ Randolph _____ County

Date: 10-28-84

Arrest Fee _____ Jail Fee _____ Mileage Fee _____

277

PROPERTY RECEIPT                     October

I, the undersigned, did execute the within warrant, on the _____ day of _____ ,

time: 2'30 ____ A.M.-P.M., by searching the premises therein described.

The following is an inventory of the property seized, hereby receipted:

4 wooden barrels
2 lengths of copper tubing (coiled)
1 stainless steel cooker
1 gallon jug of clear liquid
1 Kessler whiskey containing clear liquid
1 cooling barrel (painted black)          to Luther Winkle
1 jerry can #4 Bag of labor
1 notice of distress from wv dept of mine
    to Tucky Bug Coal Co
1 funnel (red in color)
1 gallon jug containing vinegar
1 5 gal water cooler (red + yellow)

2 bags Rye (grain)
1 bag cooler barrel
1 cool cooler barrel

Dated this 21 day of _____ , 195_

                                    Jno. M. Hershe
                                        (Officer)

Receipt of a copy of the within warrant is hereby acknowledged along with the inventory of the property
above listed.

Dated this the 26 day of _____ , time: 4 42 ____ A.M.-P.M.

SCA-M28
1st copy -- Returned
2nd copy -- Defendant                    (Person from whose premises the property was t

278

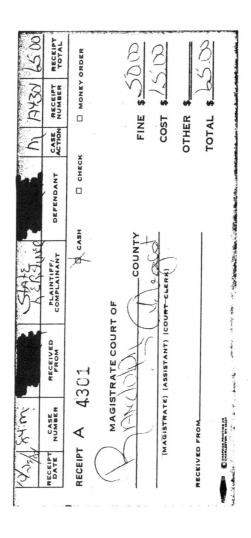

| RECEIPT DATE | CASE NUMBER | RECEIVED FROM | PLAINTIFF/ COMPLAINANT | DEFENDANT | CASE ACTION | RECEIPT NUMBER | RECEIPT TOTAL |
|---|---|---|---|---|---|---|---|
| | | | STATE PERSLAND | | M | 19430 | 65.00 |

RECEIPT A 4301

☒ CASH    ☐ CHECK    ☐ MONEY ORDER

MAGISTRATE COURT OF _____ COUNTY

[MAGISTRATE] (ASSISTANT) (COURT-CLERK)

RECEIVED FROM _____

FINE $ 50.00

COST $ 15.00

OTHER $ _____

TOTAL $ 65.00

CHAPMAN PRINTING CO.
CHARLESTON, WV 25317

279

## COMPLAINT FOR SUMMONS OR WARRANT

Complainant _Tpr W D Kershner_

Address _State Police Elkins WV_ ___ Tele 636-3101

Defendant(s) name and address:

_Box ▓▓▓▓▓▓▓ WV_ ___ ___ _WV_

Juvenile _____ Adult _X_ ___ Juvenile _____ Adult _X_

Before the undersigned Magistrate this day appeared the above complainant, and upon oath states that the defendant(s), on about the _____ day of _____, 19_83_, in the County of _Randolph_ committed the following offense(s):

_Unlawfully operate a plant manufacturing distilled Spirits 60-6-10 code of WV_

The basis for this belief that such offense(s) have or has been committed are as follows: _based on oral admission of the accused to Cpl L.E. Farben and Tpr W D Kershner that they had made illegal whiskey in the past. On May 2, 1984 this above named officers purchased 1 pint of illegal whiskey from ▓▓▓▓▓▓▓ On October 26, 1984 a moonshine still was confiscated via search warrant ▓▓▓▓▓▓▓ property near Pickens. This search warrant was found or information given to this above named officers by ▓▓▓▓▓▓▓_

I do hereby swear or affirm that the information contained above is true and correct.

_Tpr W D Kershner_
Complainant

Taken, subscribed and sworn to before me this _29_ day of _OCT_ _____, 19_84_

_William J Hechel_
Magistrate

Warrant Issued _Oct 29 1984_ ___ Summons Issued _____
(Date) ___ (Date)

SCA—M1-A ▓▓▓▓
1st Copy - Return   4th Copy - Complainant
2nd Copy - Defendant   5th Copy - Prosecutor
3rd Copy - File

280

## FACTS FOR BELIEF

That Corporal L. E. Lanham and Trooper W. D. Kershner who are duly sworn members of the West Virginia Department of Public Safety stationed at Company "C" Headquarters in Elkins, West Virginia, and assigned to work undercover on crimes requiring special investigation.

Further that the affiants were assigned by Captain M. P. Koerner, Commander, Company "C" Headquarters, West Virginia State Police, to investigate allegations that ▉▉▉▉▉▉ and ▉▉▉▉▉▉▉ were manufacturing and selling moonshine whiskey in the Pickens and Helvetia areas and that on the first day of May, 1984, Corporal L. E. Lanham and Trooper W. D. Kershner contacted ▉▉▉▉▉▉ and ▉▉▉▉▉▉▉ at ▉▉▉▉▉▉ residence and discussed making moonshine. The affiant further bases this belief on the fact that on the second day of May, 1984, Trooper W. D. Kershner purchased a pint bottle of moonshine whiskey from ▉▉▉▉▉▉. Further that on October 24, 1984, Corporal L. E. Lanham and Trooper W. D. Kershner again visited ▉▉▉▉▉▉ at his residence and was given moonshine whiskey by ▉▉▉▉▉▉ and at that time ▉▉▉▉ ▉▉▉ told the affaints that the moonshine still was concealed in a building on the property now occupied by ▉▉▉▉▉▉▉ located between Helvetia and Pickens, West Virginia.

281

282

GEORGE R. TRIPLETT, L. C.
ATTORNEY AT LAW
484 RANDOLPH AVENUE
P. O. BOX 1365
ELKINS, WEST VIRGINIA 26241

AREA CODE 304
TELEPHONE 636-7335
RESIDENCE 636-5113

April 24, 1985

In Re:  State vs. ███████████

Dear ███████:

     I  appeared on your behalf, Monday, April 22,
before Judge Nuzum and moved the still be donated and
awarded to the Helvitia Museum for historical, educational
and aesthetic purposes.

     I further suggested that it be dedicated to Major
Koerner, Judge Nuzum, James F. Cain, yourself and ████████
████████.

     Frankly, the argument flew like a lead balloon and
Judge Nuzum ruled against me that all the property
confiscated be destroyed in accordance with the Prosecuting
Attorney's petition.

     Should you have any questions, please promptly
communicate.

Very truly yours,

George R. Triplett
Attorney at Law

GRT:jlw

283

Cheat Bridge.

285

Cheat Bridge.

287

Robin and Charles Triplett, Mary Ann and Butch Triplett, and Silvia and Jeff Triplett.

# Mountain People Take
## Their Politics Seriously

Democratic primary elections in the mountains are sometimes most contentious. A young candidate during his first election for prosecuting attorney in Randolph County persuaded Susie Thompson Hedrick, a quiet, loyal Bemis Democrat to haul voters to the election polls and paid her twenty dollars.

There were thirty Democratic votes cast at Bemis and the young attorney received twenty-nine of them. Susie carried the election ballots from Elkins to Bemis and returned them to the Randolph County Courthouse after the voting polls closed on election day unknown to the young candidate he had made the "Bemis Slate."

The lawyer being extremely elated on his margin of victory at Bemis walked out of Randolph County Courthouse with Susie and continued to praised her success with the delivery of the Bemis Democratic vote for him. Susie didn't respond but as she walked away in the darkness, the victorious candidate heard her mumble, "I wonder who that double-crossin' SOB was?"

The young elected prosecuting attorney fresh out of law school possibly wasn't aware of the "goin's ons" election day at Bemis and practiced among the Celtic mountain culture. The most important election poll worker for paper ballots was the "ballot box clerk." I am told the system operated successfully as follows: The first voter took a folded blank piece of paper, same color as the ballots and wore a coat with an inside pocket. He received the proper ballot and took it to the closed voting booth that had a "drawn curtain" to vote a secret ballot. He took the folded blank sheet of paper from the inside coat pocket. He then received the proper ballot and took it to the closed voting booth that had a "drawn curtain" to vote a secret ballot. He took the folded sheet of paper from the inside coat pocket and slipped the "blank sheet" of paper hurriedly and mistakenly in the ballot box before the ballot box clerk had a chance to hand the "paper".

The first voter handed the unmarked ballot to the "pay off" man outside the voting place and received compensation either in whiskey, money or a special political favor. The outside team marked the unmarked first paper ballot for their candidates and gave it to the second voter, who dropped the first ballot into the ballot box and delivered his or her unmarked ballot for compensation. The process was repeated until the polls closed. Communications were relayed to the county political headquarters that knew almost the expected vote and candidates expected to be nominated or elected when the actual paper ballots were finally counted.

I have served as legal counsel for persons who have been elected by the "toss of a coin." Susie Thompson Hedrick was the wife of "Square Toe" Hedrick and mother of Frances Thompson Shifflett and Tom Thompson. She was the mother-in-law of Calvin Shifflett. "Square Toe" was forced to pay the Federal Revenuers $2.60 taxes on "moonshine" confiscated and destroyed after his release from the Federal prison for manufacturing "spirits".

# *P*art IV

## *R*andolph *C*ounty *F*amily *H*istory

Genealogy is mainly an incurable disease that strikes the elderly, which is unfortunate as by then all of those who could answer our questions are either dotty or dead. We should listen to the tales of our elders and even better, write them down before we forget them. The history of every family, regardless of social position or historical importance, is interesting and worthy of being preserved for future generations.

## I. *O*rigin of *S*urnames

Our surnames, like everything else, had a beginning. In England they were confined to the higher and land holding class prior to the Fourteenth Century. Many of the names familiar in the history of this country first appeared in *Doomsday Book*, written in England in 1086. It consisted of a list of land holders at that time. Its authority was not to be questioned in disputes as to title to land and for this reason was called the *"Doomsday Book"* or book of judgment. Surnames were originally written over the other name and are derived from the Latin surname or the French super nomen. Many names were derived from their baptismal ones by adding the suffix "son" to the name of the father as John-son, Wil-son, William-son, Peter-son, Richard-son, Adam-son.

The practice of using diminutives was often adopted by the

people to multiply the comparatively limited number of names at their command. The Saxon diminutives commonly used were "kin", "cock," "ock," and the Norman ones "at," "et," "on," or "in". Therefore it is ascertainable whether names so ending are Norman or Saxon in their origin.

Before surnames came into vogue it was by no means an uncommon practice to give all the sons of one family one name, as William for example. They would be called Wil-kin, Will-cock, Will-ot, Will-mot, which in the process of time has changed to Wilmoth.

The suffixes "ham," "nam," "an," and "er" were often used for man. Thus originated the name Rowan, Rose-an, being identical with Rose-man, has passed through changes in orthography, as Rows-an, until we have at present Rowan.

Likewise we have the name Cunningham, derived from Coney, Teutonic for rabbit and "ham" Norman for man. The old form of spelling Coney was Cunyng. In the regulation of the Scottish Privy Council, August 6, 1602, regulating the masters and barons of the University of Glaglow, amonst the viads mentioned were "with ane foull or cunyng or a pair of dovis and ciclyk to their Supper." Another probable origin of the name Anglo-Saxon Cyning for leader and "ham," Norman for man. Then we have Cyningham, the leader man.

The suffix lea, leah now ley is Anglo-Saxon, meaning an untilled tract of land or pasturage, used as a shelter for animals. In the origin of the name Woodley we have the Anglo-Saxon word Wudu, meaning "wood" and "lea" or "Leah," meaning land or pasturage. We then have Wudu-lea, now Woodley, meaning a "lea" on which there is a "wood".

Roman names were derived from mental or physical characteristics. Such words are Wise, Sharp, Dear, Able, Long, Crouch, and Armstrong. The romans were also partial to animals covered with wool. It is probable that such names as Fox, Wolf, and Bear had a Roman origin. A very large number of other names had their origin in the occupations as Weaver, Carpenter, Miller, etc. Surnames is some instances had their origin in the sneers of the vulgar, as is evidenced in the name Proudfoot.

**Allen**-Gaelic, exceedingly fair. In *Doomsday Book* as Alan.

**Armstrong**-Strength in battle. An ancient King of Scotland had his horse killed under him and Fairburn, his armour bearer, taking him by the thigh, set him in his own saddle. The King gave him the appellation of Armstrong. *See Scott's Lay of The Last Minstrel.*

**Ap, Mab, and Ab** are Welsh words meaning son. In the early history of Randolph we find Morgan ap Morgan.

**At or Atte** was used to describe the place of residence as John-at-Wood, now Atwood.

**Bent**-English, a plain or Moor.

**Bell**-The name Bell was taken from the sign of an inn or tavern. The sign of a bell was frequently used to designate that the house was an inn. John-at-the bell became John Bell. Belle in French means beautiful.

**Barnard**-The name Barnard is from Bean or Bairn, a child and ard, Teutonic for nature. The word Barnard, therefore, described one of a child-like nature, or affection.

**Bing**-The surname Bing is from the Danish Binge, an enclosure or a place where supplies are kept.

**Bogart**-German, Bommelgard, an orchard.

**Boseley**-The name Boseley is derived like Bosworth except that the suffixes "lea" and "worth" have reference to small estates slightly different in their characteristics.

**Bosworth**-The Anglo-Saxon words, with, worth, urth, means a small estate. This word combined with the old Norse word Bass, middle English Bose or Boose, "a stall in which cattle are kept in winter," gives us Bose-worth or Booseworth, now Bosworth. Bosworth would then mean a worth on which there is a boose or an estate on which there is a cattle stall. However, there is another probable origin of the word Bosworth. This Bos is from the personal name Bosa or Boso, found more than a score of times in the Onomasticon. In this case Bosworth means the worth or estate of Boso, getting its name from the owner.

**Bradley**-The name Bradley is from the Anglo-Saxon word Bradlea, Brad meaning broad and "lea" or "leah" a pasturage.

**Butcher**-Norse as Buoker, Danish as Boedker, German as Boettcher, Flemish as Buker or Busher, French as Boucher.

**Car**-French as Carre, meaning broad shouldered, Norse as Karr. In *Doomsday Book* as Carr.

**Cassidy**-Gaelic from cassaideach, apt to complain.

**Cheny**-French, a grove.

**Cob**-German as Kobe, Scotch as Kobbes. The name appears in the *Doomsday Book* as Copsi. The English Cob originated from Jacob.

**Collett**-The word Collett is from the ecclesiastical word Acolyte, attendant, and is from the Greek. The Acolyte was one of the minor order of clergy in the ancient church. We learn from the canons of the fourth council of Carthage that the Archdeacon at the ordination put into the hands of the Acolyte a candlestick with a taper and an empty pitcher to imply that they were appointed to light the candles of the church and to furnish wine for the eucharist. Their dress was the Cossack and the surplice. The name and the office still exist in the church.

**Collier**-French as Coulier.

**Crawford**-The name Crawford is Gaelic in its origin, and means a pass of blood. From "cru," bloody and "ford" a way. The name was first assumed by the barony of Crawford in England.

**Curtis**-The name Curtis is derived from and is an abbreviation of courteous. The name was perhaps first applied to a person noted for his urbanity.

**Daniels**-The name Daniels is from Daniel, signifying the judgment of God. The "s" added is a contraction of son.

**Davis**-French as Devis.

**Denton**-Denton is derived from "Den" a valley and "ton" a town, meaning a town in a valley.

**Dick**-Dyck, German bulwark thrown against a sea or river.

**Dilworth**-French, Diluerth.

**Dove**-Norse, Dufan, German, Dove.

**Downing**-A local name in Worchester, England.

**Ferguson**-From the Gaelic and Celtic Feor, meaning man and Guth, meaning voice or word. The two words meaning the man of the word or commander. A fierce and brave chieftain.

**Gilmore**-From their Irish, McGiolla Muire.

**Goff**-Goff is the variation of the German word Gough or Gow, being the German for the English Smith, and is, therefore, occupational in its origin.

**Hansford**-The name Hansford is derived from the Welsh words, "Han" meaning old and "ford" meaning way. The name Hansford, now Hansford, therefore means the old way.

**Harding**-Norse as Haddingr. Harding from "here" or "har," meaning an army and "ing" a meadow. A meadow in which an army is encamped.

**Harman**-The name Harman is from the German "har" originally meaning soldier and man. The name, therefore, was perhaps first applied to a military man.

**Hart**-Norse as Hyotr. In *Doomsday Book* as Hard.

**Harper**-Some names as Harper may be either German or English in their origin. Harper, meaning one who contributes to musical entertainments, would lead to the conclusion that the name is of English etymology, being occupational in its origin. However in the early records of Shenandoah Valley, the word as Herber and Herrber. This makes it probable that the name is German.

**Harris**-Norse as Harri, *Doomsday Book* as Harries.

**Hazeltine**- from Hazeldine.

**Heron**-Welsh, a hero.

**Hill**-German, Hille.

**Hutton**-The Anglo-Saxon words "tun" and "ton" mean small enclosed farmsteads or villages. In the derivation of the word Houghton, now Hutton, we have the Anglo-Saxon words "Hough" or "Hoh," meaning a heel and "tun" or "ton" meaning an enclosed village or farmstead. The name Houghton, now Hutton, was probably applied originally to a resident of an enclosed village or farmstead in the shape of a "hoh" or heel.

**Jackson**-English, Danish as Jacobson, French as Jackchen.

**Joyce**-Irish, Normandy as Joyeus.

**Kendall**-An English word derived from the two words Kent and Dale. Kentdale, now Ken-dall, meant a dale on the River Kent, so the name was probably applied originally to a people living in such a locality.

**Kelly**-The surname Kelly is derived from a Gaelic and celtic Kill or Cille, a church. The name was, perhaps, first applied to an individual who was in some manner connected with the church.

**Kennedy**-Irish, O'Ceannfhada, originally.

**Kyle**-The name Kyle is from a district in Scotland, through which the River Coyle flows.

**Kittle**-A name introduced into England, perhaps, at the time of the Norman conquest. Thor, the Supreme God of the Norsemen, is the root word of many of our surnames. The sacrificial kettle or cauldron was an important article in the worship of Thor. Thor-Kettle or Thyr-Kittle is a common name in England to this day. The word now appears in this country as Kittle.

**Long**-It is said that the name Long originated from a very tall attendant of Lord Treasurer Hungerford. The Longs were very numerous in Oxfordshire, Cambridge, England, in the reign of Edward the First.

**Lloyd**-From the Gaelic Lhuyd and signifies gray or brown.

**Marshall**-The name marshall originated in the north of England and was at first spelled Marechal. It means master of the horse.

**Maxwell**-The Maxwells took their name from a village in Roxburgshire, England.

**McLean**-The name McLean is derived from MacGilean, a highland chieftain and a celebrated warrior.

**McIntosh**- "Mac," son, and "tosh," leader. Then McIntosh means son of a leader.

**Moore**-The name Moore is from the Celtic word "morh," meaning big.

**Mullenix**-French as Molynix, from "Moulin" a mill.

**McQuain**-Irish, and is probably derived from "Mac," son, and "cairn," a heap of stones erected by the early inhabitants of the British Islands as sepulchral monuments. The name was originally McCairn.

**Phillips**-The surname Phillips is from Greek word meaning lover of horses.

**Pritt**-From the Norse Prudi.

**Russell**-French from Roussel, a stream or brook. In *Doomsday Book* as Rozell.

**Ryan**-Normandy as Royan, Danish as Ryan.

**Schoonover**-Derived from Schoonoven, a place in South Holland. The word is from "Schoon," and old Dutch word meaning fine and "hoven," a garden or court.

**Scott**-The origin of the name Scott is clouded in doubt. Scotylle, Anglo-Saxon for winnowing fan is given by some writers as the original word. Other scholars say the word meant rulers or possessors. Again it is maintained that the Scotts who invaded Argyle in 360 were so-called because the word "Scotti" meant sacred painters or sculptors, an art in which these people were proficient.

**See**-German, lake. Thunersee, the lake of Thun.

**Shannon**-The name Shannon is derived from the Shannon River in Ireland. The word was originally Shenabhanon.

**Shreeves**-Derived from "Schir," a Shire, division, or township and reeve, the Bailiff. The word then means a Bailiff of a Shire.

**Smith**-The word Smith was an occupational one; the original word was "smote," the art of striking the anvil. The name is a very common one because, at the time of the adoption of surnames, the smith made almost everything used in the arts of war and peace. A very large number of people were engaged in the trades of gunsmith, blacksmith, tinsmith, silversmith, etc.

**Stalnaker**-Derived from the German word "Stahal" or "Stahl" meaning steele, and "Nagel," a sharp point or spear. Then the original word was Stahlnagel, meaning a sharp-pointed steele spear. So the name was, perhaps, first applied to a warrior who was armed with such a weapon.

**Taggart**-Appears as McTaggart in Scotch.

**Talbott**-English, and appears in the *Doomsday Book* as spelled at present.

**Tyre**-Derived from "Tyreman," a dresser. From the fact that the Norman suffix "er" is used to abbreviate the word, it is to be presumed that it is of Norman origin.

**Ward**-From the Anglo-Saxon "weard," a watchman.

**Warner**-Appears in the *Doomsday Book* as Warn.

**Weese**-From the German "weiss" meaning white, or "waas" meaning bold.

**Wamsley**-Derived from a Lancashire township of that name.

**Weymoth**-The name Weymoth is provincial in its origin, being first, perhaps, applied to residents about the mouth of the small river Wey in England. The City of Wey at the mouth of this river, is very ancient. The Anglo-Saxon word was Wagemuth, from "wage" meaning a wave or passage way, and "muth" meaning mouth.

**White**-Derived from the Anglo-Saxon "hweit," meaning fairness of complexion.

**Wilmoth**-Derives from the baptismal name of William as explained elsewhere. Originally the name was spelled Wilmot.

Nicholas was a favorite name in the Wilmot family in England.

Sir Nicholas was Knighted in the seventeenth century in England. His grandfather was named Nicholas. It is significant that the eldest of the Wilmoth brothers to locate in Randolph was named Nicholas.

**Yeager**-Danish, huntsman. Yagere also means a sweetheart.

## II. Variation in Surnames

Individual perculiarities in pronounciation largely account for the variations in spelling of surnames. In the earlier history of the county, names were seldom written and the ear was the only guide to the spelling and in some cases the only method of transmitting names from one generation to another. Then the settler often coming direct from European countries, embraced the opportunity to simplify and abbreviate a cumbersome name. This was particularly true of German names. The object was sometimes to change the form into English. Thus we have Armikast changed to Arbogast, Hermantracht to Armentrout, Bauman to Bowman, Kromet to Crummett, Kerper to Carper, Dahle to Dolly, Herber to Harper, Herrman to Harman, Heffner to Hevener, Huber to Hoover, Loch to Lough, Roeder to Rader, Sieman to Simmons, Schaefer to Shaver, Schneider to Snyder, Sponagen to Sponaugle, Tehudi to Judy, Wetzel to Whetsell, Wildfang to Wilfong, Zwickenfus to Zickafoos.

## III. Classification of Names

The following classification of names though not free from error is in the main correct:

**A. English**

    1. Ayers

    2. Blair, Bosworth, Bell, Brown, Bradley, Barlow, Bent,

Bennett, Bishop, Bond, Boseley, Blackman, Bradley
3. Chenoweth, Cook, Channell
4. Daniels, Day, Digman, Davisson, Dawson, Denton
5. Earle, Elliott, England, Elza, Elkins, Findley, Fox
6. Goddin, Gibon, Gandy, Gawthrop
7. Haymond, Hart, Harding, Hansford, Hunt, Hutton, Harris, Henderson, Hadden, Holder, Howell
8. Isner
9. Jones, Jackson, Johnson
10. Kittle, Kelley, Kimble
11. Lamb, Lee, Long
12. Marshall, Morris, Mason
13. Porter, Powers, Payne, Pennington, Patterson, Potts
14. Russell, Roy, Reed, Robinson
15. Smith, Summerfield, Skidmore, Shreve
16. Taylor, Turner, Taft, Thompson, Triplett
17. Woodford, Williamson, Weymouth, Wamsley, Woodley, Ward, Wilmoth, White, Wilson

## B. Irish

1. Adams, Adamson
2. Burns, Bodkin, Boggs, Brady, Boyles, Beaty
3. Clark, Collier, Connolly, Cian, Coff, Cickard, Cunningham, Currence
4. Donohoe, Daugherty, Davis, Durkin
5. Ford, Ferguson, Faligan
6. Gainer
7. Jordan, Joyce
8. Keenan, Kinnan, Kee, Kennedy
9. Murphy, McLain, McAllister
10. Phares
11. Rains, Rooney, Ryan, Rowan

12. Scott

13. Wood

## C. German

1. Alt, Arbogast, Armentrout
2. Bowers, Baker, Ball, Bucket, Bowman
3. Car, Conrad, Caplinger, Crummett, Carper, Canfield, Collins, Curtis
4. Dobe, Dolly
5. Eberman, Eye
6. Fisher, Friend
7. Goff
8. Haigler, Halterman, Harman, Harper, Hedrick, Hevener, Hinkle, Hoover, Huffman
9. Judy
10. Ketterman, Kyle
11. Lantz, Lough
12. Marteney, Moyers, Marstiller
13. Riggleman, Rosencranse, Rader, Riffle, Rohrbaugh, Rinehart
14. Shaver, Simmons, Sites, Snyder, Sponaugle, Swadley, Smith, Stalnaker, See, Swecker, Schoonover
15. Teter, Tingle, Tolly
16. Vandevander, Vanpelt
17. Westfall, Weere, Wolf, Wimer, Whetsell
18. Yokum, Yeager
19. Zickafoose

## D. Scotch

1. Anderson, Armstrong
2. Collett, Cowger, Cunningham, Campbell, Crawford
3. Lambert, Logan
4. McLeary, McMullen, McClung, McLean, McDonald, McQuain, McCorkel

5. Nelson
6. Simpson, Skidmore
7. Thompson
8. Vansoy
9. Welch

**E. Welch**
1. Davis
2. Howell
3. Lewis
4. Williams

**F. French**
1. Capitio, Cassell
2. Montony, Mullenix
3. Tyre

**G. Spanish**
1. Pedro

# IV. Extinct Families of Randolph

This list includes pioneer families of Randolph County that have no descendants of the same name residing within the county. Families of the same name may live in the county, but they are not of the same strain of blood as the names here mentioned. As a rule these families pushed farther west when Randolph assumed the staid aspect of older communities: Anderson, Armstrong, Adams, Alford, Barnhouse, Bingham, Blain, Bogard, Baxter, Bell, Blain, Bond, Botkin, Btuff, Bridger, Booth, Breckenridge, Bent, Brian, Buffington, Briggs, Bozart, Bogard, Connonly, Curtright, Cade, Casto, Carpenter, Casey, Cassity, Claypool, Crane, Combs, Carney, Donohoe, Dougherty, Dolbeare, Evick, Eberman, England, Friend, Fink, Files, Gandy, Gibson, Haigler, Heath, Holder, Hughes, Hiller, Harris, Kinnan, Kozer, Lacket, Leeky, Longacker,

Mace, McLeary, McLean, McMullen, Maxwell, Myers, Maddix, Nelson, Osborn, Petty, Powell, Ralston, Rummell, Reeder, Rollins, Springtone, Stout, Steers, Slagle, Taft, Taggert, Taffee, Troutwine, Turner, Warthen, Warwick, Whitman, Whiterman, Wise, Wolf.

## *A*rbogast *F*amily

This family, numerously represented in Randolph County is of German descent, and settled in what is now Highland County, Virginia, prior to 1779. The name was originally spelled Armikast. Adam Arbogast was captain of a company of Pendleton militia in 1793.

Lemuel J. Arbogast was born in 1851 and died at the age of eighty-four in 1935. He was married to Barbara Ellen Rexrode, who was born April 23, 1853 and died July 15, 1920, at the age of sixty-seven. Both are buried in Taylor Cemetery at Bowden. They lived and resided at Revelle after moving from Pendleton County and had fourteen children, as follows:

Lemuel and Ellen Rexrode Arbogast-

1. Ellen Arbogast Vance-married Isaac Vance. Children were Lemuel Vance, Ira Vance, Nathan Vance, Harl Vance and Isom Vance.
2. Ida Arbogast-married Perry Arbogast, several children, Mason, Clara . . .
3. Tina Arbogast Powers-(first) married Mac Alpine; (second) married Burnard Powers; and (third) married Perry McLean, Belington (second marriage).

Children were: Dora Powers, a railroad trackman, Spruce, and Jade Powers, a locomotive engineer. Both Dora and Jade had several children born at Spruce. Dora and Dovie Howell Powers' children were Okareta, Wanda, Murl, Bernice, Arveda, Joyce and Jerry.

305

4. Lora Susan Arbogast Triplett, married George Washington Triplett, children, Manville, Granville, Charlie Robert, Ira William, Harry Jasper.
5. Anna Arbogast Peters-married John Peters. Children were Sam Peters, Loris Peters, Anna's second marriage was to Wirt Queen, Upshur County.
6. James "Will" Arbogast-married Ruth Coberly (sister to Harl M.Coberly). Children were John, Garnett, Wilbert "Web," Sylvia, Goldie, Opha, Howard, Troy, Violet, Mabel, Arlie, Beatrice, Harry James (___) and Wilda- 14 children.
7. Etta Arbogast Summerfield-children were John Summerfield, Mary Coberly and Icie Lindsay.
8. Earl Arbogast-married Mary Howell. Children were Fred, Daisey, Wesley, Robert and Elsie.
9. Ada Arbogast-never married.
10. Jenny Arbogast Fansler-married William "Bink" Fansler. Children were Opal, Dolly, Dessie, Ralph, Harvey, Charlie, Rachael and Rosalee.
11. Benjamin Arbogast-married Mandy Sacks. Children were John, Charlie, Denzil and Virgie.
12. Hobert Arbogast-married Florence Smith. Children were Genevieve and two sons and a younger daughter.

*Note-Two unknown-must have died during childbirth. Observe the dropped hands between the children in Lemuel Arbogast's Family Photograph.*


## ℳrmentrout ℱamily

This family is of German descent. The name was originally spelled Erhmantrout. Christopher Armentrout moved from Rockingham County, Virginia, to what is now Grant County prior to the Revolution. The immediate ancestors of the Armentrouts in

Randolph County lived in Grant and Pendleton counties.

Hiram, son of Christopher, was born in Pendleton County in 1811. He married Amanda Smith. Their children were, John W., who married Martha Dolly; Christopher, who married Pheoba Mullenix; Aaron, Mary, Martha, Isaac, Anne, Susan, Adina and Nevada.

John W. Armentrout was born in 1843 and was married in1868 to Martha, daughter of John and Susan Dolly. Their children are Robert E., Laura V., Stella C., Jasper C. and Wilbur E.

Christopher Armentrout was born in 1845. Children were Ole E., Vista G., Carrey L., Elva T., Viva and Orgie. He came from Pendleton County to Randolph County in 1872 and was elected a member of the county court in 1888. His grandfather, Christopher Armentrout, was born in Grant County in 1775. In 1792, he entered 218 acres of land in the vicinity in which his grandson, Christopher, is now a resident, but he did not occupy it. His great-grandmother, Catherine Peterson, was captured at Fort Seybert by the Indians in 1758. About forty settlers were in the fort and all were massacred but two who were held in captivity and taken to their village near Chilicothe, Ohio. Catherine Peterson was among the number spared. The Shawnee Trail by which they returned to Ohio passed through or near the city of Elkins. A brave had pity on Mrs. Peterson and gave her a pair of moccasins that she might travel with greater comfort. She remained in captivity for six years. Two hundred captives were rescued by General Boquet, who attacked the Indian towns in Ohio in 1764. They were returned to Fort Pitt. Mrs. Peterson was among the number and from there returned to her home in Pendleton County.

In 1788 Uriah Gandy sold to Christopher Armentrout 131 acres on Gandy Creek, Randolph County. The name was spelled in the conveyance "Hermantrout".

# Bosworth Family

The first of the Bosworth family to locate in what is now West Virginia were Joshua and a brother whose name is now not known. The brother, after a brief sojourn in Virginia, moved father west and located at Marietta, Ohio. Joshua Bosworth married in Massachusetts a Miss Squire and to this union were born, in the native state, the following children: Joshua, Amaziah, Squire, Parley, Harriet, who married John Phillips, of French Creek, Upshur County; Delaney, who married Alpheus Rude and moved to Illinois; Rhoda, who married a Mr. Allen and moved to Ohio.

Squire Bosworth was born in Montgomery, Massachusetts, in 1785 and died at Beverly, West Virginia in 1870. He married Hannah, daughter of Peter Buckey, in 1816. Unto this union were born John W., Squire Newton, George W., Elam B., Rebecca, who married Rev. C.S.M. See; Lucy, who married Capt. T.A. Bradford; Harriet, who married Charles See; Martha, who married McGuffin; Christina, who married William Brown; Mary, who married Adam Crawford.

Dr. John W. Bosworth married Mattie Dold. They had a child, Annie, who became the wife of Dr. Chas. Williams.

Geo. W. Bosworth married Mary, daughter of John and Ann (Conrad) Currence. Children were: Drs. John L., Albert S. and Perry.

Joshua Bosworth came to Virginia with the New England colony that settled on French Creek. He located on Turkey Run, near the Upshur-Harrison line. Among the families that comprised that settlement were the Goulds, Burrhs, Morgans, Phillips, Books, and the Sextons. They were well-educated and devout Christians and were of the best material for a new country.

Dr. Squire Bosworth, after teaching school for a time in Parkersburg and Beverly, studied medicine under Dr. Dolbear and attended lectures in Richmond, Virginia. He was for nearly half a century the only physician in Randolph County. He was clerk of the county court of Randolph County as well as deputy for a number of years under Archibald Earle. He also represented Randolph County and Tucker County in the Virginia Assembly prior to the Civil War.

Dr. J.L. Bosworth married, Rachel, daughter of Randolph and Katherine (Hutton) Crouch. Children were Mary, who married Tracy Fling, of Gilmer County, and Hallie and John Woodbridge.

Dr. Perry Bosworth married in Pocahontas County, Lucy, daughter of Joseph Samuel and Abigail (Curry) Smith.

Dr. A.S. Bosworth married in 1882, Julia M., daughter of Geo. W. and H. Keziah (Boyers) Davis. Child was Stella M., who married Blake Taylor. Mrs. Bosworth died in 1885. Dr. Bosworth married his second wife, Miss Eleanor, daughter of Henry and Elizabeth (Snyder) Weisgerber, of Baltimore, in 1894. One child, Stanley, was born to this union.

The original home of the Bosworths in England was in Leicester County, an inland town. Bosworth Field and Bosworth Market are historic places in Leicester. Benjamin was perhaps the first of the name to come to America in about 1630, settling at Highham, Massachusetts. The Bosworths in New England intermarried with the Mortons, Childs, Sturdevants and Mathers.

Squire N. Bosworth, son of Dr. Squire and Hannah (Buckey) Bosworth, was born in 1841, married (1867) Florence A., daughter of Bernard L. and Mary (Daily) Brown. Children were: Lutie Lee, Florence A., Mary Eva, Ada, Charles B., Carroll L., Hellen, Nina and Willie.

Mr. Boswroth served through the war as a Confederate soldier, belonging to the Thirty-first Virginia Infantry, of which company he was sergeant. He still has in his possession the flag of his regiment, presented by Stonewall Jackson, May 5, 1862. The flag was pierced by a shell.

Mr. Bosworth was for many years postmaster of Beverly.

Stanley Bosworth was elected prosecuting attorney and circuit court judge of Randolph County. Judge Bosworth is survived by his widow, Effie, and two daughters Jean and Julia Bosworth.


## $\mathscr{C}$rickard $\mathscr{F}$amily

The Crickards are of Scotch-Irish descent. My great-grandfather was a resident of that part of Ireland known as Ulster. He was an officer in King James army and fought at the Battle of the Boyne, July 1, 1690. The Irish forces were defeated by William III of England. After this battle many of the estates of the Irish were confiscated and divided among William's followers who were largely Protestants. Owen Crickard's great-grandfather, being loyal to Ireland and a Catholic, his estate was confiscated. Owen Crickard's grandfather resided in the County of Doun. My father, John Crickard, and his brothers came to America in 1834-1840. They settled in Augusta County, Virginia. Owen Crickard's father, John Crickard and my uncle Peter Crickard, built the Staunton and Parkersburg Pike from Greenbrier to Cheat Bridge. After the completion of this work, my father located on Shavers Run in Valley Bend District. My only brother, Peter Crickard, lived and died there. He was the father of the present sheriff of Randolph County, A.J. Crickard. Thos. Michael Plunkett, member of the British Parliament is a cousin of the Crickards of Randolph County. Owen Crickard's mother's name was Mary (Plunkett) Crickard. Owen Crickard's grandfather, Michael Crickard, took part in the Emmett Rebellion of 1803.    *-Patrick Crickard.*

John R. Crickard, son of Patrick and Amanda (Currence) Crickard, was born in 1860, married Alverda, daughter of John and Hannah (Currence) Bell. Children were: Patrick E., Nixon J., Robert B., Eva B., Peter W., Mary A., Jonas F., Anne C. and Rose P.

Mr. Crickard was educated in public schools and at Rock Hill College, Maryland. He was for several years one of the prominent school teachers of the county and served several terms as a president of the board of education of Mingo District. He was also justice of the peace of Mingo District for twelve years. In 1910, he was elected justice of the peace of that district on the Socialist ticket, giving him the distinction of being the only man having been elected by the adherents of that political faith in Randolph County. Mr. Crickard was prominent in fraternal circles and was a member of the A.F. and A.M., I.O.O.F., K.P., and M.W.W.

## Chenoweth Family

The Chenoweth family in America has descended from John Chenoweth, who came to this country from Isle of Wright in 1652. He settled in Maryland and married Mary Calvert, daughter of Lord Baltimore. William, a son of this marriage, was a member of a colony that settled in Frederick County, Maryland, prior to 1750. John, a son of William was born in 1755. He was a soldier in the Revolutionary War and drew a pension. He was in Pendleton in 1790 and entered fifty acres of land in that county in that year. The Pughs who were related to the Chenoweths and came to Randolph County with them, also entered land in Hampshire in the year 1790. John Chenoweth entered land in Randolph County in 1792, but perhaps he had been a resident of the county a few years previous.

A monument was unveiled to the memory of John Chenoweth about three miles south of Elkins, WV on the Job Daniels place October 16, 1915. On one side is the inscription: "John Chenoweth, Born November 15, 1755, Died June 16, 1831, A Soldier of the Revolution." On another side is the inscription to his wife as follows: "Mary Pugh, Wife of John Chenoweth, Born January 2, 1762, Died February 1, 1849. They were married on January 7, 1779."

311

On another side are the names of all the children as follows: "Robert, William, Mary, John, Jehu, Gabriel, Nellie."

John Chenoweth was captain of the militia in 1794; coroner in 1803; sheriff in 1810; justice of the peace in 1799. His son Robert was commissioner of the revenue in 1816; sheriff in 1827. Z.T. Chenoweth was sheriff in 1884.

Eliza Chenoweth married Jasper Wilmoth Triplett, son of Job Triplett and grandson of John Triplett. Eliza Chenoweth Triplett was the mother of Wade Hampton Triplett, George Washington "Pud" Triplett and Delphia Triplett Flint.

## Coberly Family

James Coberly was the progenitor of the Coberly family in Randolph County. He married July Vanscoy. The name is of German origin. The children of James and Julia (Vanscoy) Coberly, were Aaron Levi, born 1827, married Mary Canfield in 1846; John, born 1829, married in 1854 to Janet Gainer; Randolph, born 1830, died 1884, married in 1853 to Jane M., daughter of Archibald Wilson. Children were Helen, Martha E., John, Alfred T., Archibald, James, Wm. H., Ida J. and Julia E.

James A., son of Randolph and Jane M. (Wilson) Coberly, born in Barbour County, 1864; came to Randolph County in 1883, locating in Elkins in 1894. He was deputy surveyor four years; elected justice of the peace in Leadsville District in 1892. After studying law at State University he was admitted to the bar in 1898.

Mr. Coberly married (first) Delphia, daughter of Nicholas and Amanda (Taylor) Marstiller. She died in 1895; children were Otto Glen, who is deputy assessor of Randolph County, Cleon Edwards, Ohley Francis, and Virgil J. Mr. Coberly married (second) Mary Hannagan, of Monroe County, West Virginia.

Ruth Coberly married James Will Arbogast, son of Lemuel and

Barbara Rexrode Arbogast.

Harl M. "Cub" Coberly married Myrtle McBee and had three children, Herbert, Award and Winifred. Harl and Tom Coberly were Western Maryland railroad supervisors from Elkins to Durbin and Webster Springs. Tom Coberly married Mary Summerfield, daughter of Etta Arbogast Summerfield.

## Harris Family

All that has been written thus far is merely a prelude to the major purpose of this genealogical research, which is to focus on the descendants of Jerome Barnabas Harris, and his wife, Mary Jane Crocket[t] (aka Crocker) Kissinger Harris.

Mrs. Keifer, in her history of the Harris Family of New Jersey, wrote:

"Jerome B. Harris, son of Barnabas Tunis Harris and Rachel Marquis Harris, was born in 1836; married in 1871, name of wife not known; had six children: Lenora Harris, born April 3, 1872; Gailrod 'Gail' Harris, born April 21, 1874; Jerrold 'Buck' Harris, born January 21, 1876; Tunis 'Barney' Harris, born July 15, 1878; Mary Harris, born May 19, 1880; Raphael Harris, born March 1, 1882. Mr. Harris was a carpenter and builder by occupation. He resides at or near Beverly, Randolph County, Virginia in 1883. Is a member of the Presbyterian Church and a man much respected in the community where he lives."

This information is incomplete and has several errors.

There are two histories of Randolph County, West Virginia. One was written by H.W. Maxwell in 1898 and republished in 1961 (McClain Printing, Parsons, WV). Both of these printings are identical in wording.

Another history of Randolph County, West Virginia, was written by A.S. Bosworth and published in 1975 (McClain Printing, Parsons, WV).

The Maxwell History provides that Jerome Harris, born in 1836, is the son of Tunis and married Mary Jane Crocket[t] (aka Croker). Children: Lenora, Gaylord ("Gail"), Gerrald ("Buck"), Tunis ("Barney"), Mary, Raphael ("Raph") and William ("Poker Bill").

The other history of Randolph County, West Virginia, written by Dr. A.S. Bosworth and published in 1975 (McClain Printing, Parsons, WV) states: "The Harris Family. Jerome B. Harris, son of Barnabas Tunis and Rachael Marquis Harris, was born in 1836. He married Mary Crocket. Six children were born unto them, Lenora, Gaylord, Jerrold, Tunis, Mary and Raphael. This branch of the Harris family is descendant of James Harris, who was born in Bristol, England, in 1700. Immigrated to New Jersey in 1725. He married a Miss Boylen. A son, George Harris, was born in 1745. He married a Miss Tunis. A son, Barna[bas] Harris, was born at Pulaski, Lawrence County, Pennsylvania, in 1768. He married Ester Miller. Of this marriage Barna[bas] C. Harris was born in 1811. Barna[bas] C. Harris married Rachael Marquis, and unto them was Barna[bas] Tunis Harris, who married Rachael Marquis. Their son, Jerome B. Harris, was the ancestor of this branch of the Harris family in Randolph."

Anyone can see Mr. Maxwell and Dr. Bosworth and Mrs. Keifer had different versions of the Harris ancestry. For a more detailed early life of the Harris Family, Mrs. Keifer's article, The Harris Family of New Jersey, states: "Barnabas Tunis Harris [and his wife] Rachel Marquis [Harris] had four children: Jerome B. Harris, born April 19, 1836; Merthyan Harris [a daughter], born September 20, 1837 [died June 30, 1848]; Marquis Harris, born February 1, 1839; Samuel Harris, born July 6, 1843; Mr. Harris was a farmer by occupation and resided at or near Pulask[i], Lawrence County, PA. Was a Presbyterian in religion. He died September 9, 1871, in his sixty-first year."

Jerome Harris' mother was Rachel Marquis. The Marquis Family is an interesting family. They were French Huguenots chased

314

out of France after the Protestant Reformation. They first went to Scotland where they were adopted into the McDonald clan and from there to Letterkenny, Northern Ireland. One branch, ours I believe, married into the Margaret Kidd family, a granddaughter of the infamous pirate Captain Kidd who was hanged in Scotland in 1705 at the age of ninety-five. Another branch married into the Magruder family and they trace their lineage back to Robert The Bruce. The progenitor of the Marquis family went to Switzerland and that branch of the family was attorney general for Switzerland in 1908. Also the Switzerland family is reputed to be the owners of Nestle's Chocolate.

Mary Jane Crocket[t] (aka Crocker) was apparently quite a risk-taking lady and her second marriage was to Jerome Barnabas Harris. Little is known of the Crocket[t] (aka Crocker) ancestry, but the name is English and the Crocket[t]s may have moved into Western Pennsylvania from one of the New England states. Shortly after the birth of Jerrold C. Harris, the family decided to leave Pennsylvania and go to West Virginia to open a hunting lodge in Rainelle. They packed their things and moved by ox cart into the wilderness of West Virginia. Their thinking was one hundred years too early for hunting lodges in that area.

Their dream of a hunting lodge must have died as we find them pushing slowly north again, until they finally settle down in Beverly, West Virginia, for the rest of their lives. Their last two sons were born near or in Beverly: Raphael " Raph" Simeon Harris, born Mary 1, 1882; and William "Poker Bill" Crocket[t] (aka Crocker) Harris, born July 27, 1884.

Before the marriage of Mary Jane Crocket[t] (aka Crocker) Kissinger to Jerome Barnabas Harris, she was married to a Mr. Kissinger. They had two children, a son, whose name was John, and a daughter named Nettie. While sailing down the Mississippi River, her husband came down with pneumonia and died. Then she and her two children came to live at New Castle, Pennsylvania.

Little is known of Mary Jane's first husband. Where they were going when they sailed down the Mississippi River and why? Probably, like most pioneers, they were trying to improve their lot in life by seeking greener pastures some place else. Mary Jane Crocket[t] (aka Crocker) Kissinger Harris, by legend, is said to have been a relative of David Crockett.

After the death of her first husband, Mary Jane's parents offered her financial help, which she refused, saying, "I made my bed and I'll lie in it." The two Kissinger children were brought up with the seven children born to Mary Jane and Jerome. Mary Crocket[t] (aka Crocker) Harris was reputed to be a very strong spirited mountain woman. Jerome Harris is buried on Reservoir Hill in East Dailey, Randolph County, West Virginia.

George Harris was born in Essex County, New Jersey about 1745 or 1746. He married Hannah Tunis, (Tunisen), about 1765, by whom he had eleven children. Mr. Harris was of the old Revolutionary stock; was in the war under General Washington; was sergeant of the Second Regiment of State troops and Continental Army. Mr. Harris took part in the bloody battle of Monmouth, as did his brothers Thomas and John. During the Revolutionary War, he resided in the Colony of New Jersey. While he was in the army his house was pillaged and his stock driven off. You will find that his descendents are found in nearly half of the states of the Union.

It has been a little over a century and a half since James left the shores of England as a single man. He was the progenitor of the Harris family in the United States. Some of the oldest descendents served as soldiers in the Revolutionary War, some in the War of 1812, and some in the war between Mexico and the United States; and still later some of the younger generations served as soldiers in the War of the Rebellion, which occurred from 1861 to 1865.

It is not known for a certainty that any royal blood has ever coursed through their veins; but the wife of James Harris was of English parentage, and of the same name as the wife of Henry the Eighth, King of England. Let us look back to a little more than a hundred years ago, and step by step, along a savage wilderness, oppressed by foreign foes and assailed by murderous savages and ferocious wild beasts, suffering cold, hunger and disease, torn from kindred ties. For what purpose? To build up homes of peace and plenty for you and me. To open up a highway of light and liberty, and equal rights for us today; a country that abounds with free institutions of learning for all, and a right to worship God after the dictates of our own consciences. All this was purchased with a fortitude and suffering which we of today do not appreciate half enough; they bought all this with their best abilities; and also with their heart's blood.

James Harris was born in the city of Bristol, Somersetshire, England, close to the border of Wales, about the commencement of 1700; and immigrated to America in 1725 (or about that time).

The Harris Family is among the forty-nine "best families" selected by the American Historical-Genealogical society for whom the society has published family histories during the past several years. The Harris Family has been prominent in the British Empire and in the United States; its members having played important roles in war and peace. Family pride is a commendable trait and should be cultivated. All Harrises have just cause to be proud of their family history and traditions.

The legend persists that Miss Boleyn, who married James Harris, was a descendent of the Boleyn family that produced Anne Boleyn. There is a grain of truth in every legend, which becomes greatly exaggerated with each passing generation. Anne Boleyn was the second wife of Henry VIII and the mother of Queen Elizabeth I.

Boleyn is a place name, meaning one who came from Boulogne, France. Anne Boleyn's family immigrated from Boulogne to En-

317

gland. They were cloth merchants, who became very rich and powerful in England. When the family became wealthy and married into the best families of England, they changed the spelling of the name to Boleyn. The family name can be found in old English records previous to that change as Bullen, Bullan, Boullen, Boullan, de Boulans, Boullant, as well as many other spellings of the name. Regardless of how the name was spelled, it was always pronounced Bull-un.

The best evidence that Miss Boleyn, who married James Harris, was a collateral descendant of Anne Boleyn's family is that the spelling of their surnames is the same. In the index to New Jersey Wills, 1689-1890, the names Bolan, Boland, Boll, Bollen, Bolles, Bollis and Bolyan appear, but not Boleyn. The Boleyn Will was from Essex County, where James and his wife lived. Names, places and dates have a tendency to change from generation to generation. Information is passed down from one generation to another by word of mouth, which can account for many variations. Even when information is written down, there can be errors of spelling. What is a fact in one generation can change at a later date, for instance, when James Harris came to Elizabeth-town, New Jersey, it was in Essex County. Today, it is Elizabeth and in Union County.

Some of the descendents pushed on to Iowa, Wisconsin, Michigan, Missouri, California, Nebraska, Kansas, Texas, Indiana, Colorado, Arizona, New York, Utah, Arkansas, Minnesota, Illinois, Kentucky, Washington Territory, Nevada Territory and the Dakota Territory.

George Harris served in the Revolutionary War under General George Washington. He was a sergeant of the Seventh Regiment of State Troops and Continental Army, but most of the time served as a New Jersey Minuteman and fought in the Battle of Monmouth. George Harris's two brothers, Thomas and John, also took part in the Battle of Monmouth. George Harris lived in New Jersey

318

during the Revolutionary War. While he was in service his house was pillaged and his stock driven off.

Barnabas C. Harris married Ester Miller of Millersburg, Pennsylvania on January 19, 1796. Their son Nehemiah married Anna McGuffey, a sister of William H. McGuffey, who wrote the McGuffey Readers and Spellers. Professor McGuffey taught for many years Moral and Mental Philosophy at the University of Virginia.

Edwin Poe Harris entered the University of Virginia Medical School and graduated at the age of twenty-one and moved west and practiced medicine among the Indians in Wyoming Territory and Missouri. At the Battle of Elk Horn, he was taken prisoner by the Confederates and forced into duty as a surgeon for the wounded Confederates. He was a captain in the Second Missouri Calvary at the time. He escaped from the Confederates in April 1862. Edwin Poe Harris's second wife was Ella May Wolf. She was one-fourth Cherokee, a daughter of Judge Thomas Wolf.

Dr. Harris took as his third wife, Lou Jannett Perry, in 1884. She was a Chickasaw, who had been educated in the Eastern States. She possessed large farm properties, ferries and cattle. They had no children. He gradually reduced his medical practice to special cases, assistant surgeon for the Missouri Railroad.

Another descendent was John Harris, who amassed quite a fortune and owned 140 slaves, but the Civil War swept away almost everything he had. It is by legend that John Harris and David Crockett, who gave their lives at the Alamo during the United States-Mexican War, can be traced to the Harris lineage.

Samuel Gaillard Harris, also known as Gaylord, was the oldest son of Jerome Barnabas Harris and Mary Jane Crocket[t] (aka Crocker) Kissinger Harris. He was born on April 11, 1874. He married Estella Nelson Harmon (Harman) in 1898 or 1899. She died on October 5, 1905. They had a son and a daughter. He married Ellen May Hutton on February 20, 1906 at Marlinton,

Pocahontas County, West Virginia. They had six sons.

Many of the Harris descendents were farmers, carpenters, inn-keepers, cheesemakers, saloonkeepers, nurses, sheriffs, photographers, artists, newspaper editors, ministers, physicians, members of Congress, state legislators, soldiers (one West Point), sailors (on the Naval Academy at Annapolis), lawyers, civil engineers, dentists, wagonmakers, teachers, stagecoach drivers, manufacturers, oil businessmen and one a bishop of the Methodist-Episcopal Church.

Mrs. Keifer completed her history of the Harris Family with these words, "to gather up, compile and write such a book as this, I think I would rather do ordinary household work. When I think of the amount of time it has taken to gather up and arrange this book, I am amazed at my own perseverance."

"Gale" Gaylord and "Raph" Raphael Harris married Nelson sisters from Beverly, sisters of Joe Nelson, as their first wives.

Raphael Simeon Harris looked like Dan Rather of *CBS News*. Raphael was the son of Jerome B. Harris and Mary Crockett Harris. Allen Harris was the oldest of six sons and five daughters. Allen was a highly-decorated WWII combat infantry survivor from Gaudal Canal to Okinawa Invasion in the South Pacific.

Raphael was first married to a Nelson, who died giving birth to Allen at Beverly, and his second marriage was to Lena Bowers, daughter of John Bowers. Raphael Simeon Harris and Lena Bowers Harris' children were Geneva Catherine Harris-born June 13, 1912, married Charlie Robert Triplett on September 12, 1929, and had one son, George Raphael Triplett, born Friday, September 13, 1935, Cheat Bridge; Mabel Harris Payne-married Harry Payne. Children were Thomas Harris Payne, Jack Payne and Patty Ann Payne; Ralph Howard Harris-married Anna Mae Davis Harris, daughter of Elmer and Willa Davis, no children born to the marriage; Greta Jane Harris-married Frank Miller, one daughter, Nancy Harris Booth; Robert Harris-married Ruth Freeberger and had seven children, Robert, Jr., Ruth Ellen, Sherry, Patty, Mary, Sandy and Christopher Harris; Jeanette Harris-married Archie Beck, two sons, Fred and Daniel William Beck. Archie Beck was a Western Maryland locomotive repairman; Alice Mae Harris-married Peter Dominick Antolini and had three children, David Antolini, Joyce Antolini Hill and Sheila Antolini Scott; Jack Harris-married to Marie Coontz, no children born to marriage. Jack was a Western Maryland Railroad Conductor; James Jesse Harris-married Elizabeth Howard; four children, Kay, Lynn, Jeff and Jay Harris; Fielding Clinton Harris-never married; Raphael Simeon Harris first married Ruth Nelson, mother of Allen Nelson Harris, who married Ruth Smith, and there were no children born.

## Hart Family

The Hart family is of English descent and has been identified with the county since 1785, when two brothers, Daniel and Edward Hart, located at the present town of Beverly. Daniel settled about a mile above Beverly on Files Creek near the old Buckey mill site. They came to Randolph from New Jersey. John and Daniel Hart were soldiers in the Revolution, and were sons of John Hart, who signed the Declaration of Independence.

Joseph Hart, son of Edward Hart, was born and reared near Beverly. He became a prominent lawyer, having been admitted to the bar of Randolph County in 1837, and was also prominent in public and political affairs. He twice represented his county in the State Legislature and was president of the county court. He moved to the summit of Rich Mountain in 1855 for the benefit of his health, but continued to practice law until the beginning of the Civil War. His farm on the mountain top became the site of the Battle of Rich Mountain and his residence was between the lines of the contending forces. He died April 4, 1881.

Squire Bosworth Hart, son of Joseph and Susan (Pickens) Hart, was born near Beverly in 1841. He enlisted in Battery E. First West Virginia Artillery and served in the Valley of Virginia. After the close of the war he taught school until 1867, when he was elected county superintendent of schools, and was re-elected in 1869. In 1849 a coal mine was opened a short distance west of the summit of the mountain on the Hart farm and supplied the demand in Beverly and vicinity until the building of the railroad up the Valley. In 1868, Mr. Hart married Maria L. Organ, of Upshur County. They had one child, who became the wife of Hon. Clyde Johnson, a prominent attorney of St. Marys, this state.

William Camden Hart, son of Calvin C. Hart and Julia Hart, was born December 19, 1868; married Marietta E. Logan, daughter of William Thomas Logan and Elizabeth F. Logan. Children were: Shirley D. Hart, Logan D. Hart, Dorothy Julia Hart, Marion L. Hart, Sheffey B. Hart, and Calvin E. Hart. William Camden Hart has been constable twice and justice of the peace of Beverly District once.

Eli Triplett, who was the son of John Triplett and either Nancy Kittle Triplett or Sallie Kittle Triplett, married Margaret Hart, daughter of James Hart, and moved to Missouri.

## Isner Family

William Isner was the first of the name to locate in Randolph County, perhaps. He lived in the Valley in 1775 on lands adjoining the lands of Benjamin Wilson. Thomas Isner applied for a pension in the year 1833 on the grounds that he was an Indian spy in the Revolution. Michael Isner entered 190 acres of land in 1789 in Tygarts Valley. Michael Isner was a member of the first grand jury in Randolph County in 1787.

J. Herman Isner is the son of Jefferson Isner and Icie Triplett Isner. Icie was the granddaughter of John Triplett and daughter of Job Triplett.

322

## Pedro Family

The Petro or Pedro family was perhaps the only representative of the Spanish nationality among the pioneers of Randolph County. The names of Henry, Leonard and Nicholas Petro appear in the early records of Randolph County. Nicholas Pedro was a member of the first grand jury of Randolph County. Thomas Butcher married Susan, daughter of Henry Petro in 1807. Solomon Collett married Sarah, daughter of Henry Petro in 1815. Leonard Petro was captured by the Indians, while guarding a trail that lead into the Valley, in 1777. He was taken to Ohio and never heard from afterward. Although the name is extinct in Randolph County, the strain of blood is represented in several prominent families of the county.

## Wilmoth Family

The Wilmoth settlement was among the first permanent colonies in Randolph County. The date is fixed by the records of Monongalia County, which show that the Wilmoths obtained certificates for land on Cheat River on which they settled in 1776. These certificates were given by the commissioners of unpatented lands in 1781. They were of English descent and consisted of four brothers and two sisters. Their names were Nicholas, Thomas, James, and John and the sisters, Deborah and Susan. They immigrated from England to Virginia and thence to Randolph County, sojourning, perhaps, in Pendleton County. Thomas Wilmoth received a patent for 71 acres of land in Pendleton on Hedricks Run in 1771. The Wilmoths probably lived in Pendleton County from 1771 to 1776. For many years subsequent to their settlement on the river, the stream was called Wilmoths River.

Nicholas, the eldest of the Wilmoth brothers, married Sydney, daughter of William Currence, the pioneer and Indian fighter. The children of Nicholas and Sydney (Currence) Wilmoth were John W., Sarah, Thomas, William, Eli, Samuel, James and Currence.

Thomas, brother of the first Nicholas, married in 1798, Amy, daughter of Benjamin Schoonover. He owned the land where the stone house now stands. The stone house was built by Levi, son of Thomas. The children of Thomas and Amy (Schoonover) Wilmoth were, Absalom, John, Edmund, Levi and three daughters whose name are not remembered.

John Wilmoth, one of the pioneer brothers, married in 1799, Mary Cunningham, daughter of James Cunningham. The names of their children were Elias, Peggy, James, Prudence, Wilson, Solomon, John Adam, Mary and Dewy. James married Nancy Smith.

James Wilmoth, the pioneer, was murdered by the Indians. The date of the tragedy is uncertain, but it was probably at the time of the Leading Creek massacre. The Wilmoth settlement was apprehensive of a raid by the Indians and had sought safety at Friends and Wilson's Fort. However, James Wilmoth ventured to make a visit to the settlement, when his whereabouts was betrayed to the savages lurking in the community by the barking of a dog with him. The Indians killed him from ambush near where the stone house now stands. Susan Wilmoth married David Schoonover.

Eli, son of Nicholas and Sydney (Currence) Wilmoth, married Rebecca, daughter of Aaron Vanscoy. Their children were Archibald, Emily, Currence, James, Arnold, Louisa, Isbern, Oliver and Elizabeth.

Nicholas Wilmoth, born in 1824, son of William and Mary (Taylor) Wilmoth; married in 1853 to Eliza, daughter of Noah McLean. Children were Simpson, Haymond, Theodore, Virginia, Emiline, Minerva, Lou A. and Julia.

Benjamin F. Wilmoth, son of Wm. and Mary (Taylor) Wilmoth, was born in 1829. He was a member of the board of supervisors during the Civil War.

Oliver Wilmoth, son of Eli and Rebecca (Vanscoy) Wilmoth and grandson of Nicholas and Sydney (Currence) Wilmoth, was born in 1835. He was a member of the board of supervisors in 1861 to 1868 and was town sergeant, chief of police and city treasurer of the city of Elkins, holding one of these positions almost continuously during the first two decades of the city's growth.

Archibald Wilmoth was born in 1824 and was the son of Eli and Rebecca (Vanscoy) Wilmoth. He died in 19--. He married Caroline, daughter of Isaac Taylor, in 1847. Children were: Luceba, Alonzo F., Ella and Rebecca.

Sidney Wilmoth married Job Triplett, son of John Triplett, and she was the mother of several children, including, Jasper, Wilmoth, Oliver, Frank, William, Owen and several daughters and lived in the "Triplett Home Place" at Faulkner.

Alonzo F. Wilmoth, son of Archibald and Caroline (Taylor) Wilmoth, was born in 1854; married Nancy, daughter of Thomas G. and Emily L. Black. Children were: Emily, Josephine, Russell Woods, Edith Loraine. Mr. Wilmoth graduated from Fairmont Normal School in 1881. He was principal of the New Martinsville public schools in 1882; from 1884 to 1888 he was secretary to State Superintendent of Public Schools, B.L. Butcher. For years Mr. Wilmoth was a representative of the publishing house of Ginn & Co. He was elected court superintendent of schools in 1878 and served two terms.


## Honorable H.G. Kump Family

Herman G. Kump, son of Bejamin Franklin and Frances Margaret (Rudolph) Kump, was born at Capon Springs, Hampshire County, West Virginia, October 31, 1879. He educated in the public schools and the University of Virginia from which institution he graduated in 1903. In 1905 he received a degree of B.L. from the law department of the University of Virginia, and was admitted to the Randolph County bar the same year. He has served as prosecuting attorney since 1908. Mr. Kump married in 1907, Edna, daughter of C.H. and Fanny (Logan) Scott. Children were Cyrus Scott and Frances. Mr. Kump's father, B.F. Kump, was a soldier in the Confederate Army, his grandfather, Jack Kump, was a soldier in the War of 1812, and his great-grandfather, Jenry Kump, was a soldier in the Revolutionary War from Virginia. Children were: Cyrus, Ben, Margaret and Mary Gamble.

## Bowers Family

"John O. Bowers, born 1850 in Highland County, son of William and Margaret Catherine (Sponaugle) Bowers; Dutch ancestry; in 1875, in Virginia, he married Margaret Catherine, daughter of William and Molly (Moury) Whitecotton; children William Washington, Lawrence, Alberta, Jacob, Charles, Ludania, Ottis, Perry, Minnie, Lillie, Texie, Lena, Bertha, Clarence; farmer and teamster; has lived in Randolph County seventeen years; owns house and lot near Harman" and later moved to Glady. Lena was the second wife of Raphael "Raph" Simeon Harris. Geneva Harris married Charlie Robert Triplett, son of George Washington "Pud" Triplett and Lora Susan Arbogast Triplett. There are many living descendants of John O. Bowers. The three sons of "Pud" Triplett married granddaughters of John O. Bowers. Charlie Robert married Lena Bowers Harris (oldest daughter, Geneva). Isa Williams married Bernice Bowers daughter of "Jake" Bowers. Henry Jasper's first wife was Violet Carr, the daughter Sallie Bowers Carr and second wife was Edna Bowers, daughter of Jake Bowers.

# Family of Ira William Vance & Oda Bell Triplett Vance

Note: Isa William Vance was the son of Barbara Ellen Rexroad Arbogast daughter of Lemuel and Ellen Arbogast and a section gang foreman Oda Bell Triplett was the daughter of "Judson" Triplett. Oda Bell Triplett Vance was a sister to Owen Fansler's wife, Minnie Triplett Fansler, mother of Lonnis "Pip" Fansler.

1. Harry Vance–died at birth
2. Oliver Vance–died at birth
3. Mary Ellen Vance Kerns–married Carl Kerns
4. Isaac Vance–married Ida Mae Hodge
5. Bethel Vance Rhodes–married Jim Rhodes
6. Howard Vance–married Martha Phares
7. Charles Vance–married Rita Howell
8. Ethel Vance Howell–married Claude Howell
9. Herman "Peck" Vance–married Ruby Calain
10. Mabel Vance Race–married Cletes Race
11. Betty Vance Falute–married Jack Falute
12. Ira Vance, Jr.–married Ruth Lambert
13. Harold Vance–married Vonda Butler
14. Harley Vance–married Betty Nelson

Note: Harold and Harley Vance were twins.

15. Donald Vance–married Joann Markley
16. Donna Vance Hickman–married Dewey "Edsell" Hickman

Note: Donald and Donna Vance were twins

17. Audra Vance Armentrout–married Richard Armentrout
18. Ruby Vance–died at birth

Note: One missing

Four sons were section gang foremen and two sons-in-law were Isaac, "Ike" Howard, Herman "Peck," Charles, Claude Howell and Carl Kerns.

# Triplett Family

*George Washington's Diary* continuously contains from 1748-1799 entries of his close friendship with Francis, Thomas and William Triplett. One of the Tripletts was a surgeon on Washington's Staff. William Triplett was a builder and the main constructor of Mount Vernon for Washington. William Owen was the father of John Triplett, who was sent from Faquier County Virginia to settle the Triplett land grant from the Washington Estate.

**William Triplett.** Francis Triplett died in Fairfax in 1757, leaving several sons, of whom the two eldest, Thomas and William, appear frequently in the diary. They lived at "Round Hill," across the road from the Glebe. Thomas was a justice of Fairfax and served on the County Committee of Safety of 1774. William was elected to the Truro vestry in 1776, vice Washington, and served until 1785.

The Triplett family came from England and was among the settlers of Jamestown. William, Thomas and Francis were close friends of George Washington and appear continuously in George Washington's Diary in the Library of Congress from 1748-1799.

John Triplett was the first in Randolph County, but was born in Baltimore, Maryland. He came to Virginia when he was a boy eighteen or nineteen years old. He was married young to a Miss Kittle, who seems to have been of a different family from Abraham Kittle. To them were born fourteen children, two of whom died in infancy. Of those who lived to manhood and womanhood, Ephrain, Jacob, Moses and Job spent their lives and reared families in Randolph County. William and Loami settled in Kanawha County, where they spent their lives. Eli and James went to Missouri after marrying in Randolph County; Eli to Margaret Hart, a daughter of James Hart, and James to Deborah Harris, a daughter of Henry Harris, of Leading Creek. Ann was the wife of Archibald Ferguson, and Mary, the wife of Solomon Ferguson. Eunice was the wife of Isaac Taylor.

In April 1829, after the death of his first wife, John Triplett and Nancy Kittle were married. She was a Bennett, and came from Fauquier County, and was born in 1798. Her first husband was the brother of John's first wife. Her son by the first marriage was Major Ben Kittle, and a daughter was the mother of Lloyd and Hamilton Isner. To this union were born, Martha, who married Amasa Kittle, Rachael, who married Arnold Wilmoth, Harriet, who married William Ferguson, (John J. Ferguson is the only living child); John J., who went to Montana when the trouble between the North and South came up and died there in the eighties; Randolph Triplett was born on August 28, 1837; Hickman, who went to Nebraska, now lives in British Columbia; and Anthony, who lives near Grafton in Taylor County.

Jasper, William Owen, Oliver and Frank were the sons of Job. Elijah Triplett was the son of Jacob, and the sons of Ephraim were Milton and David.

Floyd J. Triplett, son of Randolph and Sarah (Kittle) Triplett, was born in 1863. He married Ella May, daughter of Archibald and Caroline (Taylor) Wilmoth. Children were: Eva, Belle, Samuel, Lucebia, Maria, Sallie and Clare. Floyd Triplett was the editor of the *Randolph Enterprise* and *Tygarts Valley News*, and was county clerk in 1891-1897. He was also of the editor of the Plymouth, *North Carolina Independent*.

Jasper W. Triplett, son of Job and Sydney (Wilmoth) Triplett, was born in 1842 and died in 1914. He married Eliza Chenoweth. Children were Wade Hampton, George Washington "Pud" and Delphia, who married Rev. William Flint. Wade married Louie Lambert. Children were Delphia, Mary, Helen, Preston and Revely. Grayson died in infancy. Jasper Triplett was assessor of Randolph County for twelve years.

The Triplett Home Place was built about 1800. Job Triplett,

son of John Triplett, lived in the log house until his death in 1866. The house burned about 1990. McBees currently own the original home site. Job Triplett and his family, prior to the Civil War, were bonded whiskey makers by the Government. John Triplett was born in Baltimore, Maryland. John came to Randolph County and settled on Cheat Mountain above the "S" tunnel about 1790.

Jasper Wilmoth Triplett married Eliza Chenoweth. Jasper was born in 1842 in the log house constructed by John or Job Triplett and died in 1914. Jasper was Randolph County Assessor for twelve years with his brother William Owen Triplett. Jasper also served as Sergeant, and later as Captain, for Company "A" of the 18th Virginia Calvary, Confederate States of America with two of his brothers, Oliver R. Triplett and Frank Triplett. Oliver was killed in action and Jasper was severely wounded in February 1864 at the Sinks of Gandy when they were attacked by the Home Guards of the Dry Fork, Union sympathizers, while asleep by their campfire. Jasper recognized some of his assailants as being "Arbogasts".

George Washington "Pud" Triplett married Lora Susan Arbogast, a most beautiful mountain lady with dark brown hair that touched the ground, and had three sons. The three living sons were Charlie Robert Triplett (born on April 24, 1905), Ira William Triplett, and Harry Jasper Triplett. Lora was the daughter of Lemuel and Barbara Ellen Arbogast. "Pud" was a logging teamster and made the river log drives from Upper Cheat to Point Marion, Pennsylvania.

Wade Hampton Triplett married Louise Lambert and children were: Delphia Triplett Kimble, Mary Triplett Chenoweth, Helen Triplett, Preston Triplett, (a Western Maryland locomotive engineer), and Revely Triplett.

Delphia Triplett Flint married William Flint, a Presbyterian minister and had children, William, Eliza, Robert, Mary, Elizabeth and Warren. Most all of Wade Triplett's and Delphia Flint's children attended college. Mary and Elizabeth were schoolteachers.

Elizabeth married Floyd Harrison, a Wayne County attorney and had one son, William Harrison, born September 13, 1934, and whose childhood picture hung in Buckingham Palace. William Harrison practiced law in Wayne County, West Virginia.

Robert Flint was a member of the 1918 D&E Football Team, WWI veteran and manager of Island Creek Coal Company Stores until his death.

Ira William Triplett lived in the two-story frame house above the RR tracks with numerous company trailers parked. Ira was a Faulkner welder for the section gangs from Elkins to Durbin, Spruce and Webster Springs and assigned to the Elkins yards section gang.

Charlie Robert Triplett married Geneva Catherine Harris oldest daughter of Raphael "Raph" Simeon (Simon) Harris and Lena Bowers Harris.

Ira William married Bernice Bowers, daughter of Jake Bowers and had no natural born children, but adopted Armenthea Mae Arbogast Triplett Currence, at childbirth. She married Ralph "Mac" Currence and has two sons, Gregg and Ralph.

Harry Jasper married Violet Cave, first marriage, and Edna Bowers Cook, second marriage and had no children.

George R. Triplett-Charlie and Geneva had one son, George Raphael Triplett, born on Friday, September 13, 1935, at Cheat Bridge and delivered by George Hull, M.D.

George Raphael married Frances Rossi from Coalton, a Certified Registered Nurse Anesthetist. Frances was the youngest daughter of Emedio Rossi and Agatha Saccoccia Rossi, Coalton, West Virginia. Emedio Rossi was the son of Concesio and Michaelina Rossi. Agatha was the daughter of Gustinio and Nunizata Saccoccia, Pratola Peligna, Italy.

Frances and George are the parents of three sons-George Raphael Triplett, Jr., is a graduate of Washington & Lee University, Lexington, Virginia, where he practices anesthesiology and is a graduate of the West Virginia Osteopathic College of Medicine. He married Mary Ann Sellers, formerly of Fairmont and Martinsburg. His stepson, Billy Post, is married to Lori and they have two daughters, Meredith and "Katie". Mary Ann's sister Patty married Bill Fleming, grandson of Roy Houchin.

Charles Emedio Triplett, a graduate of Guilford College and Davis and Elkins College, is a Certified Public Accountant and married Robin Queen Triplett. Robin is the first woman to graduate from Washington & Lee University. Robin graduated from West Virginia University College of Law and is employed by the Jackson and Kelly law firm in Clarksburg office. Charley is employed by Kuntz & Swisher, a CPA firm in Clarksburg.

Charley and Robin were united in marriage July 1994 in Lee Chapel, Washington & Lee University Campus, which holds the tomb of Robert E. Lee. Robin is the daughter of the late Bob Queen and Ludie Hamilton Queen, Hodgesville, West Virginia.

Charley and Robin have one son, Robert Charles Triplett, born January 20, 2002, five days before Geneva passed away. Unfortunately, Geneva only got to see Robert's photo from birth. Charley, Robin and Robert reside in Buckhannon, West Virginia.

Jefferson Lee Triplett, lawyer and Lt. Commander in the United States Navy Reserves, is a graduate of the United States Naval Academy, University of Maryland and University of Baltimore College of Law and is employed by Saul Ewing Law Firm in the Baltimore office.

Jefferson Lee is married to Silvia Gonzales Boyero, Salamanca, Spain. They were united in marriage in the Cathedral of Salamanca, Spain where Christopher Columbus received the money from Queen Isabella and King Ferdinand to purchase the ships that discovered North America in 1492. Silvia is the daughter of the late Andrew Gonzales and Ester Boyero.

Jefferson and Silvia have two children, George Andrew Triplett, born March 25, 2000 and Sofia Frances Triplett, born April 9,

2002. They reside in Annapolis, Maryland.

All three sons of George and Frances played college football at their alma maters.

# Part V
## Green Bank High School
## Class of 1953

Our 1953 Green Bank High School Class tries to meet annually and are scattered in several states. We manage to have more than sixty percent attendance at our deceased classmate, Jim "Fireball" Ryder's Restaurant in Boyer, West Virginia, where the Green Bank High School Class of 1953 "Golden Eagles" and faculty group picture proudly hangs on the wall.

We celebrated our fiftieth anniversary on July 19, 2003 and were fortunate enough to have only eight deceased classmates. The spouses of the deceased classmates continue to attend our class of 1953 celebrations.

The original Green Bank High School was torn down several years ago. The remains are the large trees and metal fence that enclose the present Green Bank Middle School and school bus garage.

## The Class of 1953
## Green Bank High School "Golden Eagles"

Betty Simmons Bennett, Frances Brewster (Frances Branock) Charles Brock, Charles Bryant, Charlotte Cassell (Charlotte Galford), Jerry "Buck" Crist, Julia "Pearl" Curry (Julia Mace–married classmate Lewis Mace), Robert "Pickle" Dill (deceased)–Robert's surviving widow, Joyce Rexroad and sister, Colleen, the auburn haired, brown-eyed "Princess" of Leatherbark, who could catch more native brook trout that her brother–Janet Gainer (Janet Starks–married classmate Robert Starks), William Gainer, Calvin Galford, Sam Galford, Jullian Gillespie, Jack "Jigger" Gragg, Donald Grogg, Donald "Markwood" Gun, Keith Gum, Thelma Hoover (Thelma Cover–deceased), Donald "Chick" Lambert, Harold "Joy" Lambert, Mildred Johnston Lambert (Mildred), Lewis Maco, Shirley "Murph" Murphy (Shirley Rexrode–deceased), Betty Jane Nelson (Betty Jane Haislop), Eugene "Sonny" Nelson, Julian Nottingham, Elva June Phillips (Elva June Ray), Howard Rada, Bonnie Rankin, Ellen Gragg Rudd, Charles "Sonny" or "Bean" Ryder, Jimmie "Fireball" Ryder, Sr. (deceased, surviving widow Violet "Tommie" Hoover Ryder), Ray Lewis Sage (deceased), Gladys Sampson (Gladys Gun-deceased), Edward Simmons, Hubert Simmons, James Simmons, Howard "Squeek" Slavins, Margaret Slavins (Margaret Woodell), Imogene Snyder (Imogene Simmons-married classmate James Simmons), Robert Starks, Ivan "Tuff" Sutton, Betty Lou Tacy (Betty Lou Meeks-deceased), Jean Taylor (Jean Wimer), Lyle Taylor, George R. Triplett, William VanDevender, Robert Ware (deceased), Naomi Wenger (Naomi Waybright), Delores Wright (Delores Price).

# Conclusion
## "A Million Dollar Childhood"

"I am part of all that I have met." Tennyson

You have read this book that *Our Proud Mountain Roots and Heritage*, and the various members of my family lineage. Most every descendent of the Upper Cheat River Basin has a very similar family lineage in their genes and DNA.

The price for freedom is sometimes painful and costly which started in Upper Cheat River Basin with George Washington's call "Rally around me men of West Augusta and we shall raise this bleeding nation from the sand."

Mountain people and their descendents have always "turned the bow of the ship to the storm" and proceeded to achieve the "Excelsior".

Mountain people are happy with a neighbor's financial or family's success and "not jealous". They want to see others get ahead and be successful.

"Worry doesn't bring happiness. Stress only brings ill health, and anxiety robs us of peace of mind."

"There is something beautiful in ever person."

"Faith is love in action."

"Anyone can be somebody to someone!"

"Internal peace of mind comes to a person who knows that he did the right things."

"Decide to do something positive today, and you will mount up on wings of faith."

By: Robert H. Schuller

The families of the Upper Cheat River Basin practiced and taught the positive hardworking sacrifice and attitude more precisely by their heritage their descendents leave in wherever they may dwell.

Each descendent of the Cheat River Basin could no doubt write with pride about their family's roots and heritage and be very similar to the informal incomplete introduction I have attempted to provide.

Charlie died in the barn lot on January 17, 1970, with his boots on. Geneva found him alone. Geneva, five days after the birth of Robert Charles Triplett, joined Charlie on January 25, 2002 under the watchful eyes of her loving personal care provider and nurse, Elsie Carrica.

Hard work, hope, faith and love were the basic principles practiced for survival and success for the Cheat River Basin "Celtic" people and their proud descendents.

I trust that many of you who have "roots" from all parts of rural and small towns in America can enjoy, relate and recall our blessed proud accumulated experiences, which have contributed to make our great nation.

One Nation Under God
With Liberty and Justice For All!

I Had A Million-Dollar Childhood
Growing Up on Upper Cheat River Basin

"Mountain Semper Liberi"

And That Is All I Have to Say About That!

# A Farewell Message

*Meetings and greetings and partings-*
*they come to us one and all,*
*They come to the man, they come to the maid,*
*they come to the children small.*
*The meetings and greetings we hail with joy,*
*But partings make sad the way;*
*So we put off farewells as long as we can,*
*And good-byes we dread to say*
*But "good-bye" just means "God bless you."*
*And that's what I'm saying to you,-*
*God bless you, my boy, God bless you, my girl,*
*And guide you in all that you do.*
*May the lessons you've learned in your school days here*
*Be such that shall help you grow*
*To manhood and womanhood brave and strong*
*To meet all life's storms as they blow.*
*By the best of success may your efforts be crowned,*
*Rich blessings be yours to the end;*
*And each day, I pray you, wherever you are*
*remember your teacher and friend.*

Roster for photo of school term 1915 from page 148. *Front row, left to right*: Jesse Coberly, Kathleen Coberly, Flora Wyatt, Sylvia Arbogast, Helen Howell, Flossie Summerfield, Carson Lambert, Russell Rhodes, Grant Kimble, Harry Howell, RosaBelle Howell. *second row, left to right*: Icie Summerfield, Louise Howell, Mabel Calain, Nell Kimble, Grace Workman, Helen Triplett, Roy F. "Son" Calain, Wilbert Arbogast, Edward Hornick, Chester Rhodes, Ira Triplett, Archie J. Coberly, _____Workman, John Summerfield and Jacob Howell; *third row, left to right*: Elizabeth Flint, Teacher Mary Vanscoy, Charley Triplett, George Calain, Lark Kimble, Garnett Arbogast, Warfield Isner, Elmer Calain, Charles Calain, Blain Isner, Clifford Howell; *fourth row, left to right*: _____, Teacher George Cunningham; *back row, left to right*: Mary Triplett, Elsie Workman, Patsy Crites, Icie Rhodes, Sally Kimble, Emma Kimble, Martha Summerfield, Marguerite Day, Delpha Triplett, Eliza Flint, Mary Summerfield and Jesse Calain.

# Bibliography

1.  Bowsorth, A.S., *A History of Randolph County, West Virginia*, Elkins, WV (N.P. 1916), (Reprinted 1975, Parsons WV: McClain Printing Company, 1975).
2.  Chapman, Odie Velta Nestor, *They Rest Quietly, Cemetery Records of Randolph County, West Virginia*: International Standard Book Number 0-87012-559-1, McClain Printing Company, Parsons, WV, 1996.
3.  Clarkson, Roy B., *Tumult on the Mountains*, Parsons, WV: McClain Printing Company, 1964.
4.  Clarkson, Roy B., *On Beyond Leatherbark: The Cass Saga*, Parsons, WV: McClain Printing Company, 1990
5.  Fitzpatrick, John C., AM., (Edited by). *The Diaries of George Washington 1748-1799*, Volume I, II, & III, Published by the Mount Vernon Ladies Association of the Union, Houghton Mifflin Company, Boston and New York.
6.  Mauer, B.B., *Mountain Heritage*, "An Informal Incomplete Introduction To Appalachian Culture" by O. Norman Simpkins, Morgantown Printing Company, 1975.
7.  Maxwell, H.W., *History of Randolph County, West Virginia*, Morgantown, WV: The Acme Publishing Company, 1898. (Reprinted 1961, Parsons, WV: McClain Printing Company, 1964).
8.  Rice, Donald L., *Randolph 200, A Bicentennial History of Randolph County, West Virginia*, A Pictorial and Documentary Sampler. Walsworth Press, Inc., 1987

**Newspapers and Periodicals**

9.  *The Log Train*, Published by the Mountain State Railroad & Logging Historical Association, Cass, WV (Volume 10, No. 4) Issue 40 *The Railroad Town of Spruce: High, Cold and Mysterious*.
    A. Sparks, Richard, *Spruce Revisited*.
    B. Childers-Cussins, Nancy Sue, *Born at Spruce*.

C. Cussins, Devane Wade, *A Childhood at Spruce*.

10.  *The Allegheny and Cheat Mountain Clubs* by H.A. Payne, Belington, WV, reprinted June 1997, Printcrafters, Elkins, WV, originally by The Roycrafters, East Aurora, NY.

## Unpublished Sources

11.  *Focusing In* by Gerald F. Harris, Rochester, NY. The Descedents of Jermane (?Jerome?) Barnabas Harris and his wife Mary Jane Crockett (Crocker) Kissinger Harris.

12.  *The Good Old Days at Spruce* by Wanda Powers Sharp, from December 1941 to 1950.

## Personal Interviews

13.  Devane "Booche" Cussins, Clarksville, Tennessee.
14.  Arlie Arbogast, Bowden, West Virginia.
15.  Willard "Peck" Vance, Bowden, West Virginia.
16.  Calvin & Frances Shifflett, Bemis, West Virginia.
17.  Eloise Mann, Elkins, West Virginia.
18.  Mary Armentrout, Elkins, West Virginia.
19.  Anna Mae Davis Harris, Elkins, West Virginia.
20.  Sheila Antolini Scott, Elkins, West Virginia.
21.  Donald Rice, Elkins, West Virginia.
22.  Roy Clarkson, Morgantown, West Virginia.
23.  H.A. Payne, Belington, West Virginia.
24.  Barbara Degler Carroll, Elkins, West Virginia.
25.  Herbert "Hub" Coberly, Elkins, West Virginia.
26.  J. Herman Isner, Kerens, West Virginia.
27.  Mary Jane Triplett Presseau, Wayne, West Virginia.
28.  Michelle Mullenax-McKinnie, Parsons, West Virginia.
29.  Wanda Powers Sharp, Elkins, West Virginia.
30.  William Keith Metheny, Elkins, West Virginia.
31.  Lars Byrne, Philippi, WV.

## Song Lyrics

30.  *Life's Railroad*
31.  *The Log Train* by Hank Williams

**Other Sources**

35. Family Trees–Heritage of Harris/Triplett/Arbogast/Bowers
36 Milepost Locations-WV Central RR, (as taken or compiled from CSX, B&O, WM documents).
37. Photos courtesty of Calvin Shifflett, Wanda Powers Sharp, Don Rice, Roy Clarkson, Lars Byrne, and the Harris and Triplett Families. William Keith Metheny collected by his grandfather Clair Metheny, J. Herman Isner, Amenthea Triplett Currence and Eleanor Currence DeMotto.

Triplett Family--*Front row:* George Andrew, Robert Charles, Sofia Frances Triplett; *middle row:* George R. and Frances Triplett, Mary Ann and Butch Triplett; *back row:* Robin and Charles Triplett and Silvia and Jeff Triplett.

# Index

Compiled by
Mariwyn McClain Smith

347

348

350

M. M., 17
Bryant, Charles, 251, 335
Btuff, 304
Bullan, 318
Bullen, 318
Burns, 302
Burner, Allen Eugene, 48, 270
 E., 245
 Eugene, 62, 91, 92, 142
 Thelma Vance, 92
Burrhs, 308
Burroughs, John, 57
Burnes, 18
Butcher, 296
 B. L., 325
 Susan, 323
 Thomas, 323
Buzzells, 26
Byrd, Lacy, 144
Byrne, Lars, vi, 19

Cain, James, 22, 66, 283
Calains, 9
 Charlie, 89, 91
 Charles, 339
 Darleau, 242
 Darlene, 89
 Elmer, 339
 George, 118, 339
 Golda, 118
 H. M. "Slim," 53, 210
 Jesse, 339
 Jimmy, 89, 242
 Lorenza, 118
 Mabel, 118, 339
 Melly, 89
 Milley, 242
 Mrs., 89
 Odbert, 89
 Roy f. "Son," 339
 Ruby, 327
Calhoun, Col., 17
Campbell, 303

Campion, Frank, 189
 Katherine, 139, 189
Canfields, 303
Capitio, 304
Caplinger, 303
 John, 34
Car, 296, 303
Carney, 304
Carpenters, 295, 304
Carpers, 301, 303
Carr, Sallie Bowers, 326
Carrica, Elsie, 338
Casey, 304
Cassell, 304
 Charlotte (Charlotte Galford), 335
 Grey, 250, 251
 Kenneth, 251
Cassidy, Mike, 182
Cassity, 304
 a Mr., 168
Casto, 304
Caudill, Harry, 104
Caves, 26
 Dick, 21
 Lee, 182
 Ronald, "Bruz," 161
Chaffeys, 26
 R., 2, 3
Champs, 9
 Bonnie, 90
 Marge, 90
 Mary, 90, 232
Channell, 302
 Marcella Triplett, 171
Chapman, "Johnny Appleseed,"
 61, 113
Chenoweths, 9, 302
 Eliza, 312
 Gabriel, 312
 Jehu, 312
 John, 311, 312
 Lemuel, 41
 Mary, 311

352

356

358

360

364

366

Ephrain, 328, 329
Eunice, 329
Eva, 329
Floyd, 329
Frances Rossi, 331, 333
Francis, 9, 328
Frank, 329, 330
Geneva Katherine Harris, 6, 25, 26, 29, 33, 41, 52, 192, 195, 197, 210, 211, 273, 326, 331, 332, 338
George, i, 333
George Andrew, vii, 332, 345, 346
George, "Buddy," 191, 192, 199, 265
George R., 48, 187, 192, 331, 336
George R., Jr., 71, 251, 283
George Raphael, 320, 331
George Raphael, Jr., 289, 331, 345
George Washington "Pud," 12-14, 145, 147, 152, 155, 157, 252, 257, 262, 306, 312, 326, 329, 330
Granville, 306
Grayson, 329
Harriet, 329
Harry, 13, 168, 212
Harry Jasper, 29, 49, 92, 252, 306, 330, 331
Helen, 118, 329, 330, 339
Henry, 260
Howard, 17
Ira, 13, 118, 123, 125, 151, 168, 259, 260, 339
Ira William, 29, 52, 252, 306, 330, 331
Jacob, 328, 329
Jack, 91
James, 61, 328
Jasper, 13, 147, 325, 329
Jasper W., 329
Jasper Wilmoth, 312, 330
Jefferson Lee, 289, 332, 345
Job, 14, 312, 322, 325, 328-30

John, 9, 322, 325, 327, 329, 330
Loami, 328
Lora Susan Arbogast, 11, 13, 29, 168, 181, 210, 256, 258, 259, 261, 262, 306, 326, 330
Louie Lambert, 329
Lucebia, 329
Manville, 306
Margaret Hart, 328
Maria, 329
Mary, 118, 329, 330, 339
Mary Ann Sellers, 289, 332, 345
Milton, 329
Moses, 328
Nancy Kittle, 322, 329
Oda Bell, 327
Oliver, 14, 325, 329, 330
Owen, 325
Paul, 151
Preston, 91, 118, 329, 330
Randolph, 329
Revely, 329, 330
Robert Charles, vii, 192, 332
Robin Queen, 332
Sallie, 329
Sallie Kittle, 322
Samuel, 329
Sarah Kittle, 329
Silvia Gonzales Boyero, 332
Sofia Frances, vii, 332
Sydney Wilmoth, 329
Thomas, 9, 328
Trotter Brothers, 60, 61
Violet, 90
Violet Cave, 331
Wade, 329
Wade Hampton, 312, 329
William, 9, 328, 325
William Owen, 171, 328-30
Willis Lavenia, 171
Wilmoth, 325
Troutwine, 305
Truman, Pres. Harry S., 255

368

Waybright, Naomi Wenger, 336
  Stan, 162
Weavers, 295
Weber, Fred, 94
Webley, Roxanne Shifflett, 20
Weere, 303
Weeses, 9, 92, 300
  Bert, 89, 91
  Enda, 89
  Jeanette, 89, 242
  Joann, 162
  Leo, 89, 01
  Mrs. Bert, 91
Weisgerber, Elizabeth Snyder, 309
  Eleanor, 309
  Henry, 309
Welch, 304
Weller, Jack, 98
Wenger, Naomi, 336
Westfall, 303
Wetzels, 301
Weymoths, 300, 302
Whetsell, 303
  Edgar, 204
  Jeff, 34
White, 9, 21, 26, 300, 302
  Blake, 123
  Dale, 89
  Edna, 57, 58
  Edna Dugger, 52, 195
  "Ground Hog," 36
  Irving, 52
  Jasper, 89, 210
  Jay, 5, 125
  Lonnie, 6
  Mattie, Lou, 89
  May, 89
  Merlin, 251
  Pauline, 181
  Russell, 39, 52, 54, 57, 58, 62, 194
  Sheffie, 89
Whitecottons, 26
  Margaret Catherine, 326
  Molly Moury, 326

William, 326
Whiterman, 305
Widney, Marguarite Kisner, 51
Wildfangs, 301
Wilfongs, 301
William, II, 310
Williams, 300, 304
  Annie, 308
  Bernice, 326
  Chas., 308
  Clayton B., 57
  Isa, 326
  Oscar, 44
  "Piney," 235
Williamson, 302
Willis, Henry, 184
Wilmot, 300
Wilmoth, a, 57, 300, 302
Wilmoth, Absalom, 324
  Alonzo F., 325
  Amy, 324
  Archibald, 324, 325, 329
  Arnold, 324, 329
  Benjamin F., 324
  Caroline Taylor, 325, 329
  Currence, 324
  Deborah, 323
  Dewey, 324
  Edith Loraine, 325
  Edmund, 324
  Eli, 324, 325
  Elias, 324
  Eliza McLean, 324
  Elizabeth, 324
  Ella, 325
  Ella Mae, 329
  Emiline, 324
  Emily, 324
  Emily Black, 325
  Haymond, 324
  Isbern, 324
  James, 323, 324
  Job, 325
  John, 323, 324

John Adam, 324
John W., 324
Josephine, 325
Julia, 324
Levi, 324
Lou A., 324
Louisa, 324
Luceba, 325
Minerva, 324
Mary, 324
Mary Taylor, 324
Nancy Black, 325
Nancy Smith, 324
Nicholas, 323, 324, 325
Oliver, 324, 325
Peggy, 324
Prudence, 324
Rachael, 329
Rebecca, 324, 325
Rebecca Vanscoy, 325
Russell Woods, 325
Samuel, 324
Sarah, 324
Sidney, 325
Simpson, 324
Solomon, 324
Stark, 48
Susan, 323, 324
Sydney, 323, 324
Sydney Currence, 325
Theodore, 324
Thomas, 323, 324
Virginia, 324
William, 324
Wilson, 324
Wilson, 302
  Alfred T., 312
  Archibald, 312
  Benjamin, 322
  Helen, 312
  Ida J., 312
  James, 312
  James A., 312

John, 312
Julia E., 312
Martha E., 312
Wm. H., 312
Wilt, Leon "Hezzy," 161, 162
Wimer, 303
  Ruth, 162
Winemiller, 28
Wise, 294, 305
Wolf, 303, 305
  Ella May, 319
  Thomas, 319
Woodell, Margaret Slavins, 336
Wood, 9, 94, 303
  Ben, 11
  Clarence, 94
  Arthur, 6
  Jim, 6
  Leah Turner, 6
  Wilson, 94
Wooden, Robert, 118
Woodleys, 294, 302 '
Woodford, 302
  Mosella Hutton, 184
Woodley, 294
Workman, 339
  Elsie, 339
  Grace, 339
Wright, Delores, 336
  Norman, 118
Wyatt, Flora, 118, 339

Yeagers, 301, 303
Yokum, 303
  Tom, 84
Young, John, 90

Zickafoos, 301
Zickafoose, 303
Zirbs, Rudy, 124
Zwickenfus, 301